A Gathering of Spirits: Japan's Ghost Story Tradition

.

A Gathering of Spirits: Japan's Ghost Story Tradition

From Folklore and Kabuki to Anime and Manga

Patrick Drazen

iUniverse, Inc.
Bloomington

A Gathering of Spirits: Japan's Ghost Story Tradition
From Folklore and Kabuki to Anime and Manga

Copyright © 2011 by Patrick Drazen

All rights reserved. No part of this book may be used or reproduced by any means, graphic, electronic, or mechanical, including photocopying, recording, taping or by any information storage retrieval system without the written permission of the publisher except in the case of brief quotations embodied in critical articles and reviews.

iUniverse books may be ordered through booksellers or by contacting:

iUniverse
1663 Liberty Drive
Bloomington, IN 47403
www.iuniverse.com
1-800-Authors (1-800-288-4677)

Because of the dynamic nature of the Internet, any web addresses or links contained in this book may have changed since publication and may no longer be valid. The views expressed in this work are solely those of the author and do not necessarily reflect the views of the publisher, and the publisher hereby disclaims any responsibility for them.

Any people depicted in stock imagery provided by Thinkstock are models, and such images are being used for illustrative purposes only.
Certain stock imagery © Thinkstock.

ISBN: 978-1-4620-2942-6 (pbk)
ISBN: 978-1-4620-2943-3 (ebk)

Printed in the United States of America

iUniverse rev. date:06/22/2011

TABLE OF CONTENTS

CHAPTER 1: TO GET THINGS STARTED

01. "Tell me . . ."

One night a policeman was walking through his usually quiet neighborhood. He was bored, he was almost asleep; his job had become almost automatic. He rounded one corner . . . and saw someone on the ground a few yards ahead. He ran forward, and saw what appeared to be a woman who had fallen. Maybe the heel of her shoe had given way, or maybe she was drunk; he didn't care. At least it was a break in the routine.

"Are you all right, ma'am?" he called out as he approached.

"Help me up, please," she said in a soft, very pretty voice. Her long hair hid her face. She reached a hand up; the policeman took her hand and helped her to her feet.

"Thank you," the woman said, raising her head. As she did so, the policeman was able to get a better look at her face . . . but instead he saw that she had no face. Where there should have been eyes, and a nose, and a mouth, there was nothing—just skin stretched smooth and blank as an egg.

The policeman fell back in shock and horror and ran up the street. He didn't even know where he was running to at first. After a minute, he saw the lights of a convenience store that stayed open

1

all night. He burst into the store, and blurted out to the older man behind the counter what had just happened to him.

The cashier looked at the policeman for a second, smiled, then said, "Tell me, officer; did she look . . . like . . . this?" The cashier waved his hand in front of his own face, and his features vanished, leaving skin stretched smooth and blank as an egg.

xxx

This ghost story, about an encounter with a nopperabou (a faceless ghost), was acted out in the 1994 Studio Ghibli animated movie known as *Ponpoko*[1]. It also appeared in print, in English, in 1904 in Lafcadio Hearn's influential ghost story anthology *Kwaidan*. In fact, this story goes back hundreds of years, and is part of Japan's long and rich spirit tradition. Stories about Japanese ghosts and other supernatural beings have been written, collected, adapted, reworked, and reinterpreted for centuries, and even the most modern ghost movies, manga (comics) and anime (animation) can refer back to ancient source material.

This book is loosely based on one of these grand and ghostly Japanese traditions, begun back in the Edo period[2]: the *hyaku*

---

[1]   To give the anime its full title, *Heisei Tanuki Gassen Ponpoko*, meaning the Heisei-Era Tanuki War Ponpoko—the last word is actually more of a sound effect.

There's also a comic twist on the nopperabou legend in Osamu Tezuka's manga *Janguru Taitei (King of the Jungle)*, which gave rise to the TV series *Kimba the White Lion*. In the manga, Leo, the son of Kimba, is exploring a human city dressed as a little girl, complete with curly blonde wig. When he loses the wig to a gust of wind, he hurriedly chases it and puts it back on—backwards. A passer-by looks at the base of the wig covering Leo's face, then runs off in terror yelling that he's just seen a nopperabou.

[2]   The Edo period lasted from 1603 to 1867; also called the Tokugawa period, since Japan's shogun for this period of over two centuries came from the Tokugawa family.

2

monogatari. Literally the phrase means "100 stories," but the assumption is that these are all ghost stories. Here's how to play: Gather some friends together one night, preferably a hot summer night, along with one hundred candles. Once all of the candles are lit, someone tells a ghost story. It can be short or long, historical or recent, frightening or humorous or morally instructive—as this book will show, Japanese ghost stories come in all sorts of flavors. When the first story ends, the storyteller blows out a candle. Then the next person tells a story, blows out a candle, and so on.

By the time the room is down to two or three lit candles, after several hours of ghost stories, everyone's nerves should be on edge. When the last person finishes the last story and blows out the last candle, plunging the room into blackness, some say that a ghost, invisible in the candlelight, will appear. Others suggest that the party-goers count off in the pitch-black room—and one extra voice will answer.

"My favorite thing about summer," writes Satsuki Igarashi, one of the cartoonists of the highly successful CLAMP manga collective, "is the ghost stories. . . . In fact, during summer breaks I would also watch a lot of afternoon TV, and the gossip shows often featured horror stories."[3] Unlike in America, where ghost stories are often told in the autumn around Halloween, ghost stories in Japan are associated with summer for several reasons, and we'll look at them in greater detail later. For now, let's just say a major reason is because of the weather; Japan, except for the northernmost island of Hokkaido, has a tropical or semi-tropical climate. The summers get very *mushi-atsui* (humid and hot), and ghost stories were found long ago to be an effective way to send much-needed chills up and down one's spine.

Prepare for a sampling of Japanese ghosts and spirits, from sources that include the world's oldest novel, the urban legends of contemporary Japanese schoolchildren, movies both classic and modern, anime, manga, and more. Some of the ghost stories will

---

[3]   Igarashi Satsuki, "Ghost stories," *NewType USA, Vol. 4,* 9 (September 2005), p. 70.

be actual ghost stories, designed to frighten and shock; sometimes, however, ghosts will appear in unlikely places—in romantic comedies, in sports anime, in domestic dramas, in school stories . . .

First, though, we have to understand the ground-rules for dealing with the reality of spirits in Japan, especially the fact that reality itself is divided into the human world and the spirit world.

CHAPTER 2: THAT'S THE SPIRIT

T. R. Reid described the years he and his family lived in Tokyo while he was Asian Bureau Chief for the Washington *Post* in his book *Confucius Lives Next Door*. The title referred not just to the sage of China who lived 500 years before Christ, but also to the next door neighbors of the Reids, who embodied so many Confucian virtues. They were an elderly couple, the Matsudas, and one day Mrs. Matsuda passed away at age 78. As Reid placed flowers on the makeshift altar that had been erected in the Matsuda living room, Mr. Matsuda turned to a photograph of his late wife and told it matter-of-factly, "Cho-Cho, it's Reid-san."[4]

It's tempting for a western reader in the 21st century to dismiss this scene as the sentimental gesture of an elderly widower. Doing this, however, misses the point. Mr. Matsuda wasn't being sentimental, or senile, or ironic. He spoke to the picture of his wife in order to communicate with the spirit of his late wife; nothing more, nothing less.

This motif pops up often in Japan's pop culture, and not always as practiced by elderly widowers. In one scene in the anime *Princess Nine*, a TV series about an elite girls' high school that creates a baseball team to challenge the boys' high schools, we see the girls' star pitcher, fifteen-year-old Ryo Hayakawa, stopping before going to school to tell her father what's been happening. It doesn't matter that her father's been dead for ten years; she still communicates with

---

4   Reid, T. R.   *Confucius Lives Next Door: What living in the East teaches us about living in the West.*   1999.   New York: Vintage/Random House, p. 90.

him through the Buddhist altar set up in the Hayakawa home (as it is in so many Japanese homes). In *Ouran High School Host Club*, the comic manga/anime by Bisco Hatori, heroine Haruhi Fujioka, another first-year high school student, consults with her dead mother via the altar in her apartment.

Similarly, in the romantic comedy manga *Ai Yori Aoshi* by Kou Fumizuki, and its anime version, the main character, Kaoru Hanabishi, has decided to take the girl he loves, Aoi-chan, to meet his mother. He picks up flowers, incense, and food, and takes them to a cemetery. He places everything in front of his mother's tombstone and matter-of-factly introduces Aoi to his mother as the girl who has come to mean everything in his life. Aoi-chan follows up on this, telling Kaoru's mother about her feelings for her son.

Kaoru, by the way, is a college junior majoring in pre-Law when we meet him; it's hard to imagine anyone more prosaic and less given to communing with spirits. Yet Kaoru and Ryo and Haruhi do not address their dead parents half-heartedly or ironically. They expect to be heard and understood in the next world.

This kind of spirit communication reflects Japan's unique spiritual heritage, which is a blend of two different faiths. First came Shinto, which literally means "the path of the gods." This animistic (based on spirits) religion has been traced back to at least the fifth century B. C. E. and has come to define Japan and its people. Shinto's creation mythology, the *Kojiki*, attributed the creation of the universe to two divine sibling gods, Izanagi and Izanami; they gave birth to, among other things, the sun goddess Amaterasu, who in turn was regarded as having created the Japanese people. For much of Japan's history, an article of faith in Shinto was that the line of Japanese emperors was descended from Amaterasu herself; this was abandoned only after Japan lost World War II and the American Occupation redefined the emperor as 100 per cent mortal.

Most important for this book, however, is Shinto's belief in kami, which can be translated as either "gods" or "spirits." It would be impossible to list all of the possible kami, since they cover all of creation; they are everywhere and in everything, making Shinto a literally all-encompassing religion. Some kami are guardian spirits of particular locations, from mountains and rivers to islands to vacant lots; some kami are associated with broader geographical areas or certain warrior clans; some kami are highly abstract, associated with the natural world or ideals such as beauty and even evil (Shinto could not imagine evil as having been the result of a separate creation).

This last type of association may be why the 1997 Studio Ghibli animated film *Mononoke-hime* (*Princess Mononoke*) was considered almost incomprehensible when it was dubbed into English as part of a deal to bring the anime of director Hayao Miyazaki to America. That deal never anticipated a film populated by giant boar kami, giant wolf kami, little potato-headed human-like kami, and the shishigami, the spirit that governs the entire natural world.

Complementing Shinto in Japan is its embrace of Buddhism; a majority of Japanese (84% according to one source) claim to believe in both religions at once. This is possible because the two faiths aren't mutually exclusive, and one point where they overlap is in the realm of the spirits.

Buddhism arrived in Japan by way of China, where a somewhat unorthodox form of Buddhism (unorthodox according to the traditional Buddhism of India, at any rate), known as Chan Buddhism, later traveled to Japan by way of Korea. With a slight linguistic shift, "Chan" became "Zen" in Japan. However, just as America can accommodate several forms of Christianity, Japan now houses several forms of Buddhism, ranging from the homespun Jodo Shinshu or Pure Land sect to the Soka Gakkai (whose liturgy at times seems a bit too close to show biz). Whatever the sect, Japanese Buddhists interpret Shinto in Buddhist terms and vice versa, with the assortment of buddhas and bodhisattvas (saints) viewed as another form of kami. This history hasn't always been one of peace and cooperation, and at times some Japanese Buddhist sects have been more militant than others, but in general Japanese Buddhists recognize the need for Shinto to underlie all aspects of Japanese society, providing a sense of history, identity, and continuity.

When it comes to the afterlife and the possibility of ghostly activity on earth, neither Shinto nor Buddhism claim a single authoritative answer. Shinto speaks of the "High Plain of Heaven" and of an unclean underworld, but doesn't go into much more detail than that. Buddhist interpretations of the afterlife vary from sect to sect and change over time, but among the Buddhist sects who preach an afterlife, they maintain that both heaven and hell are temporary. Spirits of people are born and die and are reborn on earth constantly, in a process leading ultimately to the purest of spirit, divorced from the temptations and corruptions of the physical world. Hell may be necessary to purge away some kinds of corruption, while Heaven may be a reward for work well done in one's past life, but the cycle still goes on.

Both Shinto and Buddhism recognize the place of honor given to one's ancestors, and encourage their veneration as, at the least, a matter of simple respect. It's also a practical consideration; if your ancestors didn't give birth to your parents, who gave birth to you, where would you be today? In Buddhist terms, this is part of karma, the recognition that everything that happens on earth was caused by certain events, and that every event has consequences. Your ancestors caused you to be born here and now, just as you will cause your descendants to be born; they in turn will regard you as an ancestor worthy of veneration.

In an atmosphere such as Japan's, in which natural spirits can even be found amid the skyscrapers of downtown Tokyo, and where many homes have their own Buddhist altar or Shinto "god-shelf," it should be no surprise that spirits are presumed to visit the human world. And when they come to visit from the afterlife, as they do every year, they come to party.

CHAPTER 3: SHALL WE DANCE

One principal reason that ghost stories in Japan are associated with summer is the annual summer celebration of the return of the spirits of the departed to earth. It's a holiday, complete with carnival atmosphere, refreshments, fireworks, music—and dancing. The centerpiece of the festival is the Bon Odori, a community dance.

02. My Mother, the Hungry Ghost

According to legend, Bon Odori originated when Maudgalyayana, a disciple of the Buddha, had a vision of his dead mother indulging her own selfishness in the Realm of Hungry Ghosts, gorging herself continuously but never satisfying her hunger.[5] (In this story, any food one touches in this cursed realm bursts into flame before it can be eaten.) Greatly disturbed, he went to the Buddha and asked how he could release his mother from her selfish attachment. The Buddha advised his disciple to perform a charitable act in memory of his mother. The disciple gave food to the poor and thus saw his mother's release from the Realm of Hungry Ghosts. He also began to see the many sacrifices that she had made for him in her life—sacrifices for which she had tried to compensate as a Hungry Ghost. Maudgalyayana, happy because of his mother's release after death and grateful for his mother's kindness toward him in life, danced with joy. From this dance of joy comes Bon Odori or the

---

[5]   We'll meet up with other Hungry Ghosts later in this book.

Bon Dance, a time in which the ancestors and their sacrifices are remembered and appreciated.[6]

Of course, the dead celebrated in Obon aren't exclusively parents or grandparents. Parents revisit dead children, and widows and widowers spend time again with dead spouses.[7]

Today Obon festival participants continue the old custom as they dance in traditional Japanese dress, including yukata (cotton kimono made for Japan's sweltering summers) and happi coats (short jackets). The dances may also include the use of fans, straw hats, and even local additions, such as castanets in southern California.

As the festival ends, in some places paper lanterns are painted with the names of the deceased; the lanterns are then set adrift in a river or seacoast,[8] to guide the ancestor back to the land of the dead until next year. Meanwhile, it's always possible to communicate with the deceased through praying at the altar that is still kept in many homes.

The Obon festival usually occurs in August, because it's supposed to coincide with the seventh day of the seventh month. So why August? August is the eighth month—of the Gregorian calendar. Until 1873, Japan used the Chinese lunar calendar, in which New Year's Day is movable, and falls during the thirty days after January 20, based on the first new moon after the sun enters Aquarius. However, as part of Japan's decision to modernize during the Meiji era (1868-1912), Japan adopted the medieval calendar created by Pope Gregory, even though lunar dates are sometimes still observed.

The "seven-seven" lunar date also coincides with a Chinese festival, commemorating the legendary Weaver, granddaughter of

---

[6]   http://www.scu.edu/diversity/bonodori.html

[7]   "Japanese fest offers bridge to ancestors." Shia Kapos, Special to the Tribune; *Chicago Tribune*; Jul 14, 2006; pg. 10.

[8]   Just as the ancient Greeks believed that the dead had to cross the River Styx, the old Japanese belief is that the dead have to cross the River Sanzu; hence the belief that spirits come and go to Obon by water. More later on the River Sanzu.

the King and Queen of Heaven, who had fallen in love with a mortal cowherd. They were transfigured into stars (known in modern astronomy as Altair and Vega), which from Earth seem close but are separated by the Milky Way and only able to draw close to each other on one day each year—the seventh day of the seventh month.[9] Hence the holiday's other name: the Star Festival, or Tanabata.

Much as early Christianity may have "borrowed" pagan festivals and made them over into "official" Church-sanctioned holidays, there is more than a coincidental similarity between the Chinese "Double Seven" holiday and the Japanese Buddhist Obon celebration. Both, after all, celebrate the very brief time each year that Heaven meets Earth, and those who are dead return to the land of the living—in spirit, at least. In Japan, at any rate, that time is summer, and consequently a lot of ghost stories take place during the warm weather, when spirits are presumed to be traveling the land.

xxx

For an example of what can go wrong if the proper rites aren't observed, look at *Bleach*, a manga by Noriaki "Tite" Kubo, which inspired an anime popular enough to inspire in turn (among other spinoffs) a live musical. Its teenaged hero, Ichigo Kurosaki, sees dead people, and that's the opening hook that gets him involved with the Soul Society, but all the subsequent business of Hollows and Reapers are basically window dressing. This is a case of using a ghost story to communicate to the audience what is considered important by the larger society—in this case, by Japanese society.

---

[9]   http://www.cctv.com/english/TouchChina/School/ Culture/20020725/100056.html

03. Don't forget me

Look at the story-arc in *Bleach* involving Sora and Orihime. First of all, if you're Japanese, the name Orihime is loaded. I mentioned Obon commemorating the one day a year when the mortal who loved a goddess could be with her, while they spend the rest of the year as stars in the sky separated by the Milky Way. The goddess's name in Japan was Orihime, so, of all the names that the modern schoolgirl character could have been given, this was a meaningful choice.

Sora was her older brother until he was killed in a hit-and-run. Orihime would pray for his soul daily at the Buddhist altar in their home. This gave Sora peace, knowing that she still remembered him. Gradually, though, there were other demands on Orihime's time, her prayers were less consistent, and Sora became jealous, eventually transforming into a serpentine monster. It was only when Orihime finally told her brother that she still cared for him, even though they had quarreled on his last day on earth, that—without any intervention from Ichigo or anyone from the Soul Society—Sora was able to abandon his jealousy and stop being a monster. This isn't even a subtle message; it reminds the audience not to abandon the old ways, since the spirits of the dead could take offense and cause problems in this world.

xxx

Rumiko Takahashi uses an Obon celebration in her romantic comedy manga *Mezon Ikkoku* to put a comic twist on the legend of Okiku and the plates (we'll hear more about this famous ghost in a later chapter).

An early episode of *Pokemon* has the main character (Ash in America, Satoshi in Japan) hang around home long enough to attend a local festival. However, it's more than just a festival. To those in the know, it's clearly an Obon dance.

Akachan to Boku, a manga by Marimo Ragawa published in English as *Baby and Me*, is an unlikely manga whose audience is teenaged girls, since there's hardly a female character in it that isn't in nursery school. The series found a home in Japan in *Hana to Yume* (*Flowers and Dreams*), a girls' manga magazine, and has been animated for television by Studio Pierrot in a rare Japanese-Italian co-production. The English version of the manga appeared in *Shojo Beat* magazine and in paperback anthologies published by VIZ.

It's the story of the Enoki family: widowed salaryman Harumi Enoki, his older son (ten years old when the series starts) Takuya, and Takuya's toddler brother Minoru. Still living in the shadow of the death of Harumi's wife, they muddle through as best they can. The focus is on Takuya, growing up and taking care of his baby brother, being something of a surrogate mother as well as a big brother.

Even this idyllic family tale isn't ghost-free; in this case, the ghost is not that of the boys' late mother. While the family is on summer vacation, they spend a weekend at an old traditional inn with an *onsen* (hot springs). But this story involves a special kind of ghost; we'll look at it later.

04. "Don't shoot!"

The *Patlabor* anime series started in 1988, with a series of direct-to-video episodes created by a group that included manga artist Masami Yuuki and anime director Mamoru Oshii. The title is a compressed version of the words "patrol labor," which refers to the machine suits worn by members of a special police unit in the future.

A later broadcast anime series based one episode on stories of the haunting of a rural police training camp, and set that episode in the summer, when other trainees would be away on break and the one remaining squad would have to cope with a large, empty facility. Ghostly things start happening that seem to match up with legends about a training mishap a few years earlier. It's said that cadets were sparring, while wearing the Patlabor suits (think of the machine that Ripley wore in *Aliens*, except twenty feet tall). One Patlabor was knocked down, and its weapon went off accidentally. Even though it was an oversized paintball gun, the story goes that the pellet was enough to kill a spectator, a beautiful young woman. Her ghost is seen through windows, and is heard to say, "Don't shoot!" In addition, the bath (the size of a small swimming pool) turns red; it looks like blood, but later it's found to have the chemical composition of the dye used in paintballs.

In the end, the stories about the dead girl turn out to be just that: stories. The unit's officers had devised the elaborate scheme about a ghost as a way to impress the troops, who were getting over-eager and therefore careless, with the need to be more cautious when using their suits. It certainly worked: getting the troops caught up in unearthly voices and inexplicable mysteries certainly made a deeper impression than any number of safety lectures would have.

xxx

Not every attempt to create a ghost works so well. Early in the popular anime series *Fullmetal Alchemist*, based on a manga by Hiromu Arakawa, the Elric brothers run into an apparent case of a cemetery haunting, on a holiday similar to Obon.

05. Blue Roses

Early in their search for the Philosopher's Stone, the legendary amplifier of alchemical processes, Edward Elric (who lost two limbs to alchemy) and his younger brother Alphonse (who lost his entire body, and whose soul is now anchored in a suit of armor) traveled to a village in search of Majihal, an alchemist knowledgeable about the Philosopher's Stone. They arrive at the village on the eve of a festival celebrating the dead. However, this village has some supernatural problems. Decades ago, Karin, a beautiful woman from a neighboring village famous for cultivating a rare strain of blue roses, tried to drive a cart down a washed-out road and slid to her death. Her ghost (or perhaps zombie) has recently been seen near the town cemetery. The truth is actually less hopeful for the Elric brothers. Majihal has had no luck in bringing Karin's spirit back; he had been trying to do so in order to embed it in the life-sized dolls he had built to commemorate Karin and her beauty; people see these dolls near the cemetery at night. The irony was that alchemy couldn't retrieve Karin's spirit anyway, because Karin is alive. She was not killed in the carriage accident years before but suffered a memory loss. Majihal failed to recognize her even though she was alive and nearby, because she had aged and was no longer the youthful beauty he had fallen in love with. Majihal attempted to kill Ed for revealing these inconvenient truths, but the weapon slipped and killed Majihal instead.

xxx

Rumiko Takahashi has long been meticulous in structuring not only her plotlines, but also in dressing the sets, with cues referring to the time of year as well as events meaningful to the Japanese psyche. These hints are often overlooked in the west, but are especially important to understanding the ghostly plot of one episode of the anime version of her popular manga *InuYasha,* "Soul Piper & the Mischievous Little Soul".

06. "I'm running away!"

During this episode of a series which mostly takes place in Japan's feudal past, high school student Kagome Higurashi and the dog-demon Inuyasha are in the modern world for a while during the summer. Kagome's little brother Sota is seen carrying a big "Get Well" present. One of his school friends, a boy named Satoru, was caught in an apartment fire six months ago but is still comatose and hasn't fully recovered from smoke inhalation. That's bad enough, but medical equipment in his hospital room keeps breaking down and his school friends are afraid to visit him because they think he is cursed somehow. Not one to believe in curses (even though he's on a first-name basis with the demon Inuyasha), Sota wants to visit Satoru, but he isn't old enough to ride the train by himself; Kagome agrees to take him after school.

While they are at the hospital, Kagome notices a spooky little girl dressed in a down vest (unusual clothing for summer) lurking around the hospital. Earlier, the same girl was seen attacking a group of children playing with fireworks. Fireworks may mean Independence Day in the United States, but in Japan they carry a very different, specific meaning: summer festivals and Obon.

Kagome tries to befriend the little girl, but the child, whose name is Mayu, doesn't want anything to do with her. When they reach Satoru's room, his fatigued single mother is sitting by his side. After a short visit, the equipment in the room starts to malfunction again. Kagome notices that the same little girl is kicking the machines and pulling the cords, but no one else in the room can see her. But there's also a more dangerous omen: the Tatari-mokke, a ball-shaped cat head with giant eyes, a big mouth and a long fox tail is floating outside the window.

We find out that the little girl Mayu is the ghost of Satoru's sister. She was a petulant child and had a fight with her mother just before the fire six months earlier. It was winter and they were fighting because the little girl would leave her mittens and scarf on the space heater to dry them off and keep them warm (which she had been warned was a fire hazard). Sure enough, later that day the apartment caught on fire because of the mittens on the space heater. Mom came in and saved the little brother, but didn't see that Mayu was hiding in the closet (and subsequently burned to death). Because the girl told her mother during their argument that she would "run away", which usually meant staying at a friend's house, Mom thought that the girl was out of the apartment.

The little girl thinks that "Mom loved brother, but didn't love me, so she left me in the closet to die." She also thinks that by killing her little brother, she'll be able to get back at her mom. This puts her in the long-standing tradition of a ghost powered by resentment (tatari) and a desire for vengeance, not a state that should be allowed to continue. The Tatari-mokke is a spirit that has come to collect her and take her to the afterlife once she finally turns her back on her attempts to kill her brother. Time, however, is running out for Mayu; as long as the Tatari-mokke's eyes are closed, Mayu stays a ghost on Earth trying to kill her brother; after enough time, or if she succeeds, the eyes will open and the Tatari-mokke will convey her soul to Hell. Fortunately, Mayu is made to understand by Kagome that her vengeful actions are a bad idea, causing trouble for her family in the real world and for herself in the spirit world.

Even though Kagome has never shown any official prowess as a medium, we understand why she can see and communicate with the ghost. Her family is the hereditary keepers of a Shinto temple where her grandfather is a priest. The temple is home to a gigantic tree, which in many stories is enough to make it a place of great spiritual power. The ancient well which she uses to communicate with the past is on the temple grounds. She also, thanks to having been born the reincarnation of an ancient miko (Shinto temple maiden) named Kikyo (which leads to her meeting Inuyasha), has the ability to sense the fragments of the main magical gimmick of the story, an enchanted gem called the Shikon (Four Souls) Jewel. In this case, although Kagome puts her own life and soul on the line by entering the burned-out apartment to confront Mayu, she tells the child that her mother still loves her and always has, and wants to see Mayu's spirit one last time. This is one example out of many in manga and anime that the most awesome superpowers of western heroes are often eclipsed by the compassion and kindness in the heart of a teenaged Japanese girl.

The final scene, in which Mayu bids farewell to Kagome before ascending to heaven and Becoming One with the Cosmos, takes place one week after Mayu's spirit is reconciled with her mother. On the day her brother Satoru is released from hospital, Mayu's spirit appears to Kagome; this involves an important costume change. We see her in a lovely summer yukata, the kind worn to a Bon festival. This is the most blatant cue to the audience, along with the closed eyes and smiling face of the Tatari-mokke, that Mayu has found peace.

XXX

We're getting a bit ahead of ourselves, however. There are still a lot of ghosts to cover in ancient Japan, and they're worth mentioning because, as we've already seen, many of them manage to stay around even into the 21st century. But the Tatari-mokke raises the issue that, to get safely from this world to the next world, one needs a guide.

CHAPTER 4: "I'LL BE YOUR GUIDE"

Botan—*Yuyu Hakusho*

Yoshihiro Togashi's manga *Yuyu Hakusho* (a name that can mean "Poltergeist White Paper") starts with the death of the hero: a juvenile delinquent named Yusuke Urameshi.[10] A disrespectful brawler who seldom shows up for school, Yusuke made the mistake of trying to stop a toddler from playing in traffic; the car that almost hit the child killed Yusuke instead.

Once his spirit realizes what's happened, he meets the unusually chipper Botan. Riding the oar of a boat as if it were a witch's broom, she tells Yusuke that she'll be his guide to the underworld. Not permanently; it seems that this punk's lone act of consideration has disrupted the afterlife to the point that they weren't ready for him. He therefore had the option of taking a test to come back to life. But, by going directly to Hell with Botan (whose name means the peony flower), they bypass the River Sanzu.

According to Japanese tales of the afterlife, the River Sanzu runs between this world and the next. There are three ways to cross (since "san" in Japanese means three). People with many dire sins on their souls have to swim across the deepest part of the river, which also contains nests of snakes; those with fewer sins have to cope with rapids. The sinless can cross on a solid stone bridge. This

---

10   Urameshii (with an extra "i" at the end) is a Japanese adjective; ghosts supposedly can often be heard moaning "Urameshii" (meaning, bitter or resentful, following the idea that ghosts stay alive, as it were, because of some slight or grudge.)

three-crossing arrangement sensibly takes into account that people are seldom purely good or purely evil.

xxx

Takuto and Meroko—*Full Moon-wo Sagashite*
Arina Tanemura's 2001 shojo manga *Full Moon-wo Sagashite* (*Looking for the Full Moon*) features a twelve-year-old girl, Mitsuki Koyama, who has developed a tumor in her throat. This makes it painful to sing, and singing is the one dream of her young life. (The dream is complicated by the fact that Mitsuki lives with her maternal grandmother, who never stops reminding her that she despises music in general as well as what it did to her daughter, Mitsuki's mother.)

When Mitsuki finds out that she only has a year to live, she doesn't hear the news from her doctor, but from the Angels of Death, Pediatrics Division. These spirit guides, a guy named Takuto and a girl named Meroko who in life had committed suicide, look like teenagers, move through walls, and are invisible to everyone else except as, respectively, a stuffed cat and a stuffed rabbit.

xxx

A story in the CLAMP manga *xxxHolic* doesn't seem to start out as a ghost story; true ghost stories actually occur rather rarely in this manga/anime series. But this *kaidan* is more than just a modern example of traditional beliefs. Brought from the distant past successfully to the 21st century, it achieves many of its chills in the way it sneaks up on the audience. As an added bonus, Watanuki, hapless assistant to the self-described witch Yuko, stops being his usual whining dramatic self when it really matters.

07. The Red Hydrangea

One rainy day, the main quartet of the story—Yuko the witch, Watanuki, the cute but mysterious Himawari, and the stolid Domeki—receive a mysterious request from a non-human client. The adolescent-looking girl with the umbrella is actually an *ame-warashi*, a rain spirit. When such a character appeared in Rumiko Takahashi's *Urusei Yatsura*, she was a playful child in kimono, using a giant leaf as an umbrella. Here, she has blue-tinted hair in the manga (red in the anime), a parasol, a western dress in the style known as "Lolita Goth", and a haughty disdain for humans. The spirit explains that she needs Watanuki and Domeki to perform an unspecified service; Himawari contributes two hair ribbons to the mission, and the boys follow the *ame-warashi* to a park.

The spirit leads the boys to a hydrangea bush in the park, and they immediately realize that something is unnatural. The bush is as large as a tree, and, more important, the hydrangea is showing blood-red flowers; hydrangea flowers are blue, pink, white, but never blood-red. Watanuki, holding one of the ribbons, examines the bush, but doesn't see a tendril of the hydrangea reaching out toward him, wrapping itself around his ankle, and pulling him into the plant.

What he finds there is a twilit wasteland with no markers, a foul stench, and a crying little girl who looks to be about six years old. The little girl doesn't want to go back home; tearfully she explains that she's gotten dirty and gross and nobody will accept her. Watanuki at first walks with the girl toward the source of the foul odor, which still can't be seen. A disembodied chorus of voices warns them both not to go there. At this point, a ribbon descends from above: Himawari's other ribbon, which was given to Domeki. Watanuki holds up his ribbon with one hand, and holds the little girl's hand with the other. They are pulled up and up—

Watanuki awakens at the edge of the hydrangea bush. He thought his encounter with the little girl had only taken minutes; from Domeki's point of view, ten hours had passed. Watanuki then looks at the little girl's hand, and finds that he is holding the shriveled, skeletal hand of a child's corpse.

xxx

Yuko explains that the child disappeared almost a year ago; her corpse had lain under the hydrangea during that time. This echoes the traditional Japanese belief stated later in this book: that corpses were a source of pollution. This also accounted for the unnatural growth and blood-red flowers of the hydrangea. Watanuki and the girl had been walking toward the border between the world and the after-life; specifically, to the land of those who suffered and were murdered. This accounted for the stench. If Watanuki had accompanied the girl there, he would have died; the voices that tried to stop them were the hydrangea. However, the girl's body had not yet been discovered, and (another recurring Japanese theme) her bones had to be found so that her soul could be put right. With the discovery of her body, the proper rites could be performed and her soul could then pass over.

There's one other bit of good news in this episode: Watanuki, who normally would freak out when he realized the identity of the girl and saw he was holding hands with a skeleton, kept his composure and kept his promise to the little girl. His last words to her were, "I'm very proud of you." It seems he's finally maturing as well.

The point of this explanation, and part of the point of this book, is that the Japanese audience for whom *xxxHolic* was created would already know all of this. A western audience would still be able to enjoy the chills of this story, and all of the others, but might not understand all of the symbols and details.

xxx

Rinne

For more than three decades, Rumiko Takahashi has reigned as one of the giants of manga. Beginning with *Urusei Yatsura*, with Japan invaded by boorish, obnoxious, and (in the case of Lum, sexy) space aliens, Takahashi has been one of the most consistently successful manga artists. Her career moved from strength to strength, including the Gothic chills of the *Mermaid* stories, the stellar romantic comedy *Mezon Ikkoku* and the gender-warping farce *Ranma ½*. Nobody would have blamed her if she retired after the completion of her magnum opus *InuYasha*, with more than three decades of influential and popular manga to her credit. However, she just rolled into another title, *Kyoukai no Rinne*, which, conveniently for this book, is solidly (and humorously) in Japan's ghost tradition.

The ghost of the title, Rinne Rokudo, is a guide shepherding spirits from the real world to the spirit world. He looks like a high school student—to whoever can see him. At first, this is limited to one student, whose involvement with the ghost and his tasks just gets deeper and funnier. We'll examine this manga later on.

xxx

08. "The afterlife sure seems to have a lot of rules."

Omukae desu, a five-volume manga by Meca Tanaka, takes a gently humorous approach to the problem of spirits who refuse to cross over when their time comes. Madoka Tsutsumi, a high school student studying for the college entrance exams, witnesses an argument one day between two people: another young guy named Nabeshima[11] and old Mr. Baba, whose house is a few doors away. However, Nabeshima is dressed in a giant pink bunny suit, while the last time Madoka saw Mr. Baba was at the old man's wake. Yes, once again, a student can see dead people.

---

[11] Nabeshima is a name of a family renowned for their pottery; however, the Nabeshima clan was also afflicted in legend by a demonic cat. See the "Cats and Dogs" chapter for the story of the "Vampire Cat of Nabeshima."

Nabeshima complains that, while "usually dead people can find their own way to the other side," he's got far too much work delivering spirits to the afterlife (actually shlepping them on the back of a motor scooter) to spend time on the stubborn ones who simply refuse to go. He offers a bargain to Tsutsumi: even though Nabeshima already has two assistants (a living co-ed named Aguma and a ghostly young girl named Yuzuko), Motoka can help out as a temp worker (a dilemma faced by many Japanese college students: finding a part-time job to make ends meet) by coaxing reluctant spirits to leave the world of the living, and he'll get paid in the afterlife. The payment is described as "a free trip to Heaven;" once he agrees, Nabeshima starts calling Tsutsumi "En-chan," since the kanji for his name Motoka can also be pronounced "En," and "En" is Japanese for "karma."

Back to old Mister Baba. His insistence on staying behind is simple: his only child, a daughter, is pregnant and almost due, he wants to see the child, but the spirits of the dead aren't supposed to be near a child when it's born, perhaps to avoid interfering with its own soul. In any case, he can't get to the maternity ward without a body, so Tsutsumi lets Mr. Baba use his body to view the child, as well as giving him a vote in naming the child.

09. The Ring

Megu Koike died as a little old lady, but has stayed rooted to one spot on earth and refuses to budge; getting her to leave is Tsutsumi's job. Tsutsumi, Yuzuko and the curiously silent Aguma were told to "get your butts in gear" and help Koike look for a lost ring on a riverbank. They had until sunset to find this one token that mattered to Koike.

Aguma basically sat there and stared into space, not helping to look at all. Tsutsumi asks the old lady's ghost why she had the precious ring in her pocket rather than on her finger. She admitted that the ring was a gift from someone she loved in her youth, before she got married to someone else. Back in the day, she was a servant in a wealthy family's house, and she fell in love with the young son of the family. Besides being of separate classes, which would have ruled out a romance between them, the young man was in poor health, and died shortly after Koike left their employ. First, however, he gave her a ring as a token of a love that could never bear fruit.

This triggers an outburst from Aguma. She has learned that Nabeshima isn't on this job because he's put in for a transfer to a higher-ranking job in the afterlife, and she's furious. "What am I, a bug? I don't even rate a goodbye?! All I can do now is hate him with a passion! The next time I see him, I'm gonna punch him in the nose!" When Nabeshima shows up, however, having decided not to get the transfer, Aguma hugs him rather than slugs him. "This is all I can do," the reader hears her say; "I don't know what's going to happen in the future. All I need is now." This reflects Koike's own slightly mixed emotions as she prepares to rejoin her husband in the afterlife. When asked why she's going to be with her husband when she loved the young master, Koike scoffs, "My husband kept me happy for fifty years; thanks to him, I had only one regret." In fact, she lost the ring while playing on the riverbank with her grandchildren. Just because she didn't get the romance she wanted didn't deprive her of a lifetime of happiness. Life, it seems, is more complicated than we like to think.

CHAPTER 5: A LIKELY STORY

Folktales and legends in Japan—about ghosts or anything else—are a major part of that country's literature. The foundation for these stories is a group of 45 collections, written mostly around the years 1100 and 1200 C. E., although some other major collections are hundreds of years older or younger.

The subject matter of these tales is literally universal. Some stories came to Japan from China or India; others are meant to illustrate Buddhist teachings; still others illustrate small or large events at the royal court. As time and history progress, the emphasis on some subjects grows or declines; the more modern the story, for example, the more likely it is to talk about farming.

While the stories touched on a wide range of activities, those who collected and wrote down these stories were from Japan's upper classes, since they had both the education in Chinese literary classics and the leisure time to set the stories down with the proper amount of style and grace. If there was one major difference between the legends of Japan and the stories of Greek fable-teller Aesop or the tales collected by Jakob and Wilhelm Grimm, it is this: the Japanese stories were presumed to be absolutely true; at the very least, they had to appear to be true. Many of the Japanese stories, therefore, go into great detail in describing the time or place in which they happened, no matter how outrageous the events of the story may seem to the modern reader.

The literary style of the original stories varied, with some of the tales told in proper, very serious traditional Chinese and others in more conversational Japanese (in those days, an educated courtier was expected to know both languages). Beyond that, the person who gathered and wrote down the stories (these collectors are almost all anonymous) was expected to edit and shape the stories for maximum effect, making funny stories funnier, making pathetic stories more pathetic, highlighting horror or devotion as needed.

xxx

Looking just at tales of Japanese ghosts, their stories can be put into several groups. These would include dealing with the corpse of a dead person, respecting the spirit that inhabited a body to stop it becoming a vengeful ghost, or pacifying a ghost of someone who died violently or in emotional turmoil. In some extreme cases, this would involve the change of a human ghost into a god.

Following the death of a person, the corpse traditionally was considered a source of pollution and had to be disposed of properly. Generally this meant cremation, but other methods included burying the body or, at least, hiding it in a cave or even an abandoned building.

10. The Neglected Wife

Did properly dealing with a corpse make a difference? Consider this story from the *Konjaku monogatari shuu* (*Tales of times now past*, generally just called the *Konjaku*), written around the year 1100. It's the story of a poor man living in Kyoto with his devoted young wife. They couldn't make ends meet until the man learned that an acquaintance of his had been named governor of a distant province. He went to his acquaintance in search of a position and was hired. But, because the province was so far away, he left his wife behind.

He missed her (although not so much that it stopped him from taking up with another woman). Finally the governor's term of office ended, and the man returned to his wife in Kyoto, arriving at night.

The house he returned to was in ruins, but his wife was still there, and she joyously welcomed him back. They spoke of his life in the faraway province, until they finally fell asleep near dawn, with the husband vowing to use the money he had earned to make everything right by his neglected wife.

When he awoke, he beheld the woman in his arms—except that he was holding a corpse, little more than skin stretched over a skeleton. In a panic, he ran to the house next door and asked what had happened.

"She took sick when her husband left," the neighbor said, "and died a few months ago. She had no friends or family to dispose of the body, so it's been there all this time. Everyone in town is afraid to go near the place."

xxx

That story appears in several different forms, including its retelling by Lafcadio Hearn in the book *Kwaidan* and the film of the same name; not just because it's a memorable way to creep out one's audience, but because it reminds its audience of something of vital importance to the Japanese soul. Obligation to the ancestors starts early and extends beyond the grave—and yet the grave itself is a necessary part of the equation. In episode 45 of the *Shaman King* manga by Hiroyuki Takei, hero Yoh Asakura confronts Faust VIII, a descendant of the western Dr. Faustus, who has tried to keep his murdered wife alive through magic. "Everyone dies, eventually," Yoh tells Faust. "That's what makes life precious. If you conquer death, will life still have value?"[12] (vol. 6, p. 23)

---

[12]   Yoh confronts Faust in "Chokohama Cemetery" (a thinly-disguised Yokohama Cemetery; see later), one of the few western-style

Respect for the bones of the deceased is part of the traditional Buddhist burial rite, which is why this next story is no less shocking to the Japanese than the story of the man from Kyoto sleeping with his wife's corpse. The kicker here: whether one believes the above story or not, this next story is absolutely true.

11. Barefoot Gen—His Mother's Bones

This is the story of an eight-year-old boy who lived with his family in the city of Hiroshima. On August 6, 1945 he was on his way to school when a single airplane dropped a single bomb over the city. Within a minute, everything had changed: wooden buildings burst into flame, concrete buildings were reduced to rubble and twisted metal, trolley cars were shoved off of their tracks. Some people were vaporized where they stood by the use of the world's first atomic weapon. That day, some 55,000 people were killed at once; an equal number had to wait for the end, sometimes for years, while radiation devoured their bodies. The boy's mother survived the blast, like her son, and lived to see her son grow up, get married, and start a career. When she died, everyone realized how sick the bomb had left her.

For this story to carry its full meaning, the reader first must understand the Japanese Buddhist funeral. Once the body is cremated, the ashes are not merely dumped into an urn. The family members take chopsticks and pick the largest bone fragments out of the ashes, passing them from person to person so that each has a chance to pay final respects. The last bones to go into the urn are those of the skull; even a corpse is allowed to have some dignity at the end, and not be buried "upside-down."

When the boy's mother was cremated, however, all that came out of the oven was a layer of fine ash, with no bone fragments at all. The mortuary worker explained that he'd seen this often among

---

cemeteries in Japan, where bodies are interred in coffins rather than being cremated.

those who'd lived through the atomic bombing; low-level radiation sickness gradually weakened the bones so that they were consumed by the fire.

The now-grown-up boy, however, was saddened and angry and horrified. He could not pay his final respects to his mother, since her bones were gone. In his anger and sorrow, he decided to use his career to speak out against the evils of atomic warfare that had prevented him, and so many others, from paying respects to their ancestors. The boy kept his promise, growing up to be manga artist Keiji Nakazawa, whose magnum opus was *Hadashi no Gen (Barefoot Gen)*, a semi-autobiographical account of his life in Hiroshima before and after the atomic bomb.

xxx

Of the several types of Japanese ghosts, the best-known and most easily understood is the jibakurei, a spirit who died violently or in emotional distress, which tied the ghost down to one location. The poor wife above whose husband abandoned her to take a job in a distant province is actually a fairly benign example; we'll meet many others, especially in modern tales created for manga or the movies. These spirits include the woman who threw herself down a well in grief over finding her child dead (in the manga *Ghost Hunt*), the psychic girl who was thrown down a well by her own father (in the movie *Ringu*), the dead servant Okiku whose ghostly voice can still be heard coming from the bottom of a well, and a student who died in a storm while trying to protect her sister's garden (from the manga and anime *Negima!*).

Here are a couple of stories of jibakurei. First, from the *Konjaku,* is a classic example of a sudden and violent death:

12. A Bolt of Lightning

Long before Kyoto was built, an armed soldier was going along on horseback when a fierce thunderstorm suddenly came up. The rider decided to take shelter under a very tall pine tree. However, a lightning bolt hit the tree, splitting it in two. It also split the rider and his horse in two, turning the rider into a ghost.

Since that time, the city of Kyoto grew around the spot, but, if anyone built a building on the spot where the soldier was hit by lightning, awful things usually happened. You can find the place north of Third Avenue and east of the East Tooin Palace. The building there now is called Demon Hall.

xxx

The next story appears in the *Uji shuui monogatari* (*A later collection of Uji tales*)[13], written in the early 1200s. Like the previous story, it tells you almost exactly where to find the haunted house at the center of the tale, as if daring the listener to go inside.

13. Attached to the House

The story is told of a great house near the intersection of Takatsuji and Muromachi streets in Kyoto. The woman who inherited the house from her father lived there with two servants, who were also sisters. The elder sister was married and lived with her husband; the younger entertained guests in her room at the front of the house's west wing.

---

[13]   Uji was a resort town just south of Kyoto, on the banks of the Uji River. Long famous for cultivating green tea, Uji is also the location for the final chapters of Lady Murasaki's *Genji Monogatari* (*The Tale of Genji*), which we'll encounter in chapter 9

The younger sister fell ill and died when she was only twenty-seven years old. They left her body in her room while the older sister and the rest of the household figured out what to do with it. They decided to take the body to the crematory at Toribeno. They put the body in a coffin, put the lid on the coffin, then loaded the coffin onto a carriage.

When they got to the crematory, they noticed that the lid on the coffin was crooked, and that the coffin seemed lighter. This was because there was no body inside it! They retraced their steps, and there was the younger sister's body, in her old room.

The mourners talked all night about what to do, and finally decided to try again to cremate the body. Early the next day they put the body into the coffin, put the lid on the coffin again, then waited to see what would happen. By sunset, though, they were truly frightened to see that the body was out of the coffin and back in the younger sister's room. They simply couldn't move it.

One frustrated mourner scolded the body: "This is what you want? You like it here? Then we'll leave you here!"

They took up the floor of the front room, dug a hole, and lowered the younger sister into it. They filled in the hole, leaving a large mound. Then everyone moved out of the house, since nobody wanted to stay there with the corpse of the sister. The house fell into ruin and eventually disappeared, but nobody lived anywhere near the mound. Terrible things happened to anybody who lived near it. After about fifty years, somebody built a shrine over the mound, and they say that the shrine is still there.

xxx

There are two things to note about this story. As said above, the younger sister's spirit is rooted to the spot where she died, even though there wasn't any violent trauma as with the soldier struck by lightning. The story did note, however, that, although the younger sister was unmarried and had no consistent lover, she did entertain "occasional, casual visitors." Perhaps it was memories of pleasure, rather than pain, that kept her attached to that place.

Second, we are reminded that there is a way to deal even with persistent spirits: perform a good work of some kind. Recall the disciple of the Buddha who was advised to perform good works to free the spirit of his mother from the realm of the Hungry Ghosts. Of course, you could also be aggressive about it and recruit an exorcist to deal with the spirit. Just be sure that the spiritualist you hire is strong enough to deal with the spirit, because it could turn into quite a struggle. In any event, one thing that you seldom hear in Japan, even in the 21st century, is that "there's no such thing as ghosts." Most Japanese know better.

xxx

14. The Hungry Ghost

The nature of compassion, especially in Buddhism, is to reject hatred, disgust or revulsion, as they get in the way of enlightenment. This is the case in a story from *Kwaidan* by Lafcadio Hearn; the story is titled "Jikininki," which means "man-eating spirit."

This story is set in Mino province, and tells of a Zen monk named Musou Kokushi, who lost his way in the mountains while on a pilgrimage. He continued to wander aimlessly until, just at sunset, he saw a small hut on top of a hill. He recognized it as an anjitsu, a hermitage just big enough for one person, where a Buddhist monk could pass the night in solitude.

When he got there, however, he found that the hermitage was already occupied by an elderly, fierce-looking priest. Still, Musou asked if he could stay there for the night; the old priest harshly told Musou "no," but directed him toward a small farming village in the next valley. Musou soon found a group of five or six houses and asked for the headman of the village. He was shown to a room in one of the houses, and was given food and bedding. Exhausted by his travels, he went to sleep early that night, but was awakened just before midnight by sounds of crying. A young man with a lantern came into the room, and told the monk that the young man who stood before him was formerly the family's eldest son; now, he was head of the household, for his father had died shortly before the monk had arrived. Now, according to the custom of that village, everyone would leave before midnight and not return until sunrise. "Strange things happen in a house with a corpse," the monk was told. Musou was not afraid of spirits and said that he would keep watch through the night. The young man asked him to report on whatever happened; then the family left the village.

Musou recited the funeral service for the deceased father, and sat in meditation with the corpse. In the depth of the night, as he sat, Musou saw something that made no noise and had almost no physical form. This large shadowy thing approached the head of the corpse and began to swallow it, burial robes and all. It also devoured the offerings left with the corpse; then, it vanished as quietly as it had come.

In the morning, Musou told the others what he had seen. None of the villagers were surprised about what happened to the corpse; it had been happening for many years. Then Musou asked, "Why don't you have the old priest perform rites for the dead?"

"What old priest?"

"The one who lives in the hermitage on the hillside."

"What hermitage? No priest has lived near here for years."

Musou now understood everything. He made his way back to the hermitage where he had been so rudely treated by the elderly priest; this time, though, the priest invited him in, apologizing profusely.

"There's no need to apologize. I found the village and was well received by them."

"No, I apologize for letting you see me as I truly am. I am not a priest, although I was one many years ago. I was the only priest in this part of the country, and I was kept very busy performing funeral rites. But, while I performed the rites, my heart was not in them; I would think about the food or clothing I would receive in payment. When I died, I was instantly reborn as a Hungry Ghost, as you saw last night. I beg you to perform a service of blessing for me, so that with your prayers I may finally escape this existence."

Before Musou could reply, the priest and the hermitage vanished, and Musou found himself in the tall grass, kneeling beside what seemed to be the tomb of a monk.

xxx

Some ghosts seem especially real, since they're based on figures from Japanese history. One of the favorite subjects seems to be warlord Oda Nobunaga, who ruled Japan in the late 1500s; his wars of conquest went a long way toward forging the modern nation of Japan. Whether that's a good or a bad thing depends on one's point of view.

The 2002 anime series *Mirage of Blaze*, based on a manga by Kiwabara Mizuna, is a combination ghost story and history lesson (and a story that walks up to the edge of the Boy Love genre without actually jumping in), since its mostly male, present day bishounen (pretty-boy) cast is in the middle of re-enacting one of the major disputes of Japanese history: the 16th century conflict between Oda Nobunaga and his trusted general Mitsuhide.

15. Remembering Mother

Walt Whitman said that, if you told history the right way, there'd be no need for romance novels. Certainly, the story of Nobunaga and Mitsuhide is one of the most memorable in any national history. Through an amazing act of callous disregard, Nobunaga used Mitsuhide's mother as a hostage during negotiations with the enemy, but broke his word and killed the negotiators from the opposite side. In behaving this way he allowed Mitsuhide's mother to be killed in exchange. Mitsuhide hid his outrage, bided his time, and, when his troops were later called upon to fight for Nobunaga, instead turned against him.

This TV series gave rise to a sequel OAV series: *Mirage of Blaze: Rebels of the River's Edge*. This series also looks to early Japanese history through reincarnations (some of which are gender-bending) of some of its major figures; in this case, members of the Houjou clan of the mid-1500s, who continue battling for power hundreds of years after their death.

16. The Return of Nobunaga

One of the few anime of Takashi Shiina's manga *GS Mikami* to come to the United States featured Oda Nobunaga as the villain. As it explains later in this book, ghosts do not always maintain their own identity, especially if something has powerfully affected them when they lived in this world. In this case, Nobunaga has turned from a ghost to a monster; specifically, a vampire. He drinks human blood by the pitcher (and keeps stuffing his chained-up victims with veggies to make sure the blood supply is uninterrupted.) Typical of Shiina's style, even some of the scariest bits are also openings for broad humor.

In this case, GS (which stands for Ghost Sweeper; she's an exorcist) Mikami has a harder mission than usual in killing the reborn Oda Nobunaga: he has two hearts, and must be stabbed through both in order to leave this world. Fortunately, Mikami receives a magic weapon: a spear from the ghost of Jubei Mitsuhide Akechi, whose mother was so casually sacrificed by Nobunaga and who slew Nobunaga in return. Nobunaga (in this story also called Nosferatu, recognizing his vampire nature) enlists the aid of a white spider demon named Ranmaru (after one of Nobunaga's retainers who was forced to commit suicide by Mitsuhide); by biting Mikami's face and drawing a single drop of blood, Ranmaru brings Nobunaga back to life.

Things move quickly once Nobunaga sets up his headquarters in modern-day Tokyo. The city is soon overrun by zombie victims; the Pope issues a reward of five billion yen for Nobunaga's death. Other members of Mikami's crew, including an alchemist named Dr. Kaos, his girl-robot assistant Marie and a werewolf named Pete, try to bring down Nobunaga. Mikami, in a brilliantly animated sequence, uses a stack of ofuda charms to avoid the web Ranmaru tried to trap her in and then slay him; the dying Ranmaru, however, adds his power to Nobunaga's. Meanwhile, Mitsuhide possesses Mikami's hapless apprentice Yokoshima and teaches Mikami to create a second spear to pierce Nobunaga's other heart. Mitsuhide then personally drags Nobunaga back down to Hell.

CHAPTER 6: HYAKU MONOGATARI

(ONE HUNDRED STORIES)

One pastime of ancient Japan, which still exists today in several modified forms, is the "hyaku monogatari" or one hundred stories. Here's how you play the game: get some friends together in a windowless room, or even one with windows if it's at night, and light a hundred candles. Everyone takes turns telling a ghost story. It can be short or long, have a happy ending or end up with gore and death all over the place; there are, as we can already see, many kinds of Japanese ghost stories. When the story's over, blow out one candle. By the time you get to the last couple of candles, everybody's nerves should be really on edge. And when you blow out the last candle, everyone count off; they say that there'll be an extra person in the room.

No wonder the Japanese associate ghost stories not with the gloomy autumn of Halloween, but with the hot and humid nights of summer; not only because of Obon, but because these stories were meant to bring on the chills.

The manga *Ghost Hunt* (details below) begins with some high school girls playing this Japanese ghost story game. And volume 3 of the manga takes place in a different high school that's also swarming with paranormal activity; as one student puts it, "We played hyaku monogatari to see if a ghost would really appear. Ever since then,

I've been seeing these weird silhouettes . . . I see a rope on the wall, and it's in the shape of a noose." (vol. 3, p. 23)

This is only one work among many that invoke, one way or another, the ghost story marathon. Japan's authors and artists, in a wide range of media, have called on it for centuries.

Katsushika Hokusai's *Hyaku Monogatari*

Hokusai (1760-1849) is regarded as the master of the woodblock-print medium known as *ukiyo-e*. Gifted with a discerning eye, a sure artistic hand and a one-of-a-kind imagination, Hokusai's prints have been considered the height of Japanese graphic arts, while his sketchbooks are sometimes called the first manga. In 1830 he created his own *Hyaku Monogatari*; even though it only illustrated five stories, they reflect the height of Hokusai's art—even when telling ghost stories.

One of the prints freezes a moment from the story of Oiwa: her disfigured face begins to appear on a paper lantern. Another is a picture of Okiku, her head reaching above the edge of the well where she died, searching for the tenth plate. (These very famous ghosts will each get their own chapter later on.)

Osamu Tezuka's *Hyaku Monogatari*

The God of Comics (Manga no Kamisama), Osamu Tezuka, created a manga titled *Hyaku Monogatari* which had absolutely nothing to do with old Japanese ghost stories. Drawn in 1971 and serialized in *Shonen Jump* magazine, this manga is actually a retelling of the European legend of Faust, set in Japan's Feudal Period. Things start out in a comic vein with a failed, cartoon-y samurai named Hanri Ichirui (Hanri evoking Heinrich, Ichirui meaning "first base", thus using "first" as a pun for "Faust"). Ordered to commit harikiri, the cowardly samurai balks. He strikes a bargain with a witch named Sudama: she provides him with a new face and a new name (Fuwa Usuto, another play on "Faust"). He also agrees to the terms given Faust in Johann von Goethe's drama based on the legend: if Faust were ever to declare himself satisfied with his life, he would die and his soul would go to hell.

In changing the legend's location from Europe to Japan, and telling the story in a manga, Tezuka made quite a few other changes, not least in the character of Sudama. The witch was meant to stand in for the devil Mephistopheles, but, perhaps inevitably, Fuwa Usuto and Sudama fall in love. His satisfaction with this turn of events leads to his having to commit harikiri; this time, however, he finds the courage to carry it out. As Sudama bears his soul down to hell, she rebels, releasing the soul of her beloved and watching as it vanishes into the night sky. Still, despite the title, although other supernatural events take place in the two hundred pages of the manga, there are no ghosts.

Hinako Sugiura's *Hyaku Monogatari*

The late manga author Hinako Sugiura (1958-2005) was, like the creators of the *Ghost Hunt* manga, among the most recent to draw on the "hyaku monogatari" as a source of inspiration with her final manga series, the 1988-1993 *Hyaku monogatari*.

"A hyaku monogatari are the collected writings of what was a popular pastime during the Edo period. People got together, lighted one hundred candles and told ghost stories, blowing out one candle for every story. The belief was, that when the last story was told, a ghost would appear. This series (of original stories by Sugiura) is based on that old habit and is thus a collection of beautiful Edo-style ghost stories."[14]

Describing Sugiura's manga as "Edo-style" is an understatement. Her work deliberately drew on the influence of the masterpieces of ukiyo-e woodprints. Sugiura herself, the daughter of kimono makers, usually wore kimono, and in other ways avoided the trappings of modern life. Don't look for the large eyes of manga; these eyes are classical slits.

---

[14]   http://users.skynet.be/mangaguide/au1795.html

Ghost Hunt

Fuyumi Ono's *Akuryou (Evil Spirits)* novels, written for young readers, draw on the hyaku monogatari as well in their manga incarnation (with artwork by Shiho Inada) and published and animated in Japanese and English as *Ghost Hunt*. In the beginning of the first episode, Mai Taniyama and her fellow high school students are telling ghost stories, not with candles, but with flashlights. The payoff is the same: they turn out the light, then they count off, with the possibility (maybe the hope) that a ghost will have joined the group. One extra person does appear . . . but more on that in other chapters.

Kaidan Hyaku Monogatari

In 2002 Japan's Fuji TV network broadcast an 11-week TV series, *Kaidan Hyaku Monogatari (One Hundred Ghost Stories)*. These were retellings of classic ghost stories, with the added kick of CGI (computer generated imaging) taking the special effects to a new level. These stories include the tale of Oiwa and her faithless samurai husband, the *yukionna* (snow woman), "Earless" Hoichi, Princess Kaguya, and the haunting of "Shining Prince" Genji, among others, all of whom can be found in these pages.

There's even a musical version of the game. *The Kaidan Suite* is described as a musical interpretation of hyaku monogatari, and seeks to recreate the mood of an Edo-era evening in which ghost stories were told by candlelight. While drawing from traditional Japanese musical systems and narration, the *Kaidan Suite* also borrows from 20th-century classical and jazz improvisation to capture the emotional pacing of hyaku monogatari. As in many traditional Japanese ghost stories, feminism is a distinct subtext of the suite; numerous examples are concerned with injustices against women.

Kousetsu Hyaku Monogatari

In 2003 the anime production company Geneon (formerly Pioneer) produced a 13-episode OAV series which became available in English translation in 2004. Variously titled *Requiem of the Darkness* and *Requiem from the Darkness* (both titles appeared on Geneon's own website), neither is an accurate translation of the original title: *Kousetsu Hyaku Monogatari* (*Rumor of the Hundred Stories*). This series is about the act of collecting and writing ghost stories; at least, that's how it starts.

Natsuhiko Kyougoku, principal writer for the series, is a Japanese Renaissance man, having written novels and motion pictures as well as launched a quarterly supernatural-themed magazine, *Mystery*. He collaborated for this series with two other writers of Japanese horror films, Hiroshi Takahashi (creator of the internationally famous film *Ringu*) and Yoshinobu Fujioka (who worked on one of the *Tomie* horror films based on a manga by Junji Ito), as well as Satoshi Kon collaborator Sadayuki Murai. The series is directed by Hideki Tonokatsu, who also directed a special in the *Lupin the Third* anime series.

Kousetsu Hyaku Monogatari is set in the mid-1800s, as the Edo period is coming to an end. An earnest young would-be writer, Momosuke, travels around Japan, soliciting ghost stories for his first work, a *Hyaku Monogatari*. In his travels, though, he meets three strange companions. The leader of the trio, Mataichi, is a short man who dresses as a Buddhist priest but professes to have no beliefs at all; he will do whatever he's hired to do. Nagamimi, in contrast, is a huge man, although he defers to Mataichi's leadership. They're accompanied by Ogin, a voluptuous young woman who carries a puppet.

The artwork is singular, in that it barely resembles what fans in the west have come to think of as anime. There is very little following of Japanese stylistic conventions, especially in drawings of characters' eyes, and backgrounds and people alike are rendered almost abstractly. If anything, this animation reminds the viewer of western "graphic novels" of the *Dark Knight* variety. The art lacks a distinctly Japanese quality, which has to be compensated for by the storytelling. But here, too, things don't quite measure up. There are plenty of scary events, to be sure, and it would seem that Momosuke is finding the material for his ghost stories. However, the stories don't involve ghosts at all. There are plenty of creepy and depraved events, from robbery to cannibalism, but no actual supernatural events. Until the final episodes. The eleventh story introduces a gimmick: a Weapon of Mass Destruction called a flame lance. According to the story, it was a kind of cannon given to a small island by the Heike clan, to be used in its battle against the Taira (see chapter 9). However, with the war over for centuries, the cannon exists only to be activated for the sake of general destruction. This happens in the last two episodes when a depraved nobleman finds inspiration in ancient drawings of demonic torture to use the weapon.

In the end, Momosuke tells the viewer that his *Hyaku Monogatari* were completed and published, although perhaps we are meant to wonder if his fictional ghosts could ever compare with the monstrosities of real life.

xxxHOLIC¹⁵

Early in this manga by the CLAMP collective, which started publication in 2003 and ran until 2010, and its fairly faithful anime incarnation, the four principal characters gather on a summer night for a "hyaku monogatari" session. The pivotal character, Yuko Ichihara (which isn't her real name), is a mysterious woman, something of a witch, who employs a high school student in her curious shop. The student, Kimihiro Watanuki, sees dead people, like most of his family. He wants to be rid of this family trait, however, and asks Yuko for help. She'll help him—for a price. Because he can't pay the price, she puts him to work in her shop until he's earned enough to pay for her help; until then, he still sees dead people and other spirits.

Life isn't all work and spirits; Watanuki is interested in a girl in his high school class, Himawari, who keeps her distance as if she's afraid of bad luck befalling Watanuki. There's also the school's top athlete,

---

¹⁵ Pronounced "holic" (the x's are silent), the title means "addicted to [fill in the blank]".

Domeki, who Watanuki sees as a rival for Himawari's attentions (even if Domeki doesn't see himself that way).

In volume 2 of the manga, the four gather at the Shinto temple run by Domeki's family for a ghost story session one hot summer night. The number of tales is shortened to four stories from each of the four participants, but things still get out of hand before they reach the end. Spirits begin to gather outside the room, threatening to break in through the paper screen walls; they're drawn to the room next door in the temple by the presence there of a parishioner's corpse awaiting his funeral. Domeki has a bow but no arrows; still, this is enough to keep the spirits at bay.

That's more like it. Unlike the *Kousetsu Hyaku Monogatari*, this time the ghosts are real, and threaten to break through from their realm to that of the humans. This is part of the attraction of ghost stories: the lingering thought in the back of the mind, "But what if it's true?" Besides, as CLAMP artist Satsuki Igarashi points out, "Just because you can't prove something doesn't mean it isn't real."

xxx

Sidebar: Shi

Once the quartet has arrived for the telling of ghost stories, Yuko suggests that things be shortened: each of the four people should tell four stories. This doesn't exactly make things better, and the problem is in the number four.

There are two ways of counting in Japanese, one of which is borrowed from the Chinese. In both countries, using this system causes problems when one gets to four. Ichi, ni, san; they're fine. Then comes shi—which happens to sound like the Chinese and Japanese word for "death."

Does it make a difference? According to one study conducted in 2002 at the University of California La Jolla, cardiac deaths for Chinese and Japanese Americans spike 7 percent on the fourth of each month.[16] In addition, some Japanese buildings (especially hospitals) refuse to list their fourth floor, as some American buildings don't mention having a thirteenth floor. The room numbers also leave off the numeral four, as a way of avoiding an omen of bad luck.

Like many superstitions, this one isn't easy to change. Another sound (yon) has been given to the number four, but yon has yet to replace shi.

xxx

Even ghosts aren't immune to this belief, as illustrated by this encounter from the series *Gakkou no Kaidan.*[17]

17. Dead Air

Both the old and new schools in the village of Miyanoshita are equipped with radio studios. Students with an aptitude for broadcasting can get some in-house experience with announcements, music, and interviews. Unfortunately, they also gain experience dealing with malevolent spirits. Back in the day, Satsuki and Keiichiro's mother had trapped one spirit in the broadcast booth of the old school. Unfortunately, it's gotten loose and invaded the new school.

Satsuki finds herself locked in the broadcast booth with the ghost one night. Until now, she's has a diary written by her mother detailing how all of the various spirits were subdued. This time, the book is outside the booth; she'll have to figure it out on her own.

She figures it out when the ghost starts counting down her last thirty seconds. However, the spirit skips the numbers twenty-four and fourteen. This tells Satsuki the ghost itself is superstitious, and she yells "Four! Four!" again and again until the final second has passed without the ghost getting to zero, and it vanishes.

---

[16]   h t t p : / / w w w . i n t e l i h e a l t h . c o m / I H / i h t I H /
WSIHW000/333/8014/346702.html, accessed July 27, 2007.

[17]   See the chapter on school ghosts.

CHAPTER 7: CEMETERIES IN JAPAN

Shaman King hero Yoh Asakura has grown up seeing spirits all of his life, and thinks nothing of loafing around in cemeteries and goofing off with the ghosts. However, his second battle for the position of Shaman King takes place in what the manga calls "Chokohama Foreigners Cemetery". There is, of course, a major difference between Japanese and non-Japanese burial grounds: corpses. In Japan the tombstone serves as a channel of communication with the deceased. A person's cremated ashes may rest beneath the stone, or there may be no trace of a person at all. Anyone bringing offerings of flowers or food or drink or personal effects knows that the living will benefit from these gifts rather than the dead. (In Satoshi Kon's anime feature *Tokyo Godfathers*, the three homeless heroes who find an infant abandoned in a dumpster also find an offering of disposable diapers in a cemetery.) Even if the deceased's ashes are buried there, the spirit in the other world is what's important.

The Judeo-Christian tradition, by comparison, venerates the body of the deceased and inters it, either as it was in life or in as close to lifelike as mortuary science can get. The dominant myth in the Judeo-Christian religion involves the resurrection of the physical body after death. To the Japanese, this way of doing things, keeping corpses nearby and ready to walk again, is creepy.

Chokohama Foreigners Cemetery is a rather obvious stand-in for Yokohama's Foreign General Cemetery. The similar name is the first clue; the second is the information that the cemetery was founded when Commodore Matthew Perry arrived in Japan in 1853 on orders from President Millard Fillmore. (The mission was to keep an eye on the British, with whom America had an uneasy truce after the War of 1812 and who established a major foothold in China after the Opium War of 1839.) When one of Perry's sailors died in 1854, he was entombed on the grounds of the Zotokuin Temple. While one of Perry's company is indeed buried at Zotokuin, this isn't the only version of the cemetery's founding. Two Russian sailors died in Yokohama in 1859, according to another account, and were buried there.

One of the more important foreigners buried there was Charles Richardson, a British merchant based in Shanghai. In 1862 Richardson was part of a group of foreigners who were traveling through Japan. In the village of Namamugi, which was long ago absorbed into Yokohama, the entourage of the father of the Daimyo of Satsuma, including a thousand soldiers, came down the road. The foreigners were ordered to dismount to show respect; Richardson refused, for reasons that are not clear, although Richardson was quoted as saying "I know how to deal with these people." Samurai, who by Japanese law could kill with impunity, attacked the foreigners, killing Richardson and two other men. This led to a brief but costly bombardment of the village by the British Navy in 1863 and the payment of reparations to Britain. Ironically, within a few years, the Tokugawa shogunate would end, and the Meiji period would begin its emphasis on catching up to the west in all respects.

The third clue, that about 4,500 foreigners are buried in Chokohama, establishes the cemetery as Yokohama, which has a similar number of graves.

Yokohama's is merely the most famous foreigner cemetery in Japan. There are others: in Hakodate, on the northern island of Hokkaido, where another one of Perry's crew is buried; the Aoyama cemetery in Tokyo, where some of the more illustrious dead are westerners brought to Japan during the Meiji era to give the nation a technological upgrade after 250 years of isolation; and the port cities of Kobe and Nagasaki. Nagasaki is home for the earliest known burial of a westerner: an official of the Dutch East India Company, Hendrik Duurkoop, who was buried in 1778 in a cemetery where foreigners were already being buried. That cemetery was on the grounds of the Goshinji Buddhist temple overlooking the harbor.

XXX

Christianity itself came to Japan in the mid 1500s, and the few Christian churches tended to be built in the southern part of Japan, where ships from Christian nations traded. Nagasaki is heavily populated with churches (compared to the rest of Japan), and this included the largest Catholic cathedral in Asia at the time: the Urakami Cathedral. The cathedral, and the convent of nuns attached to it, happened to be at Ground Zero on August 9, 1945, when the second atomic bomb of World War II went off.

Manga and anime set in Nagasaki often show Christian churches; examples range from the Nagasaki story in the dating sim-inspired series *Sentimental Journey* to Yoko Matsushita's *Yami no Matsuei* manga/anime about psychic investigators who happen to be ghosts themselves (more about them in the "Ghostbusters" chapter). A Christmas special in the *Ghost Hunt* manga (art by Shiho Inada, based on a series of young adult novels by Fuyumi Ono) takes place in a Christian church in southern Japan. While it may not have what the west would call a happy ending, the mystery is solved and a ghost is granted peace.

18. "Daddy will find me."

The members of Shibuya Psychic Research are offered a job at a Catholic church; Father Toujo knows the group's Australian exorcist, John Brown, and has contacted him about strange happenings at the church, including spiritual possessions. In this case, the possessed ones are children: Father Toujo has a day-care and orphanage at the church, and cares for children of various nationalities and races. The strange activity started thirty years before, as the church was being built, and Father Toujo and the children were preparing to move out of their old church. All things considered, the old priest seems rather blasé about it all, comparing the spirit possession to a game of hide-and-seek. The possessed children take on other personalities, then forget what happened when they return to themselves.

At the time the paranormal activity started, it seemed to focus on a child named Kenji Nagano. His father brought him to the church at age five, at which time the boy had stopped talking, and tapped with a stick to answer questions. (Although the manga never uses the word "autism" in describing Kenji, it suggests that this may have been part of his problem; for whatever reason, Kenji's father abandoned the boy at the orphanage.) One day the children were playing hide-and-seek at the church under construction; Kenji was never found. His spirit has persisted at the church, possessing other children more and more often.

While the group is there Kenji first possesses a young boy, then Mai Taniyama, the heroine of the series. The possessed Mai acts as if boss "Naru" Shibuya's Chinese assistant Rin is her father. When Rin gets upset and yells at Mai, she runs away; her disappearance is followed by the ghostly tapping Kenji would use to signal that he was ready to play hide-and-seek. After an exhaustive search, the former Buddhist monk, Houshou Takigawa, realizes that the children searching for Mai never look above eye-level. Sure enough, on the church grounds they find Kenji/Mai hiding up in a tree. However, finding her doesn't free Kenji's spirit. That happens when Naru goes back into the church and looks up at the angelic statues, set in alcoves high up on the walls. One of the angels seems to have one foot resting on a skull, but then the searchers realize: that skull wasn't part of the sculpture. Thirty years before, while playing hide and seek, Kenji had climbed construction scaffolding and hidden behind the statue of the angel; while he was up there, the scaffolding collapsed, trapping the unspeaking boy behind the statue, where he died. When construction was completed on the church, nobody thought to investigate the sculpture; but, when Naru and company realize the truth of the matter, Mai tells Naru, in Kenji's voice, "Thank you" before the boy's spirit leaves Mai's body.

This ghost wasn't especially malicious; Mai remembered that he "seemed pretty happy". Not all Japanese ghosts are threatening; sometimes they're just out of their place, like Kenji and the girl under the hydrangea, and may need some help getting home.

CHAPTER 8: SUICIDE

Of all of the different beliefs between east and west, perhaps the greatest difference is in the attitude toward taking one's own life. In the Judeo-Christian west, suicide is never considered an acceptable option. In the second scene of Shakespeare's *Hamlet*, the title character, upset nearly to suicide by the sudden death of his father and his mother's hasty marriage to her dead husband's brother, wishes that "the everlasting had not fixed/His canon 'gainst self-slaughter." (I, ii, 131-132) Put simply, the Old Testament commandment "Thou shalt not kill" has been interpreted as rejecting suicide as well as murder: Thou shalt not kill oneself.

Since the Bible didn't get to Japan until the 1500s, there simply is no history of specifically religious injunctions against suicide. Buddhism, with its belief in the rebirth of the soul after death, generally doesn't share the Judeo-Christian rejection of suicide. It's still not a common means of ending one's life, but is common enough: Japan, according to the World Health Organization (WHO), has the ninth highest suicide rate in the world—more than 30,000 per year.[18]

Much has been made of Japan's prolonged economic troubles, since the real estate bubble burst around 1990, as a reason to commit suicide; sensational reports have also appeared of "suicide clubs" on the Japanese internet. According to the WHO, however, things in Japan are more personal: most modern Japanese suicides seemed to

---

[18]   http://www.physorg.com/news113818898.html,   accessed November 10, 2007

be driven first by health problems, then by money problems and unemployment.

In classic Japanese lore, and even in the pop culture of anime and manga, there are many more reasons for suicide, involving everything from romance to schoolyard bullying. The Buddha, in an early incarnation as a rabbit, killed himself by jumping into a fire so that an elderly sage might find nourishment in him. Love is usually high on the list of reasons, as in this ghost tale from the 14th century collection known as *Shintoushuu (Tales of the Gods)*:

19. The Glorious Princess

Back in the fifth century, an elderly childless couple lived at the foot of Mount Fuji. One day, the old man was wandering through the bamboo grove behind their house when he met a beautiful little girl. She seemed to have no idea where she came from, so the old couple took her in. They named her Kaguya-hime (Princess Glory) because she seemed to give off a beautiful light of her own.

As she grew older, she also grew more beautiful. Word spread of this lovely woman, and men from all over the province sought her hand in marriage. At last, she agreed to marry the governor of the province. They lived together happily, but, soon after the girl's adoptive parents had died, she surprised her husband by telling him that she was not human. "I am the Immortal Lady of Mount Fuji," she told him, "and I came down to earth to bring happiness to the old couple who raised me. Now I must go home."

She gave her husband a small wooden box. "You can find me at the top of Mount Fuji; come and look for me there if you miss me. Or, look inside this box." And, saying nothing else, she disappeared.

The governor, who loved her deeply, could not be consoled. He looked in the box, which contained the special incense known as Incense to Recall the Soul. However, when he looked into the box after burning the incense, he did not see Kaguya, but only a shadowy spirit. He climbed to the top of Mount Fuji, where he found a small lake with an island in the middle. However, steam rose up from the lake, so that he could not see Kaguya on the island either. With this final disappointment, the governor walked to a cliff, held the box of incense to his heart, and threw himself off.

Still, the governor and his princess were reunited in death; the two of them became the god of the mountain. Even though there is only one god of Mount Fuji, sometimes it would appear as a man and sometimes it would appear as a woman. And, when the governor threw himself off the cliff, the box of incense burst into flame, and the clouds of burning incense became the smoky clouds that stay near the summit of Mount Fuji, symbolizing love and longing for many people.[19]

xxx

Suicide is generally considered one of those sensitive subjects in the west that are kept away from children. However, the subject often appears in Japanese pop culture, and is presented with a surprising frankness even to a very young audience. The anime series *Ojamajo DoReMi*, a sunny little comedy about a group of grade school girls who are also witches in training, has a scene in the second episode of the so-called "Sharp" season[20] that is jarring to someone who isn't ready for it. The witches have spent the better part of a day trying to care for a baby for the first time, and as fifth-graders they were worn out very quickly; they had to call for help from the mother of the main witch-child Doremi. When the exhausted Doremi comes

---

[19] Tyler, Royall, Japanese Tales. New York: Pantheon, 1987, pp. 46-47.

[20] Doremi is a Japanese name as well as the syllables for the first three musical notes in a scale. Using musical terms to name the seasons of the TV series isn't the only musical reference; one of the witches, a girl named Onpu, is also a young and popular singing idol; the word "onpu" also refers to the use of musical notes and symbols in text messages to signal a sing-song speech pattern or a happy state of mind.

home, she skips dinner and goes to soak in a hot bath. While she's in there, her mother comes into the bathroom and gets into the tub with her daughter.[21] When Doremi asks her mother if she was such a handful as a baby, the mother tells her that she had dreams of being a concert pianist, and that, when she injured her hand in an accident, she was so depressed at abandoning her dream that she wanted to commit suicide. The only thing that saved her, she said, was getting pregnant with Doremi. No matter how much Doremi cried, her mother said, she heard those cries and even regarded Doremi's kicks in utero as an encouragement: "Mother, do your best; I'll always be beside you."

One of the most popular manga in Japan in recent years had a main character who became a ghost after committing suicide. And this suicide-ghost, who befriends a sixth grade boy, was not driven to death by health concerns or romantic or financial problems, although he had recently lost his job under unfair circumstances. This man committed suicide over a game.

20. For the love of the game

Hikaru Shindo is eleven years old, doesn't do well at school; the word "slacker" applies here. At least it did, until Hikaru found a game board in his grandfather's attic while rummaging around for antiques to sell (his grades being so bad his parents cut off his allowance). The small wooden table was meant for playing go, an ancient Japanese territory-capture game. At first, Hikaru sees stains on the board that others cannot see, then hears a voice that others cannot hear.

---

[21] The subsequent revelations make sense in the context of the bath. This openness in a place where literally all barriers are down is a common occurrence in Japan, and not only in its popular culture. The Japanese describe this feeling with a made-up English-sounding word: "skinship." See Kittredge Cherry's *Womansword: What Japanese Words Say About Women* (1987: Kodansha), pp. 89-90.

Enter the ghost: Fujiwara no Sai. Dressed in elaborate courtly robes of the Heian period, he was no less than a go instructor to the Emperor and his household. A jealous rival, however, challenged Sai to a game, and not only cheated but accused Sai of cheating. Sai lost his composure, lost the match, lost his position at court and his reputation; two days later, he threw himself into the river. Death, however, was not the end.

Sai is clearly a wronged servant in the Okiku mold (Okiku's story is featured in chapter 10). But his ghost doesn't stick around in order to see justice done or to wallow in misery. Sai loved the game of go so much that he could never get enough of it. He especially longed for the chance to make one specific play, the so-called "Divine Move". However, being tied to a game board, Sai's ghost was at the mercy of whoever owned the board, even if it meant the owner seldom or never played the game.

When Hikaru lets him out and about, staying close to Hikaru by taking up residence "in a corner of his soul," Sai sometimes reacts with the amazement and even childishness of someone trying to take in centuries of change. Jet planes, push-button umbrellas, vending machines, the Internet—these are just some of the changes Sai observes and absorbs (some changes more easily than others).

Sai had previously waited in the go board for hundreds of years, until he was discovered by a very different child from Hikaru, Honinbo Shusaku.

Sidebar: Honinbo Shusaku

Honinbo Shusaku (1829-1862) is considered by many to be the greatest go player of the 19th century, if not in the entire history of the game. Shusaku was born Kuwahara Torajiro on June 6, 1829, the son of a merchant in a village north of Hiroshima. By the age of six he was already known as a prodigy. Lord Asano, the daimyo (lord) of the region, heard of the child's abilities. After playing a game with him, Asano became his patron, and allowed him to get lessons from his own personal trainer.

In November 1837 Shusaku was sent to Tokyo (then still called Edo) to become a student of the Honinbo school. Two years later, Shusaku was awarded a diploma at age 10. In 1840, during a visit back home, he was awarded a yearly stipend by Lord Asano. Arriving back in Edo in September 1841, Shusaku was given the name we now know him under. In 1844 he left for another stay at Onomichi, this time staying there for eighteen months.

In July 1846, at age 17, during his travel back to Edo, Shusaku met Gennan Inseki, of whom it is said that he was strong but had the bad luck of living in a time when there were several other extremely strong players.

Back in Edo, Shusaku was asked to become the heir of Shuwa, who was to become the next head of the Honinbo house, but he refused because of his obligations towards Lord Asano and towards his own family. After some mediation, the Asano clan relinquished its claim, so in early 1847 Shusaku could become Shuwa's heir.

Later that year, Josaku died, and Shuwa became the new leader of the Honinbo house. Shuwa was already recognized as the strongest player of the day. In 1848 Shusaku was officially recognized as Shuwa's heir, still no more than 19 years old.

In 1862, a cholera epidemic broke out in Edo, and several disciples of the Honinbo house caught the disease. Shusaku was active in caring for the sick, which resulted in his catching the disease himself. On August 10, 1862, only 33 years old, he died.

xxx

All this would seem to confirm Hikaru's original hunch: that the go board in his grandfather's attic was an antique. After all, he can see where the wood was stained by the blood of the dying Shusaku. However, he's the only one who can see those stains.

At first, Hikaru would seem to be the least likely person to help Sai reach his goal. He doesn't know anything about go; furthermore, he doesn't care. But, in order to keep Sai from pestering him, Hikaru begins taking go lessons (in exchange for Sai's help with his history homework), and is gradually drawn into the game on his own. This is another example of a common theme in Japanese pop culture: young people would do well to look to their history and revive the arts and traditions of the past.

The shifting relationship between Hikaru and Sai is the backbone of the series. Sai is eager to return to his roles as player and teacher, and sometimes throws Hikaru in over his head. But, as Hikaru gains understanding of go, he begins to assert himself, needing Sai's guidance less and less (although Hikaru is perfectly capable of getting himself in too deep at times). This leaves Sai with decidedly mixed feelings: pleased that the pupil is successful, but uneasy about his new place in this new Japan once Hikaru no longer needs him. But that's a much later installment in the story.

While Hikaru and Sai seem an unlikely couple brought together by fate, the similarly unlikely team that created the manga was brought together by an editor at *Shonen Jump*. Like Hikaru, writer Yumi Hotta knew little about go, but, while playing a game one time against her father-in-law, she thought that a manga about go had possibilities. She drafted a scenario and sent it to *Shonen Jump*'s annual Story King Award. It didn't win—and neither did the artwork of Takeshi Obata, who was a runner-up for the Tezuka-Akatsuka Award, also sponsored by *Shonen Jump*. An editor assigned to Obata found Hotta's story, and realized that the two artists would complement each other. The addition of go master Yukari Umezawa as a technical advisor completed the creative team.

The manga debuted in late 1998 and ran for 189 episodes, giving rise to a popular 75-episode anime series broadcast on Japanese television from 2001 to 2003. Once the series ended, Obata struck gold with the popular, edgier manga series *Death Note*.

Entertaining as well as educational, *Hikaru no Go* also inspired what one writer called a "micro-renaissance" for go in Japan and other Asian countries, even generating interest in go in the United States. It's a tribute to the manga/anime that, since the series appeared, anime conventions in America, in addition to spaces for screening anime, playing video games, and selling and displaying fan artwork, usually set a room aside as a go parlor.

Sai is certainly one of the most "kid-friendly" ghosts, in every sense of that word. Knowledgeable yet emotional, wise and naïve at the same time, understanding of both the game of go and the way to think while playing it, he is a ghost who poses no threat at all to Hikaru.

xxx

In another story from the anime series *Gakkou no Kaidan*[22], the suicidal ghost is hardly as benevolent as Sai.

21. The Da Vinci Code

"Da Vinci" is the name given to a ghost, formerly an art teacher who had killed himself, haunting the art studio at the Miyanoshita family's old elementary school. He had been imprisoned in a painting of the old school building by a talented student artist: Satsuki's mother. Fortunately, she left a diary detailing all of the ghosts and spirits she'd subdued and how; unfortunately, the book is a little too full. Satsuki didn't have a chance to read that, if anyone painted the same scene that Da Vinci had, the ghost might be free to strike again. When he strikes, he paints a picture of someone (usually a pretty girl) who's never heard from again.

The next day, the entire school knows about Da Vinci: overnight, bloody red paint has dripped out of the studio window in the painting of the old school building. Something similar happens to the real old school; the principal goes in to investigate what he thinks is rain water, and the kids watch the principal—until they realize that a student named Momoko is missing. Da Vinci has apparently selected her to be his next model.

The notebook says that Da Vinci can be put to sleep by burning incense and chanting a spell; unfortunately, they have no incense and the spell is smudged. The kids get a little help from other ghosts in the school: the walking Ninomiya statue, the human-faced dog, and Toilet Hanako all bring bundles of incense. Da Vinci, meanwhile,

---

[22]   For the history of this project, see the chapter on "School Ghosts".

is painting Momoko, telling her that, in a painting, her beauty will never decay. When the kids burst in, he takes Momoko into the older painting. Satsuki and her friend Hajime are the only ones who follow. But they find another student who apparently wandered into the painting; he gives Satsuki a gift, although they never met. They hear a noise, and find a radio broadcasting Japan's World Series—the 1973 World Series. They realize that the two paintings of the old schoolhouse have linked present and past. They get the ultimate proof: they meet Kayako, Satsuki's future mother, although just a fifth grader here. They head for the studio to rescue Momoko and re-enchant Da Vinci; he tries to escape by diving into the painting; however, back in the present, the painting had been tossed into the incinerator by the janitor. Da Vinci returns to the past in flames, where Satsuki and her mother are able to subdue him.

22. Mirror and Bell

Suicide can sometimes function as a way of focusing one's desires, with an effect that can outlast death. The effect may not be predictable, as noted in this story from Lafcadio Hearn's *Kwaidan*, describing an incident which legend says happened about a thousand years ago.

At that time, in Mugenyama, the priests of the local temple wanted a new bronze bell. They did what Japanese priests had done for years and years: they asked the women of the congregation to donate any bronze ornaments or utensils, which could then be melted down for the new bell. One farmer's wife donated a mirror made of bronze which contained on its back the Shou-Chiku-Bai, designs of pine, bamboo, and plumflower intended to bring good luck. The farmer's wife later realized that it wasn't her mirror alone, but had belonged to her mother and grandmother. She didn't have the money to buy back the mirror from the temple, and she could never find an opportunity to steal the mirror back. Eventually it went to the metal foundry to be melted down for the temple bell.

But a strange thing happened. No matter how hot the furnace, there was one mirror that would never melt. Word spread about this mirror, which reflected its owner's attachment to it more than her wish to donate it to the temple bell. The farmer's wife was so ashamed by this public display of her selfishness that she drowned herself. First, however, she left a letter that contained, among other things, these words: "It will be easier when I am dead to melt down the mirror and cast the bell. However, whoever rings the bell so much that it breaks will receive great wealth from my ghost."

Nobody could say how a ghost could come by such a large amount of money, or even if the statement were true. Still, once the farmer's wife was dead, the mirror could easily be melted and cast as part of the temple bell. Since that part of the suicide note seemed to be true, people felt that the rest of the letter would be true as well. And so they set about ringing the bell with the intent of breaking it. The bell was well-cast and very strong, but this didn't stop people from ringing the bell day after day, no matter what the priests asked of them. The whole exercise became so absurd that the priests finally decided to get rid of the bell themselves. One night, they cut the bell down and rolled it downhill into a swamp where it sank, never to ring again.

But this wasn't the end of the story. Some people tried to ring a version of the bell, in hopes of collecting some of the fortune that had been promised in the suicide note. One time, a warrior named Kajiwara Kagesue of the Heike clan and his lady companion Umegae were on a pilgrimage; their money had run out, and they beat upon a bronzed wash basin until it broke, calling out for the bell's fortune. A guest at the inn where they were staying was so impressed that he made the two a gift of three hundred gold pieces!

On the other hand, legend tells of a drunken farmer who heard of this couple's good fortune and tried to get some for himself. He built a clay replica of the bell and hit it repeatedly, calling for money. As he did so, a white-robed woman with wild flying hair rose up out of the ground, handed the farmer a covered jar, and told him that she was answering his prayer "as it deserved to be answered." Once the farmer held the jar, the woman disappeared. He rushed home to show his wife, and they both opened the jar.

It was full to the brim, but with what? Hearn decided that "I really cannot tell you with what it was filled." Still, the farmer was drunk and dissolute, and probably deserved whatever was inside.

23. The Temporary Suicide

One episode of Natsuki Takaya's *Genei Musou (Phantom Dream)* manga focuses on Souichi, a boy who, to hear him tell it, has had his parents on his back "since the moment I was born." His father (an attorney) and mother (housewife) kept the pressure on him to succeed and do well for the sake of the family. Failure to live up to these standards got him branded an embarrassment, as did his fascination with butterflies. The insects seemed to have an affinity for him, flocking around Souichi and, by his account, singing to him. When he failed the entrance exam to a prestigious high school and had to settle for a lesser school, the pressure from his parents became so great that he took a box-cutter to his neck and committed suicide.

Then he came back to life.

Souichi was actually being kept alive by the negative energy of demonic spirits (*jashin*). He stood a strong chance of becoming purely an evil spirit (*jaki*) unless Tamaki, the student hero of the series and a medium in training, could perform an exorcism; however, this would kill Souichi. Tamaki even contemplated exorcising Souichi without his knowing it, but dismissed that idea as showing Souichi no respect at all. Meanwhile, Souichi's mother comes on her own to Tamaki's temple and, fearful of her son's demonic power, begs for her son to be exorcised.

In the end, with his parents still unable to forgive Souichi for not being the son they wanted, unwilling to love him the way the butterflies did, Souichi confronts Tamaki, who has to exorcise his demons even if it means that Souichi dies again. Tamaki almost died himself, except that his girlfriend Asahi brought him the rosary that he had forgotten; Tamaki needed the rosary to protect himself during the exorcism. As Asahi put it, "I chose your life over Souichi's, so we'll just have to be unforgivable together." Not every dilemma has a perfect, win-win solution.

xxx

In Japanese pop culture, the word "suicide" is often followed by the word "pact;" what in the west is usually a lonely, solitary act is often shown in Japan as a partnership, if not a group activity. The word for such a pact in Japanese is shinjuu, but shinjuu has a very specific meaning that sets it apart from a simple suicide pact. It originally referred to the deaths of two lovers who were unable to marry, for one reason or another. The act thus served as a form of social protest, and became central to a number of works of romantic literature, including Japanese kabuki drama, bunraku puppet plays, and, as seen in the west, the novel *Sayonara* by James Michener. In the latter, an American serviceman and his Japanese lover face hostility and discrimination during the Korean War, and see shinjuu as their only way out. The anime film *Windaria* (also released in an edited version under the title *Once Upon a Time*) features shinjuu as the way out for two lovers who find themselves the rulers of two warring kingdoms.

Another example is found in the anime series *Gunslinger Girl*, based on a manga by Yu Aida. This series, that owes more than a bit of its plot to Mamoru Oshii's ground-breaking *Ghost in the Shell*, offers an Italian government agency that has taken young girls—all of them traumatized in one way or another—and rebuilt their bodies with cybernetic implants while reprogramming their minds to become dedicated assassins. However, as the audience had no doubt feared, adolescent girls can be a jumble of emotions. Usually their handlers, called fratelli (brothers), keep things in check. In one case, however, an assassin and her handler are found shot and killed with a single bullet each; this is especially a problem, and a potential security breach, since only a shot to the eye can kill the girls, and the agency was desperate to keep this fact from leaking.

As one of the girls explains later to the clueless grownups, this was neither terrorism nor a criminal act, but shinjuu. The assassin, Elsa, had developed feelings of love for her fratello Lauro, feelings which could not be returned. Frustrated by this situation, Elsa asked to meet with her fratello, then shot him and herself.

There are actually several kinds of shinjuu, including oyako (parent and child) shinjuu, in which the parent of a disabled child kills the child and then commits suicide, and ikka shinjuu, in which an entire family will be killed (this often happens because of poverty, and is part of an episode of Osamu Tezuka's manga *Don Dracula*; the only thing that stops the family is their chance encounter with a pair of jewel thieves). Oddly enough, the word shinjuu has nothing to do with death; its Chinese characters literally mean "center of the heart," and refer to the sincerity of the person who commits suicide. The word originally meant any sincere expression of extreme emotion, such as a woman cutting off her hair or tearing out her fingernails and sending them to her beloved.[23]

The Boy Love manga known in Japan as *Ghost!*, translated into English as *Eerie Queerie*, features a shinjuu pact that goes awry. Two high school students, a boy named Hibiki Kanau and someone he refers to only as his sempai (upperclassmen), had decided to kill themselves fifteen years earlier because they could not be together. However, at the critical moment, the sempai decided, "There's just too much for me to live for; I can't just throw it all away." He walked away from the pact, leaving Kanau to kill himself by himself.

In this case, the audience realizes that the problem is not suicide itself, but the fact that someone who pledged to kill himself backed out at the last minute. The subsequent ghostly appearance would be caused not by the original event that drove the person to suicide, but the sense of betrayal by another. This is a common theme when dealing with Japanese ghosts; we'll encounter it with classic ghosts like Oiwa and Okiku, as well as in modern works like *Hikaru no Go* and the movie *Ringu*. Generally, the act of suicide itself, as a conscious act of the will, is held morally blameless.

---

[23] http://d-training.aots.or.jp/GTJ/html/s.html#shinjuu, accessed February 21, 2007

CHAPTER 9: CLASSIC JAPANESE GHOST LITERATURE

"The Shining Prince"

The world's oldest novel (at least, the oldest surviving novel) was written between the years 1000 and 1008; an elaborate thousand-page romance written at a time when being a writer wasn't a profession but a pastime for the educated leisure class; in this case, by a member of the Japanese Imperial Court. The novel is *The Tale of Genji (Genji Monogatari)*, and its author is known to us as the Lady Murasaki Shikibu.

Shikibu (her real name is not known; possibly her given name was Takako) was born in C.E. 973 into the Fujiwara clan, one of the two major power families of Japan in the Heian era (see sidebar below). Her mother died when she was young; her father Tametoki was a provincial governor (or *shikibu-sho*) and a prominent scholar. Although the norm would have been for Shikibu to have lived with, and been taught by, her mother and her mother's clan, Tametoki gave both his son and daughter the same education. Shikibu was an eager and adept student, even studying some of the Chinese literary classics of the period, although this was not considered proper education for a female.

She married a distant member of her clan and gave birth to a daughter in 999; when her husband died two years later, Shikibu was brought to the Heian Court in Kyoto, where she was dubbed Lady Murasaki. They had heard of her writing talents, and bringing her to court allowed her to draw on court life in creating her best-known work.

Lady Murasaki did not spend all of her life at court; around 1023 she had retired to a Buddhist nunnery, where she apparently died a few years later. She couldn't have anticipated that her *roman a clef* about Heian court life would outlive the Chinese literary classics her father taught her as a child.

xxx

The *Genji Monogatari* draws on some of the events—real or fictitious—that Lady Murasaki witnessed at court, attributing them to Genji, a young noble known in the book as the Shining Prince. Although the second son of one of the Emperor's lower-ranked concubines, and therefore unlikely to ever take the throne, his sheer physical beauty—the source of his nickname—causes him to be forgiven transgressions that would be held against lesser mortals. The book is a catalogue of the various lovers in his life, including his stepmother(!) and, later, the stepmother's niece(!!); however, he never abandons any of these women, and provides for them later in life.

In addition to filmed, televised, and staged adaptations, 1987 saw a fairly faithful anime adaptation of the *Genji Monogatari*. Directed by Gisaburo Sugii, who is best known in the west for his film *Night on the Galactic Railroad*, Sugii worked for the Toei animation studio in his youth. He was an animator on *Hakujaden*, Japan's first animated feature (1958). Osamu Tezuka asked him to jump over to Mushi Pro, Tezuka's own new studio; Sugii worked on the *Astro Boy* TV series and the first anime feature to come to America, *Saiyu-ki* (one of a long line of anime inspired by the Chinese legend of the Monkey King, rechristened in this case for American audiences as *Alakazam the Great!*). Sugii's other works include *Lupin the Third: Legend of Twilight Gemini, Street Fighter II* and *Touch*, based on the very popular baseball manga of Mitsuru Adachi.

24. Genji and Lady Rokujo

Although the *Genji Monogatari* is hardly a ghost story as we understand it, Genji has an early and pivotal encounter with a spirit. Actually, his encounter is part of one of his first romances. Approaching the Lady Yugao, daughter of a captain of the guard, through an intermediary at first, the seventeen-year-old Genji finally goes to her in person. As he woos her, Lady Murasaki gives us a hint of what's to come by describing Lady Yugao as "frightened, as if he were an apparition from an old story." Still, she gives in to him, but, shortly after their affair begins, she suddenly dies.

The cause of death? The jealous spirit of another of Genji's mistresses, Lady Rokujo. She's so jealous, in fact, that her spirit leaves her body to bring about this death. She doesn't stop at one death, either. Another victim, the Lady Aoi, had her encounter with Lady Rokujo's spirit commemorated in a classic Noh play, *Aoi no Ue (Lady Aoi)*. In this case, Lady Rokujo's carriage had to pull off the road to make way for the Lady Aoi, Genji's latest amour and the mother-to-be of his child. When Lady Rokujo's demonic spirit threatens Lady Aoi, a Buddhist monk is summoned. He battles the demon, using prayers against the staff of the demon, and ultimately drives her out. The play fiddles with the original by having Lady Aoi survive her encounter with the demon. Otherwise, it's a straightforward cautionary Buddhist story, with Lady Rokujo lamenting the fleeting nature of happiness on earth (and, with a roving-eyed boyfriend like Genji, she's easy to agree with), and using Buddhist prayers to save Lady Aoi's life.

Life at the Heian court, where Lady Murasaki wrote the *Genji Monogatari*, was also the atmosphere in which Imperial Go Master Fujiwara no Sai was unfairly dismissed from his position. Driven by despair to commit suicide, that act only began his story. But for now, we're still in the library, noting some of Japan's best-known ghost writers.

65

XXX

The beginning of the Edo period (1603) saw the last of the wars which established Japan as its present-day nation. During the next two centuries of isolation from the rest of the world, other customs and arts began to appear, including the documentation of ghost stories. In the 1780s the scholar and artist Toriyama Sekien began an exhaustive study of ghosts and ghouls in which he attempted to offer the reader a full list of all known types. The project was slightly absurd, of course, since ghosts cannot be counted up in that way, and by their very nature, *obake* resist normal categorization. The first volume appeared in 1781 under the title of *The Hundred Demons' Night Parade*. Toriyama produced *The Illustrated Bag of One Hundred Random Ghosts (Gazu Hyakki Tsurezure-bukuro)* three years later, and completed two further volumes in the years that followed, ultimately compiling what remains the most definitive list of spectral types. Each volume of the set was fully illustrated with monochrome pictures, with one entire page devoted to the likeness and description of each particular spook. Toriyama's books were wildly popular in their day, and went through numerous impressions. Most modern collections of Japanese rare books have at least a few copies.[24]

XXX

Tsukioka Yoshitoshi (1839-1892) lived in the Meiji era, that transitional time when the west forced itself back into Japan, and Japan's monarchy decided that, while it had isolated the nation from the outside world for two and a half centuries, too many new technological, medical, and political advances had been made by the rest of the world. A lot of folk traditions might have been

---

[24] "Japanese Ghosts" by the appropriately named Tim Screech, from *Mangajin #40* (http://www.mangajin.com/mangajin/samplemj/ghosts/ghosts.htm), accessed June 16, 2007.

tossed aside as part of the rush to westernize; people like Yoshitoshi, however, preserved the past by keeping it alive into the present.

Yoshitoshi's father was a samurai turned merchant. At age 11 he was enrolled in the art school of the master Kuniyoshi, where he was given the name we know now. After the death of Kuniyoshi in 1861, Yoshitoshi's art ranged from prominent kabuki actors of the day to historical subjects using the woodblock prints known as ukiyo-e. His fortunes declined for several years, then revived in the 1870s, when his drawings of the 1877 Satsuma Rebellion and portraits of prominent generals made him one of Japan's most popular artists. He married and started his own school, although he was inclined to be moody. He gradually shifted to drawing for the new medium of newspapers, thus making him the last great master of the woodblock medium.

Among his series of works are "One Hundred Ghosts Stories of China and Japan," done at the beginning of his career in 1865, "One Hundred Aspects of the Moon," "Thirty Two Aspects of Women's Costumes and Manners," and the series created during the final years of his life, "Thirty Six Ghosts." These ghosts (which technically included demons as well as the spirits of the departed) include the spirit of Tomomori of the Taira clan, appearing in the waves of Daimotsu Bay, the site of the great battle between the Taira and the Heike clans. Another depicts Tametomo driving away a ghost; actually an old crone riding on another ghost's shoulders, representing an outbreak of smallpox. Yet another drawing recalls the legend of Okiku and the broken plate. We see her ghost standing before the well where her body lay, the well itself visible through her transparent kimono. The look of sorrow on her face is unmistakable, as is Yoshitoshi's mastery of his art.

A far less kindly scene occurs in Yoshitoshi's illustration of the legend of Kiyohime and the monk, which inspired another kabuki drama. Kiyohime was an innkeeper's daughter. Each year, a chaste young monk named Anchin would stop at the inn as part of an annual pilgrimage, and give a present to Kiyohime. The girl became infatuated with Anchin; however, when she declared her love, the horrified (and chaste) monk bolted from the inn and fled to the monastery, with Kiyohime in hot pursuit. So deep was her obsession that, when she reached a flooded river, she turned into a snake and swam across; Yoshitoshi's print shows the transformation. When Anchin saw this, he hid himself under the bell of the temple; Kiyohime, however, still in serpent form, wrapped herself around the bell, and the bell grew hot enough to kill both the monk and the obsessed woman.

One of the finest of the series is based on the legend of Kuzunoha the fox-woman. One of many similarly themed Japanese legends, the story is of a legendary astrologer of the Heian court, Abe no Yasuna, who rescues a fox from a hunt. Later he meets and marries a beautiful woman, who bears him a son, then leaves three years later. On the third night after she leaves, the nobleman has a dream in which his wife reveals that she was the fox whose life he saved. She thanked him by becoming a human, marrying him, and bearing a son, but she could not stay with him; a fox, after all, does not live as long as a human. This story has been the basis for kabuki and bunraku puppet plays.

Yoshitoshi's picture of this scene is of the moment of Kuzunoha leaving. Her young son hangs onto her kimono, as she passes out of the house. We cannot see her face, since it is already outside, but she casts a shadow on the paper screen wall: the shadow of a fox. It is at once chilling and poignant, and a prime example of the ambivalent mix of emotions so common in Japanese storytelling and in ghost stories in particular. In performances of the play, the departing spirit sings lines of great tenderness and sorrow:

"Last night I slept with my husband on one side of me and my beloved son on the other; I did not know it would be my last night. This must mean that my fox powers have grown weak because of my love for humans. I must go now."

xxx

The best-known chronicler of ghost stories in Meiji Japan wasn't born in Japan: Lafcadio Hearn (1850-1904). Born of an Irish father and a Greek mother, he lived in Greece, Ireland, America, and the

West Indies, working as a journalist and writer, before moving to Japan in 1889. Hearn became a teacher, married the daughter of a samurai, and was adopted into her family under the name Yakumo Koizumi. Although he died at age 54, his influence has continued, primarily through his collections of Japanese ghost stories. Published under the names *In Ghostly Japan* and *Kwaidan*, the latter collection of legends inspired Masaki Kobayashi's landmark 1965 film of the same name. In addition, Canadian born director Ping Chong created a puppet show in 1999 titled *Kwaidan*, and another Lafcadio Hearn puppet show in 2002, *OBON: Tales of Rain and Moonlight*. And the 2005 Irish play *The Dream of a Summer Day* mingled Hearn's life with some of the ghost stories he retold.

Foremost among the Hearn legends is the account of Earless Hoichi. It was mentioned above that Hoichi was the monk who sang so compellingly of the battle of Dan-no-Ura that the ghosts of the Taira and Minamoto combatants came to hear him. Playing to an audience of ghosts almost proved fatal, however, so, when Hoichi had to perform again for the spirits, the monks painted Buddhist sutras all over his body to protect him from the ghosts. He gained the name "Earless Hoichi" because the monks forgot to paint sutras on one ear . . .

Another classic Japanese ghost story, one which has recurred again and again, is that of the *yukionna* or snow-woman. In Hearn's version, a woodcutter is trapped in a blizzard, where he is found by the snow-woman. She takes pity on him and decides not to kill him; however, if he tells anyone about their encounter, she would indeed slay the woodcutter.

As time goes by, he marries, and his wife asks him about his past. Even as he starts to tell her about the encounter in the blizzard with the *yukionna*, the audience knows that he's sowing the seeds of his own destruction. There's no need to tell you who his wife turns into . . .

Kobayashi's film version of Hearn's tales is at once modern, edgy, and as traditional as kabuki. The presentation is stagy, stylized, expressionistic, yet they still carry the power to give the audience chills.

xxx

Japan's best-known literary award is the Akutagawa Prize, awarded generally twice per year (although in some years three prizes have been awarded, and in other years, such as the first three years of the postwar Occupation, no prize at all was given). The award has been given since 1935 by the literary journal *Bungei Shunju*, and is named for the young author who took his own life in 1927 at age 35.

Born the son of milkman Toshizo Niihara in 1892, Ryunosuke Akutagawa's mother suffered a mental breakdown shortly after the birth, dying while he was still a child. He was sent to live with the Akutagawas, relatives on his mother's side. He landed a teaching position at Tokyo University (then called Tokyo Imperial University) when the previous teacher was forced to resign after stating his belief in clairvoyance.[25] He worked as a journalist, but his short stories quickly gained him attention. In his thirties, after a stressful trip to China, he began suffering hallucinations. As he described in an essay which serves as his suicide note, Akutagawa said that he was driven by "a vague sense of anxiety about my own future;" presumably, although it's never stated, he feared he would succumb to his mother's insanity. He also wrote that "I am left with little appetite for food and women. The world I am now in is one of diseased nerves, lucid as ice. . . . I do not regard (suicide) as a sin, as westerners do."[26] He attempted suicide twice in 1927, succeeding the second time.

Not known as a writer who specialized in the supernatural, two of his stories nonetheless formed the basis for *Rashomon*, a story in

---

[25] http://www.st.rim.or.jp/~cycle/KAPPAE.HTML, accessed November 4, 2006. One of the hallmarks of the Meiji era in Japan was the aggressive belief in western science, dismissing traditional Japanese spirit-worship and folk practices about ghosts and monsters as evidence of a feeble mind.

[26] http://en.wikisource.org/wiki/Ryunosuke_Akutagawa_suicide_note, accessed November 4, 2006.

which the dead are allowed to give testimony at inquest through a medium.

xxx

Most of these stories are still alive in Japanese culture, one way or another. Even the cyber-adept generation of the 21st century gets exposed to the ghosts of old Japan at an early age—and manga and anime are among the ways younger generations are exposed to traditional ghosts.

xxx

Sidebar: Taira/Heike Wars

The battle of these two clans not only makes a compelling history in itself, but has inspired many compelling works of fiction. In speaking just of ghost stories, the dispute between the Taira and Heike clans figures in "Earless Hoichi," as written by Lafcadio Hearn and filmed as part of the brilliant ghost-story anthology film *Kwaidan* (1965).

As for the battle itself, it ended a dispute between the two clans that had gone on for almost thirty years. The two families were actually related, both being distantly descended from younger princes of the Emperor unlikely to ever succeed to the throne, and both families hired themselves out as mercenary armies to shore up any local nobility seeking to protect its turf. The two clans' competition for power was just one clashing point; culture was another, with the Heike perceived as educated sophisticates living to the west of Kyoto while the Taira were the rural rough-and-tumble type suited to the wilderness east of Kyoto. Perhaps it was inevitable that the two would clash.

The Taira at first had enough armed force to expel the Heike, but time changed the equation: by 1181 the Taira patriarch Kiyomori had died, and the Heike armies were now led by Yoshitsune, an infant at the time of the first battles, and a prototype of the bishounen warrior (see my book *Anime Explosion*). When the naval battle at

Dan-no-Ura turned against the Heike, the figurehead boy Emperor Antoku was taken by his grandmother, who jumped into the sea, drowning them both. The boy's mother, Tokoku, also attempted suicide, but was rescued by some of her troops. She was brought to Kyoto, and lived her remaining six years as a Buddhist nun.

Is any of this important in a book of ghost stories? Yes, because these are critical events in Japanese history, because any period piece in pop culture is built on a historical foundation, and because a reader needs to know at least the bare bones of the history to get the full flavor of the story. For example: Nobuhiro Watsuki's popular manga *Rurouni Kenshin* and its anime incarnation draw on the 19th century Meiji Restoration and the resistance of the *Shinsengumi*, for example, in the same way that Margaret Mitchell's novel *Gone With the Wind* draws on the Civil War. The Japanese anime audience brings knowledge of the history into the theater or to the TV screen or to the manga magazine; western viewers who don't have the knowledge just aren't getting the whole picture. It's rather like watching a John Wayne western while knowing none of the history of the west. In the case of the Taira/Heike feud, some two dozen Noh dramas touch on one aspect or another of the history; enjoying or even understanding these plays without understanding the historical background is almost impossible.

CHAPTER 10: OKIKU OF THE PLATES

Our next two ghosts—both also of women who were wronged in life, like Lady Rokujo—have been immortalized in kabuki theater, but their stories existed in legend long before they appeared onstage.

25. "six, seven, eight, nine . . ."

The first example takes place at Himeji Castle, one of the three major medieval Japanese castles to survive World War 2. Designed in 1346 and built in several stages until 1618, the castle is on Mount Hime in the south of Honshu, Japan's main island, west of Osaka-Kobe. It's one of the favorite location shots for Japanese and Western movies and television programs set in olden times, serving as a principal site for films as varied as Akira Kurosawa's *Ran, The Last Samurai,* and *You Only Live Twice.* Yet it was also as the site of the events in the kabuki play *Bancho Sarayashiki*[27] that the castle is remembered in Japan today. Also, it shows the problem of folklore having to sort through different versions of the same story.

On the grounds of Himeji Castle is an old stone well identified as Okiku's well. Okiku, according to legend, was a maid in service to the lord of the castle. According to some versions, she harbored a deep love for the lord which could never be spoken because of their

---

[27] Note that the ghost-based manga and anime *Yuyu Hakusho* by Yoshihiro Togashi features Yusuke Urameshi, a delinquent student at Sarayashiki Junior High School. This is only the first allusion in that manga to classic Japanese ghost motifs and tales.

different social standings. A third party turns this from a romance to a ghost story: Tessan Aoyama, a samurai also in service at Himeji Castle. He lusts after Okiku (even though in some versions of the legend the samurai is already married), but Okiku resists his advances. In other versions of the story, Aoyama is plotting treason, and Okiku heads off the plot. The common factor: Aoyama, looking for revenge, engineers Okiku's death.

He does this with a set of ten plates, family heirlooms for which Okiku is responsible. Again, different types of plates appear in different versions of the story. Usually the plates are Japanese or Chinese, although they were also said to be rare and expensive Delft plates from the Netherlands. Whatever their origin, one of the ten plates is stolen by Aoyama. According to some, he used the plate for extortion, refusing to return it unless Okiku becomes his mistress. In other versions, the plate is broken and Okiku is blamed. The result is always the same: seeing no other way out, Okiku commits suicide by throwing herself into a well on the grounds (although, variations being what they are, another version has Okiku tortured to death and her body thrown down the well). According to legend, at night on the grounds of Himeji Castle, a woman's voice can be heard coming from one of the wells, counting; when she gets to nine, she then lets out a scream of fear and sorrow.[28] It was said that the lord who ordered Okiku's death was driven to madness by her ghostly cries.

Still, manga artist Rumiko Takahashi had some fun with the legend in her romantic comedy *Mezon Ikkoku*. The manga episode "Ido no naka (In the well)" was later animated for the 1986-1988 TV series as episode 29, "Slapstick autumn fest. Inside a well with Kyoko!"

As part of a summer festival "ghost walk,"[29] the young widowed boarding-house landlady Kyoko Otonashi has agreed to hide in a shallow

---

[28] http://www.artelino.com/articles/ghost_story_okiku.asp, accessed December 18, 2006. Yet another variant of the story has a friend of Aoyama exorcise the ghost of Okiku by hiding near the well; when the ghost counts to nine, he jumps up and shouts "ten!"

[29] Traditional ghosts sighted back in the Edo period that still appear in modern ghost walks include the Karakasa (a paper umbrella

well, dressed in classic kimono (if anyone is brave enough to look in) and counting the plates like Okiku's ghost. Yusaku Godai, the college student tenant smitten by his lovely landlady, has also volunteered to be there, agreeing to be made up as a *nekomata*[30] cat-spirit, but his hopes for getting some romantic time alone with Kyoko are dashed by the other boarding-house residents. Both Godai and the good-looking tennis coach Mitaka get shoved into Kyoko/Okiku's well, which is just deep enough to keep them from climbing out on their own. Of course, since Godai and Mitaka are both after Kyoko's romantic attentions, they don't exactly cooperate to solve their predicament, for fear of leaving the rival alone with Kyoko. As the manga episode ends, the other boarding-house residents start piling into the well, which definitely wasn't built for more than three people. Kyoko and Godai end up having the same thought, yet in very different ways: Godai, who's now squeezed up against his beautiful landlady like commuters on a packed subway train, happily thinks, "I could die now;" Kyoko, hot and sweaty and cramped, is thinking, "I wish I was dead."[31]

XXX

Okiku's story, in all its variations, sets up one of the most common ghost themes in Japanese culture: that a person's ghost can stay on earth to protest its innocence after having been mistreated. However powerless the victim may have been in life, she finds considerable power in the afterlife. This is especially true of Okiku's sister in haunting, and one of the star ghosts in Japan, Oiwa.

---

which hops about on its handle), the Rokurokubi (a person with a long rubbery neck), the Chochin (a ghost whose head is a paper lantern) and the Nopperabou (a person with a blank face—no features at all; we met this spirit on page one).

[30] Find out more about these spirits in the "Cats and Dogs" chapter.
[31] "Ido no naka" in Takahashi Rumiko, 1984, *Mezon Ikkoku*, vol. 6, Tokyo: Shogakukan, pp. 165-184.

CHAPTER 11: OIWA AND THE YOTSUYA KAIDAN

One of Japan's most enduring ghost stories is only about two centuries old, although the type of ghost was certainly familiar by the time it was written. The Kabuki drama *Yotsuya Kaidan*[32] was first written and performed in 1825. Its author, Tsuruya Nanboku, said it was based on a true story. True or not, there is a tomb (the Oiwa Inari, or Oiwa Shrine) in Tokyo's Myogyoji Temple that is still believed to hold the remains of the woman at the center of this story; her date of death is given as February 22, 1636. Anyone who plans to stage *Yotsuya Kaidan* traditionally goes to Oiwa's tomb and pays their respects, just to make sure the production isn't cursed. There are legends about ill-fated productions of *Yotsuya Kaidan*, just as there are legends about the "curse" associated with Shakespeare's *Macbeth*. One actress is supposed to have been killed in a car crash, a stage light fell from the ceiling and injured several actors, one member of the crew of another production is supposed to have committed suicide . . . Other rumors maintain that if you visit the shrine out of morbid curiosity and not to pay proper respects to

---

[32] Yotsuya started as a farming village on the outskirts of Edo (now called Tokyo). As the city of Edo grew in the early 1600s, more people moved to Yotsuya, especially after 1658, when a disastrous fire swept through Edo and Yotsuya was one of the few neighborhoods that was spared. Now a part of the Shinjuku section of Tokyo, the name Yotsuya literally means "four valleys."

Oiwa that the visitor's right eye will be disfigured like hers was; but that's getting ahead of the story.

Yotsuya Kaidan was not only one of the best-known Kabuki dramas, it was also one of the first to be filmed, in 1912. The silent film, which was remade three times in the silent era alone, contains elements still present in Japanese horror movies today. In 1949 the film was one of the biggest postwar features; the first full-color version was made in 1959. There have been at least fifteen different film versions, including the 2006 anime; the 1994 film *Chushingura kaiden yotsuya kaidan*, released with the English title *Crest of Betrayal*, directed by Kinji Fukasaku, was actually a double-header, a remake of *Yotsuya Kaidan* within a remake of *Chushingura*, also known as *The 47 Ronin*. This time around, when the shogun is tricked by a treacherous nobleman into dissolving the estate of a loyal noble, scattering the loyal lord's group of masterless samurai (ronin) in the process, one of those scattered was named Iemon.

Iemon, the real villain of *Yostuya Kaidan*, which is in its own way a Japanese version of the ancient Greek story of Medea, is a ronin (a samurai whose master in this case has died). Iemon wants to marry a wealthy woman. Since he's already married, he arranges for the death of his wife. She (rather, her angry ghost) gets revenge, but this is only a small part of a much richer drama. Each scene of *Yotsuya Kaidan* could serve as its own play, but they are all interconnected, and establish overwhelmingly that Oiwa was a victim long before her ghost set out to curse others. (It also shows that Jerry Springer and his modern-day friends have no monopoly on dysfunctional families.)

By the way, if you read about an elaborate stage effect here and wonder whether it's possible—it definitely is. Kabuki started in the Edo period (the 1600s), and they've had time to develop complicated and effective special effects machinery. The most important machine is the kabuki stage itself, or *butai*: a rotating circular stage equipped with trapdoors. So, when the script says that the ghostly arms of Oiwa reach out of a washtub on the stage, that's exactly what the audience sees. And much, much more.

26. "You killed my father, and now me . . ."

The first act sets up the relationship between Oiwa, elder daughter of Yotsuya Samon, and Tamiya Iemon. Samon and Iemon were both in the service of Lord Enya, who died after his finances went into decline. Iemon had married Oiwa, but then Iemon began embezzling from Lord Enya, bringing about the financial troubles that caused his master's physical decline and death. Samon learned of Iemon's embezzlement, and forced his daughter Oiwa to divorce Iemon. Shortly thereafter, Samon is attacked by some homeless men, and Iemon rescues him. He asks Samon to let Oiwa be his wife again, but Samon, still angry at Iemon's embezzlement, refuses.

Samon's other daughter, Osode, has found work at a brothel to make ends meet; she's achieved a major reputation for her services, under the name Omon. One man, Naosuke, wants to marry Osode, but she doesn't like him; besides, she already has a fiancée (actually, her husband, although this is kept secret), Yomoshichi, who is currently missing. Like Samon, Yomoshichi was part of Lord Enya's household, thrown out of work and into poverty by his lord's death. While Osode and Naosuke are visiting one night, during which Naosuke gives Osode a purse of money, Yomoshichi shows up at the brothel to buy Osode's freedom. When Yomoshichi happens to find Naosuke's money, Naosuke (who was hiding in the next room) confronts them. After Yomoshichi gives Naosuke back his money, he leaves with Osode, while Naosuke follows at a distance.

Next we meet yet another former retainer of Lord Enya, named Shozaburo, disguised as a homeless man. He is waiting in the dark of night by a roadside shrine to meet with Yomoshichi, so that they could organize other former retainers of Lord Enya (including Samon) to carry out a vendetta. Yomoshichi trades clothes with Shozaburo, then goes off with a message for other conspirators. When Shozaburo is alone, Naosuke kills him, believing him to be Yomoshichi; then, he mutilates the victim's face to slow up any investigation.

Meanwhile, Samon shows up in order to tell the displaced retainers that Iemon's stealing caused Lord Enya's death. Before he can do this, however, Iemon kills Samon. After this second murder, Osode arrives looking for Yomoshichi and Oiwa shows up looking for her father. They discover the two corpses and begin crying and lamenting (remember that the body of Shozaburo is believed to be that of Osode's beloved Yomoshichi). Meanwhile, the two murderers, Iemon and Naosuke, realize that they have a mutual interest in the situation. They vow to avenge the deaths of Samon and Yomoshichi if Oiwa would return to Iemon and Osode would marry Naosuke. This state of affairs at the end of act 1 clearly suggests that no good can come in act 2.

Time has passed between the two acts. When we next see Oiwa, she has given birth to Iemon's child and then contracted a debilitating illness. Iemon has a family but no money, and his desire for Oiwa has turned to contempt. Iemon waits to meet with Kohei, a henchman who has stolen a powerful, potentially lethal medicine. Meanwhile he has to put up with other visitors; because of their untimely arrival, Kohei is bound, gagged, and shoved into a closet. These visitors including Takuetsu, the manager of the brothel where Osode formerly worked, the money-lender Mosuke, and Omaki, employed as a wet-nurse by Ito Kihei, a neighboring lord. She has also brought Oiwa some medicine for her condition. Omaki pays Iemon's debt to Mosuke, then suggests that Iemon accompany her to her lord's house to thank him for the medicine for his wife. This leaves Oiwa alone with Takuetsu (and Kohei, still tied up in the closet). When Oiwa feels faint, Takuetsu accidentally gives her the medicine Kohei had delivered. The scene ends with Oiwa in extreme pain.

Iemon, meanwhile, is received warmly by Ito Kihei. His granddaughter Oume has told grandfather that she's in love with Iemon, so grandfather decides to get Oiwa out of the way for his granddaughter's sake. He knew exactly what the medicine he gave to Omaki would do to Oiwa. What it has done is cause one side of her face to be swollen and disfigured, while her hair starts falling out in great bloody clumps. At first, Iemon rejects the idea of marrying

Oume, but, between Ito Kihei's offer of money and Oume's threats to kill herself if she doesn't get Iemon, he caves in.

Iemon goes back to Oiwa to break the bad news to her: not only is he leaving their marriage, but he's also giving up seeking vengeance for her father Samon (who he murdered). Iemon's first attempt at leaving Oiwa involves trying to convince Takuetsu to rape Oiwa, giving Iemon an excuse to leave, but Takuetsu refuses. Takuetsu instead tells Oiwa that the medicine came from Ito Kihei's servant Omaki. Oiwa tries to prepare to go to Ito Kihei, but in trying to attack Takuetsu inadvertently slashes her own throat; Iemon returns with some friends, finds his wife's body, and blames the death on Kohei, his former servant and owner of the sword that killed Oiwa (never mind that Kohei's been bound and gagged in the closet since the second act began). Iemon cuts the heads off of both Oiwa and Kohei and the bodies are thrown into the river. (In some versions of the story, Takuetsu takes the place of Kohei as scapegoat.)

Events immediately move to the wedding of Iemon and Oume. The severed head of Oiwa's ghost, however, shows up in the original play for the honeymoon; film versions of the play have Oiwa's full corpse, nailed to a door, appear to accuse Iemon. In his fear and guilt, Iemon kills Oume. When he goes to speak to Ito Kihei about this, Iemon sees the ghost of his former servant Kohei instead, and kills his new (dead) wife's grandfather, thus slipping further into madness.

And that was act two.

The third act begins in late afternoon with Iemon as a fugitive wanted for murder. He runs into his mother Okuma by the Onbobori Canal. She's carved a wooden tombstone for Iemon, thinking that, if people believe her son is already dead, the authorities will stop hunting for him. Together they set up his fake tombstone.

After Okuma leaves, Iemon runs into Naosuke, who has still been stalking Oiwa's sister Osode. Naosuke sees the tombstone, figures it to be a joke and throws it into the river. It gets fished out a short way downstream by Oyumi, the older sister of Oume. After the murder of her grandfather and younger sister, Oyumi and the family servant Omaki were forced to live penniless and homeless.

When Iemon realizes who Oyumi is, he pushes her into the canal. As the sun sets, the bodies of Oiwa and Kohei float down the canal. Iemon lashes out at them but, because they're already dead, there's nothing he can do.

The fifth and final act takes place in an abandoned house (or temple) at Hebiyama. Iemon has taken refuge there, driven to madness by the ghosts and memories of what he has done. The neighbors try to exorcise the ghost of Oiwa, but she will not be denied her grudge now. The ghost of Oiwa is joined by the living: Yomoshichi, the beloved of Oiwa's sister, and Ohana, the widow of Iemon's former servant Kohei. They are poised to take their own vengeance as the curtain falls.

All things considered, the living visitors were just frosting on the cake; Iemon was amply punished in his life for his own misdeeds, being plagued by the ghosts of his victims as well as other phenomena; in the 1959 version, *Tokaido Yotsuya Kaidan*, Iemon sees snakes everwhere. It's an open question whether being haunted to madness was "enough". Still, this is similar to the variation in the story of Okiku and the plates in which the lord of the manor was driven to madness by Okiku's ghost moaning in the well. There are, in Japanese ghost stories at any rate, things worse than death.

xxx

If you've kept track, this synopsis skipped over act 4; so do most modern productions of the play, although in some even shorter versions Iemon throws himself into the canal at the end of act 3. The fourth act, however, is where the ghostly happenings begin in earnest, touching on lives other than Iemon's, and reflecting attitudes that go beyond, and add another dimension to, the basic ghost story. Act four begins with Naosuke having married Oiwa's sister Osode, the former prostitute. Things aren't settled in this household, either: Osode refuses to consummate the marriage with Naosuke, she has to take in washing and sells incense to survive, and in this act ghostly hands reach out of the washtub to strangle Naosuke. Osode finally submits to Naosuke's amorous demands, only for them to be interrupted by her beloved Yomoshichi, who Osode (among others) thought was dead. She tricks both men into killing her, having already written a suicide note explaining the secret problem: that Naosuke her stalker was actually her brother. When Naosuke finds out, he kills himself. Meanwhile, the ghost of Kohei appears to a member of the ronin seeking revenge against the downfall of their former master Lord Enya. This ronin, Matanojo, is disabled and contemplating suicide. The ghost of Kohei gives him the poisonous medicine that disfigured Oiwa. Matanojo, however, is miraculously healed by it, and this good deed allows Kohei to be reborn into Paradise.

This is an example of how, as Patrick Macias noted, "Japanese horror films . . . traditionally fold in the concept of karma, drawn from . . . Buddhism. Rarely do bad things happen to someone without a good reason. Often a curse, a misdeed in the past needs resolution—and there will be no peace until the balance is restored."[33] With so much relentless depravity in this story, from embezzlement to incest, from murder to rape, the act of Kohei's ghost healing Matanojo is a rare glimmer of light, and perhaps should be left in productions of *Yotsuya Kaidan* as a reminder to the audience that not all ghosts are evil, and that their deeds may even lead to salvation.

xxx

Along with the various film and TV versions of the *Yotsuya Kaidan*, an anime version is now available. It was adapted into a four-part television anime as part of the series *Ayakashi*. The adaptation, directed by Tetsuo Imazawa (who's worked on TV anime series as different as the historical romance *The Rose of Versailles* and the wrestling story *Kinnikuman*, plus movies and OAVs), is a fairly faithful one, although it is still missing the hopeful fourth act. It does include all of the set-pieces for which the play is famous: Oiwa's ghostly arms reaching out of Osode's washtub, the lantern that turns into Oiwa's face, and so on. The fourth episode also includes one new device that would be hard to duplicate onstage: rats, a wave of them, attacking Iemon at the end

---

[33] Macias, Patrick. "Mysterious and Spooky: Inside Japanese Horror Films." *Shojo Beat*, Volume 2 #3, pp. 275-276.

of the production, much as he was plagued by visions of snakes in the 1959 film version.

Also in the series are pictures of some of the kabuki effects machinery, photos of the Oiwa shrine, and explanations from the narrator, author Tsuruya Nanboku, who died in 1829. Among his comments to the audience are explanations for the medicine that afflicted Oiwa (which he says was probably not a drug at all but smallpox), a prosaic explanation for the "curse" of the play (with so much stage machinery, he essentially says, accidents will happen—which doesn't explain why the producer of a recent and successful revival committed suicide during the run), and a rather minimal explanation for the play's popularity: that people want to see justice brought about by destiny in this manner. Certainly, in the modern world (whether in Japan or anywhere else) it seems that justice is hard to find and karma takes its own time punishing those who need to be punished.

Of course, the vengeance of Lady Oiwa is far beyond anything that would be handed out by mere mortals. In Japan, Oiwa is the classic example of an *onryou*, a ghost (more often female than male) who appears for one reason: vengeance. Onryou are often victims of circumstance, like Oiwa; powerless and subject to manipulation by the men in their lives. In death, however, it's a different story.

The look of the onryou has become standardized thanks to kabuki theater and the movies. They have three things in common: a white burial shroud, white faces, and, most important, black disheveled hair. This last trait is actually another bit of shorthand symbolism; disordered hair is the sign of a madwoman, and the message can't be much clearer: you can't reason with her. You can't come up with excuses. You can't appeal to tenderness or mercy. You might as well try talking with the great white shark in *Jaws*.

Onryou have significant powers, except that, like Oiwa, they do not directly attack the person most responsible for their grievous condition. Okiku's ghost likewise didn't attack her former master, but her lamentations drove him mad. Oiwa also drove the faithless Iemon to madness. After all, killing him would not only have been too easy, it would have simply repeated the bad karma caused by Iemon's own killings.

All of this probably sends a mixed message to the modern-day audience: as frustrating as it may be to let things go through channels, or just forego vengeance altogether, do you really want to take a chance on the alternative?

CHAPTER 12: NOH DRAMA

Ghosts are a standard, almost required, part of Noh[34] theater, which was a synthesis of courtly and folk performances. Ghosts have been featured Noh performers since Noh was standardized in the 14th century, during the Muromachi period. Of the thousand or so Noh plays that were written, half no longer exist in writing, but those that do often feature some sort of ghost. One reason few Noh plays survive in writing is the way in which Noh was rehearsed and performed: the soloists would rehearse on their own, under the tutelage of an older master. The only time the full cast would get together would be for the performance itself. In other kinds of theater this would seem to be a recipe for disaster, but the slow and stately nature of Noh helps preserve the production.

An evening of Noh theater is actually a set series of moral-lesson plays mixed with music, dancing, and singing, beginning with the *shugen*, a celebration of the Shinto spirits that have ruled Japan since its creation. Next comes the *shura*, a battle-play in which the ghost of a famous warrior (a major character or *shite,*[35]) appears onstage to a visitor, often a wandering priest (known as a *waki*). The shite is, more accurately, a maeshite if it's human in appearance and a nochijite if it appears as a spirit. The warrior spirit is suffering because, no matter how distinguished he was on earth and how honored he was on the field of battle (and that battle usually is the Heike/Taira feud which culminated in the 12th century naval battle

---

[34] The name is short for *saragaku-no* theater.
[35] Pronounced shih-tay, unlike the Irish epithet which is spelled the same way and rhymes with "kite."

at Dan-no-Ura—see chapter 9), he failed to realize a higher form of honor. The third section is the *kazura* or *onnamono*. The central spirit here was once a member of court or other high-ranking woman whose soul still haunts the earth, in repentance for some deed or other. This is followed by the Oni-Noh, focusing on realistic people and showing that redemption is possible. Two other sections, extolling traditional virtues and again praising the gods, round off the evening.

27. The Flutist and the Warrior

The ghost play *Atsumori* is one of the Noh dramas based on the history of the Heike wars, and features a ghost slain in battle. The battle is very specific: the battle of Ichi-no-Tani, which took place in C.E. 1184. Atsumori was a youthful samurai of the Taira clan; he's shown onstage as more of a poet than a warrior. The young samurai even insists on carrying his flute into battle. This is incomprehensible to Kumagai Naozane, a veteran fighter for the Heike clan. Kumagai defeats and slays Atsumori, although he has his misgivings.

These misgivings come out in the Noh play, which begins with a monk, Rensho, who is actually Kumagai, on a pilgrimage back to the battlefield at Ichi-no-Tani. For years since the slaying of Atsumori, Kumagai has lamented his actions; after all, Kumagai had a son roughly the same age as Atsumori, who was wounded in battle. He also regretted having to fight someone clearly not prepared for the hardships of war. This is brought up in the first act of the play, as Rensho meets and spends some time with a young man who was also a flutist.

After an interlude (called a kyogen) in which a performer reminds the audience of the circumstances of the story, Rensho is shown praying for the repose of Atsumori's soul. The young flutist from the first act reappears, revealing himself to be the spirit of Atsumori. He is indeed not able to rest in peace, because his soul is still tied to this world by the emotional circumstances of his death. The ghost of Atsumori reenacts his death, and expects Kumagai to reenact his part in slaying Atsumori. This time, however, the warrior-turned-monk refuses to relive his past, and the ghost of Atsumori declares that Rensho is not his enemy. Unlike so many vengeful ghost stories, in which the survivor still tries to maintain that he was in the right, the two leading characters here actually want to achieve the same thing: peace for Atsumori's soul.

28. Modern Western Noh: "The Gull"

Arts stay the same, and change; this paradox has examples in every culture and country. The Noh theater tradition would seem to be a museum piece, but it's been used for modern storytelling as well. A 2006 Canadian piece seems to be especially appropriate for the conventions of Noh, including its ghosts.

The Gull was written by Daphne Marlatt and tells the story of two Japanese-Canadian brothers. As happened on the west coast of America in 1942, after the Japanese bombing of Pearl Harbor, Canada also forcibly relocated its Japanese population at the beginning of World War Two. For the fishermen Waki and Wakitsure, exile didn't end until 1950, when they were able to go to the village of Steveston, a suburb of Vancouver, British Columbia, on the north bank of the Fraser River. On their way back to rebuilding their lives, they encounter a part-human, part-bird spirit, who turns out to be the spirit of their dead mother; she exhorts them to return to their Japanese ancestral home of Wakayama-ken instead of staying in Canada. This character is solidly in the Noh tradition: "Ghosts who refused to leave until they were heard by the living symbolize unresolved emotional conflicts that continue after death."[36] In addition, *The Gull* fits into Noh's Buddhist heritage; playwright Marlatt was brought up in Penang, Malaysia, by a Buddhist nanny.

Marlatt also notes a parallel in her work to another typical aspect of Noh:

---

[36] http://www.kyotojournal.org/10,000things/043.html, accessed January 7, 2010

Traditional Noh plays are highly allusive and often weave quotes from the classical poetic repertoire or from other Noh plays into their texts. That's one of the features of Noh that I find very contemporary and I wanted to keep it alive in my play. However, I realized that quoting from those sources would mean nothing to a Western audience so I chose instead to weave in some lines from poems by the contemporary Canadian poets Roy Miki, Joy Kogawa, and Roy Kiyooka.

Noh drama isn't the only medium creating new buildings out of old material; this happens a lot in anime and manga.

CHAPTER 13: KAIDAN
KASANEGAFUCHI

Yoshihiro Togashi's manga *Yu Yu Hakusho* is the story of a high school delinquent, Yusuke Urameshi, who (when he felt like it) attended Sarayashiki Junior High School. The name of the school evokes the story of Okiku and the ten plates. The manga also has another echo to a classic kaidan in Yusuke's mortal enemy (at first, anyway) Kuwabara, who sort-of attends Kasanegafuchi High School.

The "Ghost Story of Kasane Swamp" (*Kaidan Kasanegafuchi*) was written in the late 1800s by Sanyutei Encho (1839-1900), an author and performer whose works include *Botan Doro* ("The Peony Lantern;" see chapter 23). He lived and worked in the Meiji era, when Japan was rushing to catch up technologically with the west, and the intelligentsia of Japan declared that a belief in ghosts and demons and nature spirits was "the result of mental illness." I suspect that, whether he believed in the rush to science and technology or not, Encho seemed to relish trotting out the often lurid ghost stories for which he is remembered.

Kaidan Kasanegafuchi has been filmed a number of times; the first version in 1926, directed by Kenji Mizoguchi. Other prominent versions appeared in 1957 (directed by Nobuo Nakagawa, who two years later would direct the full-color and brilliantly staged *Tokaido Yotsuya Kaidan*) and 1970; a film version simply titled *Kaidan (Ghost Story)* directed by Hideo Nakata, director of *Ringu,* was released in

2007. This was Nakata's first period piece, and by most accounts it's a fine and scary production.[37]

29. A Curse for Father and Son

Some ghost stories center around money; many of them center around love. This one involves both. The chain of misery and bad karma begins when an 18th century samurai, Fukami Shinzaemon, borrows some money from a blind merchant (in some versions a masseur) named Soetsu. Shinzaemon, however, takes his own time in repaying the loan; one winter night, Soetsu leaves his wife and his young daughter Rui at home and goes looking for Shinzaemon to collect on the debt.

Unfortunately, Shinzaemon not only decides to cancel his debt by killing Soetsu but has the body dumped in Kasane swamp. Soetsu's spirit calls down a curse on the samurai's family, a curse which has echoes of *Yotsuya Kaidan* and other classic tales.

Shinzaemon's mind is twisted by the curse, he fails to recognize his wife when he sees her and instead slashes her throat. This further maddens the samurai, and he takes his own life. However, this is not the end of the story.

The story resumes twenty years later, with Shinkichi, the son of Shinzaemon, now grown up and working as a servant to a wealthy man. Shinkichi has found love with a young woman named Hisa, but theirs is a bittersweet forbidden love; Hisa is the daughter of Shinichi's wealthy employer, and the social distance between them makes it impossible for them to be together except for occasional secret meetings. When a wealthy samurai asks for Hisa's hand in marriage, Shinichi sneaks into Hisa's room one night. They are caught, and Shinichi is dismissed as a servant.

However, he is taken in and cared for by a somewhat older woman who has been interested in him for some time. This older woman

---

[37]   Nakata has also directed a live action movie based on the *Death Note* manga, titled *L: Change the World*.

is Rui, a music teacher and daughter of the blind moneylender murdered by Shinkichi's father. Both Rui and Shinichi are unaware of this connection between them; only an elderly servant is aware, and she hasn't told anyone.

Even though he too is unaware of this connection, Omura, an Iago-like samurai who knows that Hisa is still interested in Shinkichi, befriends Shinkichi and talks him into eloping with Hisa, then "accidentally" leaves information about the elopement in a letter where Rui can find it. Omura was hoping that Rui would see to it that Shinkichi was arrested at least, preferably beheaded, thus giving Omura free access to the music teacher. However, the curse is still alive. Rui barges in on the couple and tries to kill Hisa herself; instead, she falls down a flight of stairs.

Rui doesn't feel the extent of the damage caused by the fall until later. Omura brings Shinkichi another note from Hisa requesting a meeting. Shinkichi is torn between fleeing to his lover and staying by the woman who gave him a home when he was orphaned. Finally, though, he tells Rui he's going to get her instrument and leaves her; Omura comes back to mock Rui about her faithless Shinkichi.

This is the moment when Rui decides to look at her face, and finds that the mirror has been taken out of the room. She goes to a water barrel and, when the ripples stop, sees herself: half of her face is torn up and distorted, in an echo of Oiwa in *Yotsuya Kaidan*. The elderly servant knows that now is the time to tell Rui about her parents and those of her beloved. As she dies, Rui leaves a threatening note for Shinkichi: "I will haunt your wife to her grave."

And she does. Shinkichi and Hisa know that they have to leave town; unfortunately, the road out takes them through the Kasane swamp, where the dominoes seriously start to fall. Shinkichi's mind is turned by the ghost of the abandoned Rui, and he kills his beloved Hisa. The duplicitous samurai Omura then kills Shinkichi. The ghost of Rui rises up in the swamp, threatening Omura but not killing him. She leaves that to the ghost of Soetsu, the blind moneylender whose murder started the whole tragic cycle.

CHAPTER 14: PRINCESS OF THE DARK TOWER A/K/A TENSHU MONOGATARI (STORY OF THE CASTLE TOWER)

Izumi Kyoka (1873-1939) didn't really exist. It's the pen name for a prolific and talented writer of the Meiji era, Izumi Kyotaro. His output included novels, short stories, and plays for the Kabuki theater, including *Tenshu monogatari* (1917). He was introduced to Kabuki through his mother's family: his mother's father had been a musician and his uncle was a renowned Noh actor, Kintaro Matsumoto. At age 18 Izumi became an apprentice to Koyo Ozaki, one of the great writers of the day. By 1895 he had published his first major success, the novel *Yakoujunsa* (*The Night Watchman*), and remained a prominent writer until his death. His health almost always compromised by one illness or another, Izumi's work is known for its use of the supernatural (more than half of his writings deal with ghosts or spirits) and dealing very little with jazz, machinery, or other aspects of "modern" life and literature. In a time when Japanese literature focused on young girls being romanced (in reality or fantasy) by older men, Izumi's works often turned on an older woman aiding a younger man; *Tenshu monogatari* is, in a sense, one such work.

Only a handful of Izumi's works have been translated into English, and it can be argued that *Tenshu monogatari* isn't one of those works. Even though it was animated following a screenplay by Yuji Sakamoto and directed by Hidehiko Kadota (previously an animator on two of the *Dragonball Z* movies) as a four-part story along with two other ghost stories (the classic *Yotsuya Kaidan* (see chapter 11) and the original *Bake neko* (coming up in chapter 15)) by Toei in 2006 for broadcast on Japanese television under the collective name *Ayakashi*, the story was modified a bit from Izumi's original.

30. Because of a falcon

In this version, the ghostly princess Tomihime and her retinue of ghostly women live at the top of a tower in Shirasagi-jo castle. Just as humans are warned in these stories not to meddle in the affairs of spirits, the ghostly women (who range in age from old crones to little girls) know that they must not deal with the world of humans—except that their diet largely consists of human flesh. They eat people, as Tomihime explains, "to escape the pain and suffering" of their immortal state, which places them in the Hungry Ghost tradition. Part of the curse of being a Hungry Ghost is that one eats but is never satisfied; often, what one eats is human flesh and blood—or something even more disgusting.

This story, however, is based on a love affair between Tomihime and Zushonosuke, a falconer for the decadent Lord Harima. One day, while looking for a strayed falcon, Zushonosuke spies Tomihime bathing in a pond—and the dominoes begin to fall, not only for the love affair between the human and the ghost, but also for Zushonosuke's rebellion against his master in the name of love. Tomihime also must rebel, for the sake of her love for a mortal; the "life" of a ghost is formal, stilted, and repetitive, like life at court, and some have seen this story of defiance of tradition as a social comment by Izumi. Of course, it also works as a chilling tale of supernatural love.

It's ultimately an ill-fated love, as we knew from the beginning. Zushonosuke and Tomihime try to set up housekeeping among the humans, but, returning to the castle for Lord Harima's falcon, Tomihime has to attack one of her ladies, who "dies" of her wounds. Zushonosuke is sent back to the village alone, where he takes up with an old girlfriend, Oshizu. In a moment of jealousy, Oshizu tells Lord Harima that his missing falcon is still at Shirasagi-jo, held captive by an evil spirit. Lord Harima sends a thousand men to storm the castle, but Tomihime and the others, including Zushonosuke, destroy them all, even as the castle is destroyed in the process. At the end, we see the falcon that started the entire story circling above the ruined castle; now, however, it has been joined by two others, meant to be the spirits of Tomihime and Zushonosuke . . .

One fascinating aspect of this anime is the constant appearance, just on the edges of the frame, of stone figures of monks and (occasionally) demons, often barely visible in the tall grass. The monks represent Jizo, a Buddhist saint (bodhisattva) believed to protect children both in this life and the afterlife; in recent years, Jizo statues are erected by those who have abortions in Japan as a way of apologizing to the fetus and praying that it will be born under better circumstances. There are also statues of the Chinese goddess of compassion, Kannon (the Japanese name of Kwan Yin). Many of these statues are draped with a bit of red cloth; these were garments of dead children, brought to protect the statue in hopes that the Jizo will protect the spirit of the dead child.[38] The sheer number of these statues in the area around Shirasagi-jo indicates that the humans had lost a great many children, possibly to the swampland, possibly to the ghosts of the castle.

There is one other detail in the anime that dates the events: candy. In particular, a sweet candy called by the Japanese "konpeitou." This is actually a loan word, from the Portuguese "confeito" (confection, candy). It's one of several Portuguese loan words (like the word for bread, "pan") that came to Japan along with Portuguese sailors in the latter half of the 1500s. Unlike the Portuguese sailors, the words stayed in Japan.

---

[38] http://www.onmarkproductions.com/html/jizo1.shtml, accessed August 12, 2007.

CHAPTER 15: CATS AND DOGS

We've looked at *Yotsuya Kaidan* and *Tenshu Monogatari*, two of the three anime ghost stories that make up the TV series *Ayakashi*. The third is in many ways completely different from the other two. Before we touch on the third story, which deals with a demonic cat spirit, it's worth remembering that a number of Japanese ghost stories revolve around common pets.

Not all ghosts are human, but that doesn't make them monsters, either. If all living things have spirits, then those spirits at the moment of death also move from our "real" world to the spirit world. Sometimes, though, it's no easier for the pets than for their owners.

Take the case of Kazumi Ryudo, son of a Buddhist exorcist and a member of the Holy Student Council at Saito High School. In a school where the ghostly activities are never-ending, it's all Kazumi can do to get through one day in the comic anime series *Haunted Junction*[39] without being possessed by random spirits—even those of dogs and cats. We often see the boy-monk scratching behind his ear with his foot, or with his back arched and screeching like a frightened feline; usually a punch to the head sets the invading spirit free.

More about cats later; dogs are another matter.

Dog-gone

Dogs have a special role in Japanese folklore. People used to believe that dogs could see ghosts and spirits that were invisible to humans. Thus the best protection against the wiles of a kitsune

---

[39] More about *Haunted Junction* in the chapter on school ghosts.

(fox spirit) or tanuki (a dog that resembles a raccoon; it and the fox are believed to be magical animals) was a faithful dog's watchful eye. The step from having the second sight to entering the spirit world was a short one, however. In Japanese legend, Inugami (Dog-God) is an invisible creature that can be summoned by a witch to fulfill various destructive purposes. But the witch has to be careful—the Inugami can possess her and take over her body and soul.[40]

The three pet stories coming up next focus on the positive rather than the demonic: on the devotion dogs show their masters—except that one of them has a surprise ending.

31. Because even a dog should rest in peace

In *Yu Yu Hakusho*, street-fighting punk Yusuke Urameshi is killed trying to save a child from a traffic accident. To earn his way back to the land of the living, he has to undergo a number of trials, the first of which involves a boy named Shota and his old dog, Jiro. Shota is so upset about Jiro dying that he doesn't want to go to school; he'd rather wait for the end with his dog. This, however, isn't the way it's supposed to be; Yusuke's guide to the underworld, Botan, points out that, even after death, Jiro's spirit circled the house looking for Shota. Yusuke's task: to break Shota of his clinging to Jiro, which is actually doing the dog's spirit more harm than good by holding him to this world.

Yusuke appears to Shota in a dream, disguised as the Lord of Hell (complete with penciled-in mustache), leading Jiro on a barbed wire leash and telling Shota that his concern for his pet made Jiro lose his chance for peace in the afterlife. Yusuke goads Shota into a fight (which was just about the only thing Yusuke understood when he was alive), which Yusuke throws in order to get Shota to let Jiro's

40   http://www.ainurin.net/japan/nihonken/photos/photo_27.html, accessed July 26, 2007.

spirit go, rather than cause it to remain attached to the earth by fretting and fussing over it. "I'll miss you, but I'll do my best," he tells Jiro's spirit as it ascends into the sky.

Ghost stories are a reminder that, even on the canine level, destiny applies to all things, and death is part of that destiny. If a soul is frozen to a spot, even out of good but misguided emotions like love and faithfulness, destiny cannot go forward.

32. Mission accomplished

The title of Yukiru Sugisaki's manga series *Lagoon Engine* is an elaborate pun based on the names of its two main characters: the sons of the Ragun family, Yen and Jin, ages 12 and 11. The manga ran in the Japanese magazine *Asuka* and its sequel, *Lagoon Engine Einsatz*, was briefly printed in translation in *New Type USA*. *Asuka* is nominally a *shonen manga* magazine, aimed at an audience of adolescent boys, and therefore should focus on action adventure and macho themes. There are a lot of *shojo manga* touches to this title, however, which suggests at least a crossover to the girls' market. *Lagoon Engine* especially shows the influence of CLAMP, the women manga artists collective, and suggests that *Lagoon Engine* is one of a growing number of crossover manga, capable of appealing to both boys and girls.

The Ragun brothers are still in elementary school, but have been studying their father's business of becoming gakushi (the kanji literally means music masters, but the kanji "gaku" can also be pronounced "raku" and carries the meaning of comfort or relief). As exorcists, their job is to bring comfort to ghosts and other evil (or merely tormented) spirits. In order to comfort the spirits, the brothers have to subdue them, and to subdue them, they have to state the demons' true names. This is a motif that appears elsewhere in manga and anime; the 1988 *Vampire Princess Miyu* OAV series[41] shows the eternally teenaged vampire of the title subduing one evil

---

[41] As well as the 26 week TV series created in 1997.

spirit after another by stating its name. (I presume that stating its name strips away its illusory disguises and reveals the spirit for what it is. At the very least, it's a tipoff that the ghost-chaser can see the otherwise invisible or disguised quarry.)

The brothers are aided by other spirits called koga, vaguely resembling little stuffed unicorns. And if you think that's cute, you should see the first ghost that appears in this series: the ghost of a little puppy. It had gone on its own to see its owner, a classmate of Yen's who has had to spend two years in the hospital. The puppy, named Tom, bit through its leash and went to the hospital to see its owner, but had gotten hit by a car before it could get there. Since then, its spirit haunted a temple near the hospital looking for its mistress, tugging at the stockings of little girls it believed to be its owner. It took the two brothers to put the clues together and realize that the puppy wanted to see its owner one last time before its soul moved on to the afterlife.[42]

This story and the next present an image of the faithful dog that has been a Japanese icon for decades. The details may vary, but these stories would surely remind Japanese readers/viewers of perhaps that country's best-known dog, Hachiko (see sidebar).

33. Whose ghost is it?

As they travel in search of tournaments, the episode of *Pokémon* with the English title "Just Waiting on a Friend" has Ash, Misty, Brock, and their various pokémon stop at a house, standing alone in the middle of the forest, seeking shelter for the night. Inside they discover the owner of the house: Lakoko, a girl with a pet Ninetails. This pokémon (none of them have names except for their species) is a fox type, but this animal has a particularly Japanese trait, as its name

---

[42] There is a negative side to this happy ending, reminiscent of the story of Jiro. Tom was supposed to move on once he saw his owner one last time. Tom, however, stays at the hospital, and begins to change...

suggests: nine tails. This is common in a *kyuubi-no-kitsune* (literally, nine-tailed fox), a powerful fox demon (a nine-tailed fox spirit possessed Naruto at birth, in the manga by Masashi Kishimoto, and in the *Digimon* anime series one of the fighting forms of the fox-like Renamon is a nine-tailed fox named Kyuubimon), and suggests the animal may be more than she seems.

Brock (as usual) is instantly smitten by Lakoko's beauty, and for once she likes him in return. Brock blurts out that he wants to marry her and Lakoko surprisingly agrees. Brock rushes to hug her; instead, he goes through her. Ash and Misty get scared and suspicious; just then, a fog appears and Ninetails mysteriously blasts them out of the house. Ash and Misty sneak back in and find what seems to be a decades-old picture of Brock in the house. Also there's a diary apparently written by Lakoko, except that it's over 200 years old. Misty and Ash try to stop Lakoko from keeping Brock with her, suspecting that she is a predatory ghost.

Ash and company finally discover the truth: there is no Lakoko. Ninetails is actually 200 years old. The owner of the house (who bore the uncanny resemblance to Brock) went traveling on business years ago, leaving behind his staff of servants (including Lakoko) and his pokémon Ninetails. He was never heard from again. One by one the servants died or left the house, until the last two in the house were Lakoko and the Ninetails. Because of her age and experience, this Ninetails developed psychic abilities to the point that she was still alive after two centuries. Ninetails created an image of Lakoko to keep her company, but when she saw Brock she hoped that if this lookalike of her old master stayed, everything would be as it was before. With the breaking of her old pokéball during a scuffle with Ash, Ninetails is free to be wild and not restricted to the mansion anymore.

So there was no ghost at all; just a highly-evolved psychic pokémon. But the episode's worth including here because it sounds so many of the themes of the classic *kaidan*. The beautiful, powerful, and clearly not-human maiden asks a mortal to stay with her forever, and he very nearly accepts. Of course Ash and Misty would presume that the human was a ghost causing everything to happen; who would imagine that a pet could bring all this about? This particular pseudo-ghost story, though, like the two that precede it, would also resonate with any Japanese child who's heard the story of faithful Hachiko.

Sidebar: The Faithful Hachiko

Shibuya is a neighborhood known today as a popular gathering point for Tokyo's young people. But long before loose socks and platform sandals, before Yoyogi Park and the Shibuya 109 shopping mall, Shibuya had another claim to fame: a dog named Hachiko.

The year was 1925. Professor Eizaburo Ueno walked to Shibuya Station every morning, accompanied by his loyal akita, Hachi, nicknamed Hachiko. Hachiko didn't ride the train with his master to the Imperial University (now known as Tokyo University), but when Professor Ueno returned every day at 3 p.m., the dog was always at the station waiting for him.

However, on May 21 of that year, Ueno died of a stroke while at the university. Hachiko went to Shibuya as always to meet his master, but 3:00 came and went, and the professor didn't arrive. So Hachiko waited. And waited.

The akita must have known something was wrong, but nonetheless he returned to the station every day at 3:00 to meet the train. Soon people began to notice the loyal dog's trips made in vain to meet his master. Ueno's former gardener, the Shibuya stationmaster, and others began feeding Hachiko and giving him shelter.

Word of Hachiko's unaltered routine spread across the nation, and he was held up as a shining example of loyalty. People traveled to Shibuya simply to see Hachiko, feed him, and gently touch his head for luck.

The months turned to years, and still Hachiko returned to Shibuya Station daily at 3 p.m., even as arthritis and age took their toll. Finally, on March 7, 1935 — nearly ten years after last seeing Professor Ueno — the 12-year-old akita was found dead on the same spot outside the station where he had spent so many hours waiting for his master.

Hachiko's death made the front pages of major Japanese newspapers. A day of mourning was declared. Contributions poured in from all over the country to memorialize the dog that had won the hearts of the nation. Sculptor Takeshi Ando was hired, with the money that had been contributed, to create a bronze statue of Hachiko. It was placed on the exact spot where Hachiko had waited for so long.

Within a few years, however, Japan was at war, and any available metal was melted down to make weapons and ammunition. Not even Hachiko's statue was spared. However, after the war, in 1948, Ando's son Teru sculpted a new Hachiko—the statue that stands outside Shibuya Station to this day.

This is not the only monument to Chuken ("loyal dog") Hachiko to be found in Tokyo, however. Aoyama Cemetery contains a memorial to Hachiko on the site of Professor Ueno's grave. Some of Hachiko's bones are reportedly buried there, but in fact, Hachiko can still be seen—stuffed, in the National Science Museum, northwest of Ueno Station. March 7, the anniversary of his death, is the Chuken Hachiko Matsuri (Loyal Hachiko Festival).

Hachiko was given life on the big screen with the *Hachiko Monogatari (The Story of Hachiko)* in 1987. The screenplay by Kaneto Shindou was adapted for a 2009 English-language telling of Hachiko's story. *Hachi: A Dog's Story* was directed by Lasse Hallström, whose films include *The Cider House Rules* and *What's Eating Gilbert Grape?*; the cast of western actors includes Richard Gere, Joan Allen, and Jason Alexander, and the movie was filmed not against the backdrop of 1920s Tokyo but in a historic station in Woonsocket, Rhode Island. Almost the only use of the original story is that Hachiko is an akita. The movie was released with very little fanfare and mixed reviews.

With so much attention being paid to Hachiko, it's no wonder that there are no ghost stories about this loyal dog. Spirits can get disgruntled when they are neglected, or when the proper rites have been slighted. Hachiko will never have anything to worry about in that regard. (Elsewhere in this collection, we hear repeatedly from ghosts who have been neglected.)

Back in Shibuya, Hachiko's statue sits in a noble pose, forever waiting for his master. And, appropriately, his statue, the best-known landmark and meeting place in Shibuya, is where hundreds of people every day sit and wait for their friends.[43]

Enough of Man's Best Friends; ghostly cats are completely different.

xxx

While dogs are part of the cycle of twelve animals in Chinese astrology and Buddhist lore, cats appear irregularly. They are in the Vietnamese version of the Chinese zodiac, replacing the Hare.[44] The Cat and the Hare share many of the same capricious, mysterious qualities, and it's no wonder that there are legends of demonic and ghostly doings surrounding Japanese cats.

34. The Vampire Cat of Nabeshima

---

[43] In the comic romance anime known in Japan as *Gals* and in the west as *Super G.A.L.s*, based on a manga by Mihona Fujii, the *kogals* (trendy young Japanese urbanite girls) who are the stars of the series are shown in the opening credits (and often in the series) not just in Shibuya Park, but at the statue of Chuken Hachiko. That statue also plays a brief role in Rumiko Takahashi's *Mezon Ikkoku*. Mitaka, the handsome tennis coach, wants to woo the widow Kyoko, but he's deathly afraid of dogs, including hers. Trying to conquer his fear begins with trying to touch the Hachiko statue.

[44] The usual translation of the Chinese zodiac animal is "rabbit," and often the words "rabbit" and "hare" are used interchangeably in the west. However, they're two different species, and, while rabbits are domesticated, hares are wild and famously unpredictable, as in the saying "as mad as a March hare." In my opinion the notoriously independent cat fits the Hare more than the Rabbit.

This is actually a relatively recent story, dating from the Sengoku era (1568-1615).

xxx

A long time ago, the Prince of Hizen had in his house a lady of rare beauty, called Otoyo. Among all his ladies she was the favorite, and none could rival her charms and accomplishments. One day the Prince went out into the garden with Otoyo, and remained until sunset, when they returned to the palace, never noticing that they were being followed by a large cat. Otoyo retired to her own room and went to bed. At midnight she awoke with a start, and became aware of the huge cat watching her; when she cried out, the beast sprang on her, tearing out her throat. Then the cat, having scratched out a grave under the veranda, buried the corpse of Otoyo, and assumed her form.

The Prince knew nothing of all this, and never imagined that a monster had slain his mistress and assumed her shape. As time went on, the Prince's strength dwindled away; his face became pale; he looked like a man suffering from a deadly sickness. Seeing this, his wife and his councilors became alarmed; they summoned physicians who prescribed various remedies for him, but these only seemed to make him worse. He suffered most of all in the night-time, when his sleep would be troubled by hideous dreams. His councilors appointed a hundred guards to watch over him; but, towards ten o'clock at night, the guards were seized with sudden drowsiness, and one by one every man fell asleep. Then the cat came in and attacked the Prince, feasting on his blood until morning. Every night the same thing occurred, with no one the wiser.

At last three of the Prince's councilors determined to see whether they could overcome this drowsiness; but by ten o'clock they too were fast asleep. The next day their chief, Isahaya Buzen, said, "Surely the spell upon my lord and his guard must be witchcraft. Let us seek out the chief priest of the temple and beseech him to pray for the recovery of my lord." They went to the priest Ruiten of

Miyo-in and hired him to recite sutras so that the Prince might be restored to health.

One night at midnight, when he had finished his religious duties and was preparing to sleep, he heard a noise outside in the garden, as if someone were washing himself at the well. He looked down from the window; and there in the moonlight he saw a handsome young soldier; he washed and then stood before the figure of Buddha and prayed for the recovery of the Prince. Ruiten looked on with admiration; and the young man, when he had finished his prayer, was going away; but the priest stopped him.

"I am Ruiten, the chief priest of this temple, praying for the recovery of my lord. What is your name?"

"Ito Soda, and I serve in the infantry of Nabeshima. Since my lord has been sick, my one desire has been to assist in nursing him; but, being only a soldier, I am not of sufficient rank to come into his presence."

When Ruiten heard this, he shed tears in admiration of the fidelity of Ito Soda, and said, "Every night the retainers who sit up with him are all seized with a mysterious sleep, so that not one can keep awake."

"Yes," replied Soda, after a moment's reflection, "this must be witchcraft. If I could sit up one night with the Prince, I would see whether I could resist this drowsiness and detect the demon."

The priest said, "I will speak with the chief councilor of the Prince of you and your loyalty, and will intercede with him."

"I am most thankful. I am not prompted by thought of self-advancement; all I wish is the recovery of my lord."

The following evening Ito Soda accompanied Ruiten to the house of Isahaya Buzen; the priest went in to converse with the councilor.

"I think that I have found a man who will reveal the monster; and I have brought him with me. He is one of my lord's foot-soldiers, named Ito Soda, and I hope that you will grant his request to sit up with my lord."

"Certainly, it is wonderful to find such loyalty in a common soldier," replied Isahaya Buzen, after a moment's reflection; "still, it is impossible to allow a man of such low rank to watch over my lord."

"Then why not raise his rank and then let him guard?"

"Let me see this Ito Soda: if he pleases me, I will consult with the other councilors, and perhaps we may grant his request."

The next day the councilors sent for Ito Soda, and told him that he might keep watch with the other retainers that night. So he took his place among the hundred gentlemen who were on duty in the prince's room.

Now the Prince slept in the center of the room, and the hundred guards sat surrounding him keeping themselves awake. But, as ten o'clock approached, they began to doze off as they sat; and despite trying to keep one another awake, they all fell asleep. Ito Soda took a small knife which he carried and stuck it into his own thigh. For awhile the pain of the wound kept him awake; but little by little he became drowsy again. Then he twisted the knife round and round in his thigh, so that the pain became extreme.

As Ito Soda watched, suddenly the sliding-doors of the Prince's room opened, and he saw a figure coming in stealthily; the form was that of a beautiful woman. Cautiously she looked around her; and when she saw that all the guard were asleep, she smiled an ominous smile, and went up to the Prince's bedside, when she realized that in one corner of the room a man was still awake. This seemed to startle her, but she went up to Soda and said, "I am not used to seeing you here. Who are you?"

"My name is Ito Soda, and this is the first night I have been on guard."

"How is it that you alone are awake?"

"There is nothing to boast about."

"What is that wound on your knee? It is red with blood."

"I felt very sleepy; so I stuck my knife into my thigh, and the pain of it has kept me awake."

"What loyalty!" said the lady.

"Is it not the duty of a retainer to lay down his life for his master? Is a scratch such as this worth thinking about?"

Then the lady went up to the sleeping prince and said, "How fares my lord tonight?" The Prince, worn out with sickness, made no reply, but Soda was watching her eagerly, and made up his mind that if she attempted to harm the Prince he would kill her on the spot. But whenever she drew near to the sick man, she would turn and look behind her, and there she saw Ito Soda glaring at her; so she had to go away again, and leave the Prince undisturbed.

At last day broke and, when the other officers awoke and opened their eyes, and saw that Ito Soda had kept awake by stabbing himself in the thigh, they were greatly ashamed.

That morning Ito Soda told Isahaya Buzen all that had occurred. The councilors all ordered him to keep watch again that night. At the same hour, the false Otoyo came and looked all round the room, and all the guard were asleep, excepting Ito Soda, who was wide awake; and so, being again frustrated, she returned to her own apartments.

Now, since Soda had been on guard, the Prince's sickness began to get better, and there was great joy in the palace. In the meanwhile Otoyo, seeing that her nightly visits bore no fruits, kept away; and from that time the night-guard were no longer subject to fits of drowsiness. This coincidence struck Soda as very strange, so he went to Isahaya Buzen and told him that Otoyo was a demon. Isahaya Buzen reflected for a while, and said, "Well, then, how shall we kill the thing?"

"I will go to the creature's room, as if nothing were the matter, and try to kill her; but in case she should try to escape, order eight men to lie in wait for her outside."

Having agreed upon this plan, Soda went at nightfall to Otoyo's apartment, pretending to have been sent with a message from the Prince. When she saw him arrive, she said, "What message have you brought me from my lord?"

"Oh, nothing in particular. Be so good as to look at this letter." And as he spoke, he drew near to her, and suddenly drawing his dagger cut at her; but the demon, springing back, seized a halberd, and tried to strike Soda. Soda fought desperately; and the demon, seeing that she was no match for him, threw away the halberd, and from a beautiful woman became suddenly transformed into a cat, which, springing up the sides of the room, jumped onto the roof. Isahaya Buzen and his men who were watching outside shot at the cat but missed, and the beast escaped.

The cat fled to the mountains, causing havoc among the people, until at last the Prince ordered a hunt, and the beast was killed. The Prince recovered from his sickness; and Ito Soda was richly rewarded.

xxx

A ghostly cat movie premiered in 1958 that, in some ways, shows a clear western influence, and in others shows the completely unique cinematic sense of its director, Nobuo Nakagawa. He lived from 1905 to 1984 and directed almost a hundred films in those eight decades. Many of these were horror films, with names that should by now be familiar, including a version of *Yotsuya Kaidan* and of *Kasanegafuchi*. Nakagawa's *Borei Kaibyo Yashiki (Mansion of the Black Cat)* reflects, for good or ill, the dominant source of horror movies at that time: England's Hammer Studios, with their costumed dramas, over-the-top acting by the likes of Peter Cushing and Christopher Lee, and tendency to push the edge of the envelope on what was then acceptable displays of sexuality. *Borei Kaibyo Yashiki* has elements of both old and new.

35. A Cure Worse Than the Disease

Though Dr. Tetsuichiro Kuzumi runs a successful private practice in the city (presumably Osaka), he has decided to move to the more rural southern island of Kyushu in the hopes that his wife Yoriko's tuberculosis might clear in the fresh air. With the help of Yoriko's brother, they move into an old and somewhat dilapidated mansion (*yashiki*) large enough to accommodate both their residence and the new medical practice.

But from day one Yoriko gets very bad vibes from the old mansion and repeatedly sees a very old woman intent on strangling her. Despite her attempts to tell her husband of her experiences, he is all too eager to dismiss them as mere hallucinations brought about by her illness and the stress of moving. It's not until the nurse also begins seeing the old woman and Yoriko is found lying unconscious that Tetsuichiro begins to open his mind to other possibilities.

Finally, after Yoriko's brother admits that the mansion has a spooky reputation, he and Tetsuichiro visit the local monk who calmly divulges the entire demonic history of the house. [45]

This movie is basically a "frame" story. Dr. Kuzumi of Osaka is so concerned about the health of his wife Yoriko that they relocate to the island of Kyushu in the hope that she'll get better. The reason why she doesn't get better is the core of the movie.

Nakagawa employs a radically creative stylistic flow as the narrative moves from present to past to present again. The film makes clear that the central portion of the film is to be understood as a "jidaigeki" or historical piece, presumably from the Edo era. The prologue and epilogue take place in the present day and amount to narrative bookends to the lengthier and more substantial middle. Rather than cast the present in color and the past in older hues, Nakagawa saves his use of color solely for the jidaigeki where the crimson red of blood and the ghastly pale of monstrosities come through all the more powerfully, while the prologue and epilogue are filmed purely in black and white, as if to imply the present somehow lives under the shadow of the past; at the very least, modern life is far less interesting than the 17th century when the house got its reputation. The result is quite striking and, as hinted at above, caught contemporary audiences thoroughly off guard due to its counter-intuitive approach.

The tale here falls squarely within the genre of tragic ghost story, and centers on classic Shinto animism wherein the departed souls of humans and animals indeed may merge in the afterlife, resulting

---

[45] http://www.sarudama.com/japanese_movies/mansionghostcat. shtml, accessed February 17, 2010.

in a formidable breed of monster. (A more recent example of this can be found in *Ju-On* where little Toshio has absorbed the spirit of his departed black cat.) Here Nakagawa depicts a ghostly triad comprised of one part cat, one part cursed human soul, and one part *onryou* or spirit intent purely on revenge.

The central portion of the narrative depicts the tragic and unfortunate chain of events which lead to the formation of this formidable monster and the generational curse which follows. Those in the present merely experience the ghostly results of the far more colorful past.

36. Hello Kitty

A lesser-known and very different ghost-cat movie worth mentioning is *Kuroneko (Black Cat)*[46], a 1968 film written and directed by Kaneto Shindou. The story is fairly straightforward: during feudal times, a woman and her son's wife are tending the family farm while the son is off fighting in a war. This leaves them vulnerable: no sooner does the film begin when a band of twenty ragtag soldiers take over the house, eat all the food, rape the women and burn down the house. Once the fire has died down, we see a black cat licking at the blood on the neck of the (relatively unmarked) corpses.

The spirits of the women and the cat merge; the women become vengeful ghosts, luring samurai to their deaths in their hut in the forest, which now appears to be a luxurious mansion. The samurai, all of them low-class louts who have been elevated in rank because of the war, expect a night of pleasure and are found in the morning with their throats ripped out by some wild beast. One fearless samurai is sent to investigate, and, wouldn't you know it, he's the son/husband

---

46   The full title of the movie is *Yabu no Naka no Kuroneko (The Black Cat in the Grove)*. The reference to a grove reminds us of "In a Grove," one of the short stories by Akutagawa that was the basis of *Rashomon*.

of the two ghosts. His wife, Shige, not only recognizes him, but abandons her desire to kill all samurai, and swears to enslave herself to the Lord of the Underworld if she could take bodily form again and spend seven days with her husband. The mother's vengeance, however, is not so easily stopped.

Watching this film reveals that the director has completely internalized manga into his narrative style. Most of the scenes are freeze-frame reaction shots or establishing looks at locations. Like manga, the movie is in black and white. Movement usually takes place within the frame of vision, without characters entering or leaving the scene. Several times in the film, a ghost is shown somersaulting through the air against a black background, in an imitation of the "time-lapse photography" way of drawing certain manga action scenes. It scans very much like a moving comic book, and makes *Kuroneko* one of the strongest statements that manga would become a dominant part of Japanese popular culture.

37. "So you were a kitten?"

There's a brief incident at the beginning of "The Heaven to Which You Will Someday Return," the first chapter of the one-volume manga *Heaven's Will* by Satoru Takamiya. Mikuzu Sudou can see spirits, but has been generally overwhelmed and is afraid to deal with them. She learns a hard but necessary lesson from Seto, a boy who looks stunningly like a girl. Specifically, he looks like his sister, who "died because of me;" he claims that her spirit is in a fan, and he wants to go to the extreme of having a sex-change so that he can "die" while his sister can "live again." Mikuzu can't go along with this self-destructive gesture.

While they're talking, a small demon attacks Mikuzu, who knows a few defensive blocks against demons but little else. Seto picks up the demon, saying "Nothing will be solved like this." Using the fan, clearing away the surface of the demon like peeling off layers of cellophane, Seto reveals that the demon was once a kitten. It then rises up into the air, dissolves, and Becomes One with the Cosmos.

Mikuzu, who saw only the scary surface of the demon, starts to cry. Seto asks her: "Do you finally understand how stupid it is to simply be afraid?" Mikuzu was too afraid to look beyond the surface; this object lesson serves her well as she goes on to deal with, among other things, a possessed piano and a vampire who transforms into a wolf.

38. The Boy Who Drew Cats

This is one of many Japanese stories translated into English and published by Lafcadio Hearn. Technically, this may be more a monster (youkai) story than a ghost story (kaidan), but it definitely features a haunted temple and battling spirits. And blood; lots of blood. This story would be right at home during a hyaku monogatari.

This story happened in a small rural village many years ago. A farming couple had a great many children, and both the boys and the girls were able to pitch in and help. The youngest son, however, wasn't much help around the house or in the fields. He was short and not very strong, and his parents soon realized that his destiny would be in studying rather than in farming. So he was sent to the village temple to be an acolyte to the priest.

But, even here, the boy didn't quite fit in. Even though he was quick-witted and obedient to the priest of the temple, he had one bad habit: he liked drawing cats. He sketched cats in the margins of papers, on the edges of books, and even on the wall screens. He drew cats sleeping, playing, hunting, and they all seemed to be almost alive. Still, this wasn't why he was sent to live at the temple and study with the priests. The old priest repeatedly asked the boy to stop drawing cats, but it seemed the boy couldn't stop.

Finally, the old priest took the acolyte aside and said, "Maybe one day you will be a great artist, but I doubt that you will make a good priest. You will have to leave this temple. Before you leave, though, I want to give you some good advice; you haven't always paid attention to what I have to say, but this is very important. It is this: at night, avoid the large and keep to the small."

111

The next day, as he prepared his small bundle of clothes, he thought and thought about what the old priest said. Still, he could make no sense of it. This just helped the boy feel even worse: he felt he was letting his parents down by being sent home from the temple. Then he remembered another temple, in a village about twelve miles away. He decided to go there to see if they would be willing to take him as an acolyte. It was better than returning in failure to the family farm.

By the time the boy got to the temple in the neighboring village, the sun was setting. Strangely, the temple only had one or two candles burning in its many rooms, and there was no sign of priests there. Still, the boy ate the little food that he brought, drew a few of his beloved cat sketches on the walls, and prepared to sleep in the deserted temple. Just as he was about to fall asleep, however, he remembered the words of the old priest: At night, avoid the large and stick to the small. So, leaving the large room where he planned at first to sleep, the boy made himself a nest inside a closet. After drawing another couple of cats inside the closet (because he truly could not help himself), the young boy went to sleep.

However, he was awoken in the middle of the night by the loudest, most frightening noises. There was shrieking and screaming, noises made by nothing human. The boy was glad he remembered the priest's words to avoid the large, even though he also realized that he was trapped by whatever was rampaging through the temple. All he could do was sit tight and wait until morning—or until the thing found him.

Finally, the boy could see through a crack in the door that the sun had come up. All was quiet, so he cautiously opened the door to the closet. The first thing he saw scared him almost to death, for every inch of the floor of the large room was covered with blood. A quick search of the temple showed where it had come from: the deserted temple had been invaded by a demon shaped like a rat—except that this rat was as big as an ox! What could have killed it?

Then the boy noticed something when he looked at the cats he had drawn the day before. In every picture, the cats' teeth and claws shone red with blood.

112

The news spread quickly through the village, and the boy found out the history of the temple. He heard how the rat demon had attacked the temple years ago, killing off or driving out the priests who lived there. He heard that many brave warriors had gone to the temple to try to slay the rat demon; none of the brave warriors were ever heard from again.

But people did hear of the boy, who grew up to become a famous artist.

xxx

The 11-week 2006 anime TV series *Ayakashi*, also known as *Samurai Horror Stories*, told two old and famous ghost stories and one original one. Since it had to live up to the impact of *Yotsuya Kaidan* and the *Tenshu Monogatari*, the third, original story needed to be something special. It is, in terms of both visuals and scares.

Bake Neko (Demon Cat) was written by Michiko Yokote (a veteran of television anime from *Cowboy Bebop* to *Naruto* to *xxxHolic*) and directed by Kenji Nakamura, who worked as a production coordinator on projects as different as the *Sailor Moon* movies and the *Serial Experiments Lain* series. However, the impressive look of these three episodes is the work of designer Takashi Hashimoto, whose career goes back to the nineties with his work on *Giant Robo*, *Armitage III*, and *Macross Plus*. This time, however, the look is like nothing you've seen before, which in anime is saying something.

39. "At first, I only meant to keep her a few days . . ."

The story, set in the Edo period, starts as the Sakai family, prominent but cash-strapped, is about to marry off their daughter, mainly for the infusion of money from the groom's family. As she steps over the threshold, however, the bride-to-be drops dead—and she isn't the only one. A passing merchant, known only as the Medicine Seller, shows that he has other talents as well; to protect the Sakai family from the title demon cat which is preying on them, he scatters *ofuda* on all of the walls. This just buys them some time, however; before he can fight the demon, the Medicine Seller needs to know the family's darkest secrets, to understand why the demon cat has a grudge against these people. The first explanation—that the head of the family and his son used to test newly purchased samurai swords on cats—just wasn't convincing. As the pattern has already established, for successful exorcisms the whole truth, and nothing but the truth, must come to light; when it does, the outcome isn't pretty.

Twenty-five years earlier, the head of the Sakai household stole a young girl on her way to be someone else's bride. He seduced her in a room in his estate, and, while he claimed at first that she seemed to care for him, things soon took a nasty turn. He ended up imprisoning the girl in his house, raping and abusing her at will. She refused to eat for a time, but her captors didn't realize that she was giving her scraps of food to a kitten that was in the room with her—her only source of comfort and companionship. She ultimately died of starvation, telling the cat to escape, and find some way to avenge her.

Which it did. The cat came back as a *bakeneko*, a demonic cat. It's a creature with a long and interesting history. Some of that history appears in the Inō Mononoke scroll, a collection of folklore from the Hiroshima area. The *bakeneko* also appears in *Shrine of the Morning Mist,* a manga by Hiroki Ugawa largely inspired by the scroll; the manga/anime version of Ugawa's *bakeneko* character sometimes looks human, sometimes like a cutesy feline/human hybrid (the "catgirl" of many, many manga/anime), and sometimes like a hybrid that's far more menacing than cutesy. The *bakeneko* could also be confused with the seemingly similar *nekomata*, a kind of *bakeneko*; both are cat demons, but the *nekomata* has learned to walk upright and is noted for having two tails. In Rumiko Takahashi's *InuYasha,* demon hunter Sango has a pet *nekomata* named Kirara, which turns from a cute little two-tailed kitten into a giant cat as big as a tiger, with fiery paws and the ability to fly. On a more earthy note, the Nekomata are also a low-level Yakuza (organized crime) gang in the manga/anime *Gokusen.*

The Medicine Seller ultimately slays the demon cat afflicting the Sakai family, but by then they could no longer deny their sordid past, and the chambermaid Kayo, who alone seemed to have any kind of good sense, fled the house. The Medicine Seller at the end finds the corpse of an old dead cat, while the spirits of a girl and a kitten, long imprisoned in the Sakai mansion, finally reach the outside world.

Bake Neko proved so popular that the Medicine Seller became part of a separate anime series in 2007, called *Mononoke*.[47] In this case, the Medicine Seller travels across Japan, getting involved in murder mysteries and in doing so encounters a variety of ghosts and demons. Once again, Michiko Yokote is the writer, Kenji Nakamura is the director, and the unique visuals are by Takashi Hashimoto. The multi-episode stories are *Zashiki warashi* (see chapter 17), *Umibouzu, Nopperabou* (the faceless ghost we encountered in the first pages of this book), *Nue* and *Bakeneko*.

There are touches of humor among the thrills of *Bake Neko*, but the episodes build quickly and relentlessly in tension and pacing as we try to find out what really happened before the cat spirit takes its revenge. If it's possible, the story feels as if it's exceeding the speed limit—the mounting sense of terror and danger is that palpable.

---

[47] There is no connection between this twelve-episode series and the 1997 movie written and directed by Hayao Miyazaki, *Mononoke-hime* (*Princess Mononoke*). The name Mononoke-hime (Princess of evil spirits) was a derogatory nickname that the people of Tatara-ba gave to San, the feral child in the movie who constantly disrupted their attempts to mine iron ore and turn it into firearms, polluting the sky, earth, water, and nature spirits in the process.

CHAPTER 16: BEYOND THE ANIMAL KINGDOM

Buddhism, as is fairly well known, allows for the migration of souls from one body to another. This isn't limited to the same species; a soul may, in this scheme of things, be reborn from an animal to a human or vice versa. This sets one of the *Rinne* stories of Rumiko Takahashi in motion.

40. I want my princess

The ghost in this case is of a medieval Japanese warrior, decked out in the armor of the 1500s. You can tell he was killed in battle because he has arrows sticking in him. You can also tell he's an ochimusha—a coward—because the arrows are sticking in his back. The logic is inescapable: the man was running away from the battle when he was killed.

But that doesn't explain why he has lingered on earth for hundreds of years. There is a bit of unfinished business: he was engaged to be married to a girl he called Hime (princess), has been waiting to find her again, and now believes that he has done so. Consequently, he's haunting a high school student named Kaori Himekawa who he's convinced is his one-time fiancée. He keeps appearing to her in dreams, trying to get her to drink saké as part of a Shinto wedding ceremony.

To solve the problem, the spirit named Rinne consults an ungakyo—a mirror which shows a person's past lives. By setting the ungakyo to 1573, the year the warrior was killed, it reveals that the student named Himekawa was at that time—a sea turtle. Checking out other members of the cast of characters in this story, Rinne examines the high school's middle-aged, rather large nurse and finds that, on the year in question, she was a carp. Finally they locate the person who was the soldier's beloved Hime, who is currently the boys' physical education coach Suzuki. Not realizing he was once Hime, the coach asked the soldier, "Haven't I met you somewhere?" The warrior's response: "You have the wrong guy." As the story says, after that, it didn't take the ochimusha long to pass on; he'd put a lot of extra baggage behind him.

XXX

A story dating from the 1600s has quite a mix of ingredients, including sacred trees and political corruption.

41. Death by Tree

A famous fire in 1658 destroyed one-eighth of the city of Edo, the new capital of the nation which would be called Tokyo. One nobleman, the Daimyo Lord Date Tsunamune of Sendai, had built seven houses, but lost them all in the fire.

Lord Date Tsunamune wanted to rebuild his palaces with a splendor that would almost match the houses of the Shogun. (For obvious reasons, he couldn't rebuild them as more splendid than the Shogun's.) He appointed a nobleman to see to things, Harada Kai Naonori; he in turn met with a lumber broker named Kinokuniya Bunzaemon. The broker pointed out that, because of the fire, good lumber was hard to find; Harada replied that money was no object.

Kinokuniya was only concerned about one piece of wood: a single beam cut from a camphor tree for the ceiling beam of

Lord Date Tsunamune's main house. Most of the camphor trees, however, were old and regarded as sacred. The one tree that would best suit the purpose was in the forest of Nekoma-myojin, and was the responsibility of one of the Shogun's retainers, named Fujieda Geki. He in turn met with four local village elders and, over dinner and drinks, determined that none of the four elders could read or write. This suited Fujieda Geki. All four of the elders told Fujieda Geki that the large camphor tree in question could not be touched, but they also agreed to put their seal to whatever document Fujieda Geki wrote. And Fujieda Geki was now assured that he could write the lumber permit any way he chose, regardless of the respect and veneration in which the local people held the camphor tree.

The next day, Kinokuniya sent a crew to the forest in question, four days travel away, with the vaguely worded permit signed by the seal of all four elders. The local caretaker questioned the four elders, who thought they had exempted the large camphor from being cut, although the permit didn't read that way. When he realized what had happened, Hamada Tsushima, the caretaker of the camphor tree, committed suicide, stating before he did that his spirit would enter the camphor tree, so that he might have revenge on the corrupt Kinokuniya.

Eventually the crew brought down the camphor tree, but it was difficult: the men could not move the felled tree at all, and, whenever they came close to it, the branches would lash out at their faces and bodies. The fallen tree's branches swung so quickly and powerfully that members of the crew suffered broken limbs, and some were crushed nearly to death.

In the middle of all this, with word spreading on the inability to take lumber from the famous camphor tree, a messenger from the Daimyo arrived, ordering the lumber crew to leave the camphor tree alone and return home; the four elders, on the other hand, were summoned to court so that they might commit suicide to atone for their foolishness.

As for the corrupt contractor Kinokuniya, he stated that he was sick and hid in his rooms. A servant was sent to look in on him, and a barber came to see him; shortly thereafter, Kinokuniya was found dead. The head of the crew sent to harvest the camphor tree, a man named Chogoro, did penance by building a new shrine for the fallen camphor tree and hiring a new caretaker to replace Hamada Tsushima, who had committed suicide. At last report, the fallen camphor tree and its new shrine are still there.

xxx

Sometimes, a ghost can turn into something completely non-animal.

42. Returning as a "Bug"

According to a legend from the *Konjaku*, an epidemic struck Japan in the ninth century C.E. Everyone, from the emperor down to the common people, developed a terrible hacking cough. However, nobody knew just what it was, and everyone feared that it could turn into something lethal.

One evening, a cook was on his way home from work; he cooked for a nobleman but did not live with him and his staff. Along the way, he met a tall and frightening nobleman, dressed in a red cloak and formal headdress. He didn't know the dire figure, but knew enough to kneel and bow before him.

The noble spoke: "I used to be Ban no Yoshio, a counselor who committed a serious crime against His Majesty, lost his post and died in exile.[48] In death I became a spirit of pestilence. But I still feel that I owe much to my country for the favors that I enjoyed while I was at court. I have something important to tell you.

"Heaven had decided that there would be a dire sickness this year that would kill all who contracted it. I petitioned to have the

---

[48]   Tyler, p. 38. Ban no Yoshio was a real courtier, who was exiled from court to Iyo province in the year 866, where he died two years later. Iyo province is the old name for Ehime Prefecture, along the coast of Shikoku, the smallest of Japan's four main islands.

fatal epidemic become a coughing fit instead. Please let people know that they need not be afraid." After he had spoken, the noble spirit vanished.

The cook did as he was asked, telling people about Ban no Yoshio and the nature of the sickness then sweeping through Japan. People were relieved that the illness was not serious, although it seemed strange that Ban no Yoshio, who certainly could have appeared to anyone, spoke to a cook.

xxx

Another memorable case chronicled in the *Konjaku* tells a cautionary tale of a hermit monk who allowed the beauties of an empress to so possess him that, at death, he immediately left human form.

43. A Lustful Demon

This story started with the serious illness one summer of the beautiful Somedono Empress.[49] Doctors and monks tried to heal her but failed. Finally, the emperor heard of a powerful hermit monk who lived in the Katsuragi Mountains of Yamato Province.[50] The emperor and his father-in-law summoned the monk, who no sooner started praying for the empress than one of the empress' ladies-in-waiting began yelping, screaming, and running through the house. Finally she was cornered, and a fox crawled out of the lady's kimono. Once the fox was captured, the empress regained her health.

---

[49]   The Somedono Empress lived from 829 to 900.

[50]   Yamato Province is located on the Nara peninsula south of Tokyo; in the sixth century A. D. it had been the seat of Japanese government, and the name Yamato used to be synonymous with Japan itself.

A few days later, while the hermit was still at the home of the emperor, he caught a glimpse of the empress in a light summer kimono. With this brief glimpse of feminine beauty, the hermit monk fell hopelessly in love with the empress. He rushed to embrace her, but the ladies-in-waiting sounded the alarm, and the hermit was thrown into prison. In his cell he would pray to die, be reborn as a demon, and have sex with the empress in that demonic form. The emperor banished the hermit back to his home in Yamato province, where, still consumed with desire for the empress, he starved himself for more than ten days. When he died, he changed in that instant into a demon: a monster standing eight feet tall, with black skin, eyes like brass bowls, tusks like a boar, and a bald head. He wore only a loincloth.

This was how he appeared to the empress, as he had desired. As her ladies-in-waiting fled in terror, the empress, whose mind was turned by the demon, welcomed him into her bed. This repeated itself daily, with the demon appearing in broad daylight to be the empress' lover, leaving only around sundown.

The emperor called in other holy men to subdue the demon, and, for a time, it did not appear. However, one day, when it had been days since the demon had appeared, he returned as the entire court watched. He went to the empress's bed chamber; she followed him as if the rest of the court wasn't there; then they came out again and, as the *Kojaku* put it, "brazenly performed an unspeakable act."[51]

The moral of this story originally was that noble ladies should safeguard their virtue and not allow themselves to be approached by hermit monks. For this book, however, the point is that the spirit is very flexible after death, and one might assume any of an infinite number of shapes, not necessarily limited to humans or even animals. There are, as we shall see, even good ghosts.

---

[51] Royal, pp. 178-180.

CHAPTER 17: HOUSEHOLD GHOSTS: ZASHIKI

While some spirits—human or animal—can be malicious, others are nice and even helpful. Ghosts stay in the human world not just in order to inflict rough justice as payment for bad karma. A few ghosts even bring good luck; the trick is to recognize them as such.

44. "Brother, poor brother"

The Enoki family (a widower father and his two sons) are featured in Marimo Ragawa's manga *Akachan to Boku (Baby and Me)*. In one episode, they spend a summer weekend at an old inn complete with its own *onsen* (hot springs). The little old lady who runs the inn at first calls older son Takuya "Tadaomi"; we find out later it's because he resembles an ill-fated boy by that name who died at a young age of tuberculosis. Tadaomi's little sister Kikuko was killed shortly thereafter when a building collapsed.

Kikuko, however, has hung around the *onsen* in spirit, and at first she's only visible to Takuya, who caught a cold and developed a fever, and his toddler brother Minoru. We'll see a little later that (in the pop culture, anyway) ghosts can be perceived while one is undergoing surgery, suffering delirium, or otherwise detached from this world. Minoru's case reflects the traditional Japanese belief that, between birth and age seven, a child lives partly in this world and partly in the spirit-world where the child's soul dwelt before it was born on Earth. By age seven, the child is accepted as fully in and of this world.[52] This explains not only the very unusual things little children sometimes say and do—such as saying that they remember things that happened before they were born—but also its parallel belief that elderly people over the age of seventy begin losing their souls back to the spirit realm in preparation for death, as a way of accounting for some forms of senile dementia.

Kikuko's spirit is unsettling to Takuya because Kikuko herself was unsettled in life. When her brother developed tuberculosis, he knew that it was contagious and that he needed to be isolated, so Tadaomi, who previously had been kind to Kikuko, became angry and short with her, hoping that she would grow angry and leave him alone, and avoid catching the disease; in doing this, he was still being the loving big brother by looking out for her, thinking that she was still too young to understand what was happening. All this did, however, was confuse the child, who ended up both hating and loving her big brother and couldn't reconcile the two sets of feelings. In the end, Minoru's unfailing love for his ill big brother causes Kikuko to remember her love for her brother despite his abuse. She apologizes to Takuya, believing him to be Tadaomi; he accepts her apology by patting her on the head. In the final scene, the fever breaks, the Enoki family checks out of the inn, and Minoru happily waves goodbye to the ghost of Kikuko, presumably before she Becomes One with the Cosmos and is reunited with her beloved big brother. However, she may have another part to play, especially if she hangs around the inn as a zashiki.

The story can be read to mean that the main reason that Kikuko was still haunting the inn was because she did not have a *yasashii* (kind, compassionate) spirit. When she appeared to Takuya, she

---

[52] This is one of the reasons for the Shichi-Go-San (Seven-Five-Three) festival in November commemorating those birthdays for Japanese children. The tradition goes back to a time when infant mortality was a severe problem, and the holiday notes not only the child's survival but its entry into humanity. http://www.japaneselifestyle. com.au/culture/shichi-go-san.html.

tells him, "Brother, poor brother, it's so sad; you're going to die soon." The look on her face, however, is anything but sad. Still remembering his mean behavior toward her, she looks very happy delivering the news of his imminent death. As the old lady tells Takuya, "Kikuko was still angry with her brother when she died." But if she were *only* angry, then Tadaomi's death would have been sufficient. The conflict had to be resolved for her to find peace, and, Japanese pop culture being what it is, the conflict was resolved in favor of love, kindness, and compassion.

XXX

Kikuko would have been a good candidate to become a zashiki. Legends of zashiki warashi (the name literally means "room child") vary from place to place, but, despite its human appearance, it isn't a particular person's ghost. Rather, it's a good luck spirit who appears and behaves in a child-like manner. Generally speaking, the zashiki warashi blesses whatever house it occupies, and a house which loses this spirit falls on hard times. There are minor ghostly happenings that come along with the good luck—music coming from empty rooms, footprints appear in ashes—and usually only children or family members can see the spirit. It must be acknowledged and respected, although too much human attention can drive it away.

It's worth noting that the ghostly little girl was still at the inn when the boys and their father left. Since zashiki warashi can be either boys or girls, it's possible that this ghost has stayed around to bring luck to a family that needed it.

45. One Hundred Hiccups

One story in the Boy Love manga known in Japan as *Ghost!* and in English translation as *Eerie Queerie* records a zashiki encounter. The cast members of this manga by Shuri Shiozu attend an exclusive boys-only high school; in one episode the students go to a rural hotel for a four-day field trip. The old landlady[53] at the equally old inn at first denies that the inn is haunted; the students, however, have already heard rumors that severed feet wander the halls at night, or that they might encounter a woman in a bloody kimono. A few oddities do occur, but they're far tamer and seem like traditional poltergeist tricks: pebbles fall from the ceiling, and at dawn all the pillows in the room where the boys sleep have stacked themselves into a pyramid. Mitsuo also gets a severe case of hiccups, and hears a voice telling him that he will die if he hiccups one hundred times without stopping.

The supernatural activity is actually by a zashiki warashi, whose presence brings good luck to the inn—if only by reputation. Landlady Okiku admits that simply the rumor of a zashiki at the inn, which has had to compete with more modern tourist hotels, has brought more business, if only from curiosity-seekers. It's been a balancing-act, however. The zashiki would flee the inn with too much attention or the wrong kind; Okiku took it on herself to scout out playmates for the zashiki, which explains Mitsuo's non-lethal case of hiccups.

The reader is told that this particular legend survives in the Tohoku region of Japan, the northernmost prefectures on the main island of Honshu.[54]

XXX

---

[53] The landlady's name is Kikuno, but asks to be called Okiku, the name of one of Japan's most famous ghosts. At one point, the students find Okiku using a whetstone to sharpen a very large knife—the same image which terrified Minoru when he heard the story of "The Three Ofuda" (see chapter 20).

[54] Oddly enough, although the manga refers to this story as taking place in Michinoku Prefecture, there is no such prefecture; Michinoku is an old name for Fukushima Prefecture.

46. "Who are you?"

An adult manga story by an artist who uses the pen-name "Senno Knife" is titled "Zashiki Bokko." In this case, the spirit is a female, who watches over and blesses a small mountain inn next to an *onsen*. The word "bokko" is an archaic reference to a young woman. This particular spirit, who goes by the name "Koyuki" (child of snow) is interested in Masao, the youngest son of the family that owns the inn; he's been away at college for four years, and the family is afraid he'll follow the path of his brothers. "Once you go to the city," they tell him, "you'll never want to come back here."

Unknown to his family, he has an incentive to come back: Koyuki, who he met in a cave in the hot springs. He discovered her there one day, attractive and nude, and she told him, "When the time is right, I'll do it with you." The night he returns from college, just as Masao decides to look for Koyuki, she comes to his room and takes him down to the onsen cave. They strip and have sex. Masao fleetingly wonders, "Koyuki, who are you?" before realizing "It doesn't matter who you are, if you could always be by my side." In the end, Masao decides to stay at the inn. We can certainly understand the incentive.

47. For a potato chip

In *Jigoku Sensei Nube*, a manga with artwork by Takeshi Okano and story by Sho Makura, fifth grade teacher and part-time exorcist Meisuke Nueno begins one episode on a Sunday morning; with no school and bored to death, he heads for a pachinko parlor where he uses his exorcist abilities to manipulate the game and clean up, winning a lot of prizes (mostly alcoholic). On the way home, though, he gets hit by a falling tool from a telephone lineman. His luck swings from bad back to good when he sees, over near a garbage dump, a very little girl, looking like a doll in traditional kimono. He immediately recognizes her as a zashiki warashi and offers her a potato chip, which she happily accepts. Nueno chats happily with the spirit, which none of the passers-by can see.

The next morning, the zashiki warashi is waiting in Nueno's classroom, sitting on the teacher's desk. He announces a pop quiz, and all of the students get perfect scores. He puts them through gym class, and even the smallest and weakest students do perfectly. It seems the zashiki warashi is still trying to help. The last straw comes when Ritsuko Takahashi, a very pretty teacher, walks up and asks Nueno out on a date.

Nueno takes the zashiki warashi up onto the roof of the school, feeding it chips, and then has to break it to her: she made the entire class happy inside of ten minutes, but people have to seek out their happiness, and can't have it given to them. In short, he says, they don't need her. He knows he's hurt her feelings, but all he can do is watch as she runs off of the roof.

Sometime later, as school is letting out, a student dashes out into traffic in front of an oncoming truck. He would surely have been hit and killed, if not for the zashiki warashi; she caused a five-car pile-up, but saved the student. Nueno sees the zashiki warashi, asks if it's exhausted from saving the student's life, and offers some of his own psychic energy to her. This is all it takes to make her happy again. She disappears. Nueno is surprised when snowflakes start falling; warm snowflakes. He looks down the road and sees the zashiki warashi (having taken one last chip) happily running down the road, presumably looking for someone else to help.

48. Gift Exchange

Finally, we see a zashiki warashi (actually more of a zashiki bokko) in the CLAMP manga and anime *xxxHolic*, created for young adults (a seinen manga) and published from 2003 to February 2011, making it one of CLAMP's longest-running titles. It's the tale of Kimihiro Watanuki[55], a high school student whose highly developed psychic abilities (a family legacy) enable him to see spirits. This poses a problem; he's basically a good guy, and can't help trying to aid whatever spirit he finds; most of the time, though, he considers his gift a nuisance. He stumbles across the curiosity shop run by a self-described witch named Yuko Ichihara; she offers to remove his ability to see spirits—for a price. Since he can't meet the price, he agrees to work at the shop. The catch, of course, is that he's going to keep seeing spirits until he earns enough to pay Yuko's fee (she never explains until the end how much it is or how far along Watanuki is to earning the right amount; this makes her kind of a spiritual loan-shark).

This particular ghostly encounter (the manga version) starts late on the night of February 13. Even after working during the day for Yuko, she orders him to make chocolate pudding cakes for herself and her two childlike assistants. As Watanuki rather loudly reminds Yuko, she didn't have any ingredients for a chocolate pudding cake, so he had to go out shopping first—in cold and rainy weather—before he could start cooking. By the time he's finished, it's midnight, the start of Valentine's Day. Yuko sends the leftovers to clients in another dimension, but is happily frank in admitting that she sent the gift on Valentine's Day so that her clients would feel the need to reciprocate on White Day.[56] Watanuki is still bitter about the whole thing, since the

---

[55]   The name of the hapless hero of *xxxHolic*, Watanuki, literally means "the first day of the fourth month." It's also something of an in-joke for CLAMP. April 1 is the birthday of Sakura Kinomoto, the heroine of *Card Captor Sakura*, the birthday of both Sakura and her beloved Syaoran in *Tsubasa Chronicles*, and the supposed birthday of Sakurazuka Seishirou in an earlier CLAMP series, *Tokyo Babylon*. More important, CLAMP was officially formed on April 1, 1989.

[56]   In Japanese society, receiving a gift gives one an obligation to reciprocate with a similar gift. The first commemoration of modern Valentine's Day in Japan was as a sales gimmick created by a Japanese chocolatier in 1958, in which women were encouraged to give chocolate to their beloved. In 1965 a Japanese marshmallow

Valentine tradition in Japan has girls cooking chocolates to give to boys they like. He feels better, however, when he realizes that he can take the last leftover cake and give it to the cute but mysterious Himawari, on whom he's had a severe crush ever since he first saw her.

But things do not go according to plan. First, Himawari isn't in school on Valentine's Day, having caught a cold. Moreover, the pudding cake, and even the accompanying cup of hot chocolate, are devoured instead by Domeki, star athlete and apparent rival with Watanuki for Himawari's attention. To make matters worse, on this day when girls are supposed to give chocolates to guys, Watanuki hadn't received any chocolate at all; Domeki, meanwhile, has to carry his gifts home in a shopping bag. Their argument is interrupted by a young girl, who looks to be about twelve years old, wearing a parka and hood over her dress. She speaks as if she had meant to give a chocolate gift to a special person, but has apparently misplaced it. Suddenly, however, she reaches through Domeki's coat and into his stomach, pulling the pudding cake out, whole again.

Domeki, who is descended from a line of Shinto priests but hasn't had much experience with spirits, faints dead away. Watanuki can only watch as the girl, looking ready to burst into tears, rises up off the street and floats away. Just at this moment, Yuko happens by; she declares that the girl didn't just take Domeki's snack but also his soul. Watanuki, realizing that it was his fault Domeki got involved, wants to put things right even if he doesn't much like Domeki. Yuko whistles up her Mokona,[57] who arrives at once flying a bird as big as an elephant.

---

company created White Day (formerly Marshmallow Day) one month later to balance the equation. These days, the White Day gift of choice is flowers rather than candy. See (http://web-jpn.org/kidsweb/calendar/february/valentine.html, and http://web-jpn.org/kidsweb/calendar/march/whiteday.html, accessed March 2, 2007.)

[57] The chubby rabbit-looking Mokona has appeared in a number of CLAMP projects, but was originally in the series *Magic Knights Rayearth*.

Yuko tells Watanuki to use the bird to find the girl; Domeki's soul must be restored to him by sundown.

Watanuki quickly sees the girl, silhouetted against the rising moon. No sooner does he get close to her than he's attacked by five cherubs in trench coats, riding snowboards through the sky. They threaten Watanuki because "You made her cry!" Watanuki falls off of the giant bird, but is rescued by the girl spirit. She rescued Watanuki because she meant to give him the pudding cake; she didn't seem to realize that she'd taken Domeki's soul out of him when she took the cake. With that, she floats away, as do the cherubs, who threaten Watanuki one last time to never make her cry.

Yuko explains that the girl was a zashiki, while the cherubs were karasutengu—crow spirits who usually hide in the mountains away from the pernicious influence of humans. However, the zashiki was a girl, doing what Japanese girls did on February 14: she gave a gift of chocolate to a boy she found to be admirable: Watanuki. This softened the blow somewhat for Watanuki; after all, not only had he baked it in the first place, but he had to give it back to Domeki to restore his soul. Even when Himawari returns to school after her bout with the cold, things don't get better: she gives a box of store-bought chocolate to Watanuki, and an identical box to Domeki. Yuko tried to console him by reminding him that he'd also gotten chocolate from the zasshiki, even though he'd had to give it back to Domeki. (When this manga episode was animated for television, the date was changed from Valentine's Day to the Obon festival, which made the zashiki seem confused rather than simply naïve.)

The zasshiki appears again in the anime version on March 14, dressed in kimono, and this time Watanuki's prepared, giving the spirit a set of hairpins for White Day (in the manga Watanuki finds her, months late, in a strange world, where he may unwittingly be serving Yuko as bait). Interestingly, her crush on Kimihiro is understood to be natural, even in the spirit world.

CHAPTER 18: SPIRITS, SICKNESS AND SURGERY

We've already had examples of hauntings as part of sicknesses, in or out of hospitals, places where souls become detached from their bodies on a regular basis. This is a concept built into the Japanese kanji used to describe the phenomenon. The word ikiryo means "the spirit leaving the body."[58] The reasons for the move, however, can vary. Lady Rokujo had an out-of-body experience when her lover Prince Genji got interested in another woman. Here are a few more examples; the first is an elaborate ghost story featuring one of the classic characters of the God of Manga.

xxx

Black Jack: Clinical Chart 6: Night Time Tale in the Snow "Lovelorn Princess"

49. Can a surgeon heal what's wrong with a ghost?

---

[58] "Heroes and Villains", July 22, 2009, by Mike Montesa, in http:// www.therumicworld.com/blog.php, accessed July 26, 2009.

> In my travels I've witnessed both life and death. On rare occasions I've also encountered incidents for which I have no explanation; events that seemed to defy reason. As a doctor I place my faith in knowledge, which both time and science have proven to be true. When I am faced with things that scientific knowledge can't explain, I find myself filled with wonder and awe. I am reminded that man's knowledge is still far from perfect, and believe all men of science need such reminders.

So begins the sixth OAV featuring one of Dr. Osamu Tezuka's most popular characters: the super-surgeon known as Black Jack. He receives a commission one day by mail to heal the wife of Saburo Taneda, who lives in a small village in the mountains. The request—which had been delayed in the mail for two years—was accompanied by over 3.7 million yen in cash as a retainer.

When Black Jack and his child assistant Pinoko arrive in the mountains during a blizzard, they seek shelter in a Buddhist temple—and are immediately whisked back to feudal times. Black Jack now must heal a princess whose malady is symbolized by an elaborate serpent tattoo that circles her body. He also gets caught up in a romantic extended triangle: a princess is in love with one of her retainers, a soldier whose lower social position prevents them from being together. At the same time, the princess is also sought after by Mr. Rokushouji, a wealthy Imperial bureaucrat who abandoned his first wife to pursue the young and beautiful princess. The first wife, Lady Kaoru, has gone to the temple, shaved her head, and become a Buddhist nun, but has not forgiven her husband for abandoning her; she sets her own plot in motion with the assistance of Abumaru, a young man who is loyal to her. Things do not end well: ultimately, the princess, her beloved retainer, the bureaucrat, the Buddhist nun, and the nun's devoted young man are all dead.

This ghostly encounter, which by unfolding around Black Jack seems to echo the "Earless Hoichi" episode of *Kwaidan*, may seem like a digression from the doctor's real business. However, once the older drama has played out, Black Jack finds himself back in the present day. He locates the ailing but still living Mrs. Taneda, whose husband was killed in a construction accident shortly after he sent the money to Black Jack two years earlier. Her condition can be cured, but only in a hospital with proper surgical facilities. As they leave, Black Jack meets Mrs. Taneda's neighbors, a woman and her teenaged son—who bear a strong resemblance to the Lady Kaoru and her young devotee Abumaru, just as Mrs. Taneda resembles the princess and her husband resembled the soldier. And what of Mr. Rokushouji, the wealthy bureaucrat whose cold abandonment of his wife helped set the feudal tragedy in motion? At the beginning of the anime, Black Jack has to ask directions to the village from a trucker hauling logs. We never see the trucker, but, by going back to the beginning and replaying this scene, we realize that he is speaking in the voice of Mr. Rokushouji.

In essence, the older tragedy had to play itself out, presumably again and again, with the ghosts of those involved until things could be resolved properly through the intervention of someone like Black Jack. Unlike Hoichi, Black Jack was not a mere spectator to a ghostly pageant; the ghosts showed him what they had done to cause such enduring bad karma, which he had to fix, just as he surgically healed Mrs. Taneda. The whole story is summed up—although the viewer may not realize it at first—by Lady Kaoru; when Black Jack apologizes to her (the Buddhist nun who ran the temple where Black Jack took shelter) for his unexpected visit, she simply says, "All of us become lost in our travels from time to time." Some, it seems, become lost because of their actions, and some become lost in order to help others find their way home.

xxx

Black Jack also ran into another patient who wasn't exactly human.

50. On a snowy night

The story takes place on the night of a raging blizzard. Black Jack is home alone when there's a knock at the door of his isolated house. He answers; nobody is outside. He shuts the door, and finds two people suddenly in his house: a man and a woman, in modern dress. The woman asks Black Jack to operate on their mother. "I'm not a regular doctor," he tells them, and demands a fee of ¥30 million. No sooner does he ask than the money is on the table, in cash. The young people are talking to the doctor's examination table as if their mother is on it; Black Jack can't see anyone there.

He goes through the motions of trying to operate on someone who he can't see, while his visitors tell him he's doing a brilliant job. Finally he declares that he's finished and the mother will be fine. The woman finally tells Black Jack about the patient: name, Aya Matsumoto, age 45, and that the two are her children; their names are Eiji and Maniko. Mother was to take a tour of the northern island of Hokkaido, until her passenger jet was struck by a missile from a nearby military base; it crashed to earth, setting off a fire in the nearby village's *shitamachi*.[59]

It's only after Black Jack defends his invisible patient to some local hunters and police that the voices of Eiji and Maniko return. They invite Black Jack to accompany their mother on a journey much farther than Hokkaido; when he refuses, the millions of yen blow out the door and into the snowy night.

XXX

We've already seen how, in *Akachan to Boku*, a character can open the door to the spirit world when fever or other illness weakens the connection to the real world. Another example appears in *xxxHolic*, the manga by CLAMP and its animated version. On a hot summer night Yuko arranges for four people to tell ghost stories; it was supposed to be a *hyaku monogatari* session, but cut down to four stories told by each of the four participants—sixteen

---

[59] Literally the "lower city," the term used to refer to a city's slums or lower-class area.

stories instead of the full hundred. However, the spirits are so active that the partiers don't even make it to the fourth story. Nobuhiro Watanuki gets to tell only one story, and, in the manga, his turns out to be elegantly creepy:[60]

51. Just Two Students Chatting

One time in grade school, Watanuki was resting on a bed in the nurse's office; he had a bad headache and "was really out of it." As he lay in bed, alone in the office, he heard a voice ask, "Hey, mister, are you all right?" The voice came from a child who was outside the window, looking in. Watanuki said that he just had a headache, and they spoke for a while. Watanuki had no idea who the boy was, but it was a large school and it was easy to lose track of people unless you see them all the time. After a while, the child waved, said "Take care of yourself," and was no longer standing at the window.

It wasn't until he was feeling better that Watanuki realized something: the nurse's office was on the third floor of the school. There was no balcony, no fire escape, no ledge, no tree—nowhere someone could stand and look in through that window and have a conversation.

XXX

Ghosts have also been known to appear in medical anime/ manga in another circumstance: when a character is undergoing surgery due to a life-threatening condition. While they are under anesthetic, a character is seen as on the border between the worlds of the living and the dead, especially if that character has almost given up the will to live.

---

[60] When this manga episode was animated for television, the writers provided three completely different stories for them to tell, perhaps thinking that knowing in advance what the characters will say would dull the chills.

Two examples out of many:

Kodocha is an abbreviation of the phrase *Kodomo no Omocha (Children's Toys).*[61] This girls' manga by Miho Obana ran in *Ribon* magazine from 1994 to 1998 and was later animated into a popular series. The story centers on child actress and idol Sana Kurata and her attempts to have a "normal" life (as normal as possible, anyway, between hosting her own TV series, her mother being a reclusive novelist, and her mother's assistant being a transvestite). She has been seeing Akito, a classmate who's something of a loner, in no small part because he's been made to feel guilty because his mother died giving birth to him.

At one point in the manga, Akito is knifed in the woods by a disturbed student named Kazuyuki; by the time they get back to civilization, Akito has lost a lot of blood. He has also nearly lost the will to live, but during the surgery he's encouraged to keep fighting by the spirit of his mother. Even though he never met her, he recognizes her as such.

Actually, we see that he's almost met her. Kazuyuki had become obsessed with Akito's popularity, and had hoped to receive at least some of that reflected popularity by arranging for the two of them to commit the mutual suicide known as shinjuu. When Akito refuses, Kazuyuki stabs Akito in the arm; by the time they get back to civilization, Akito is dying from his wound. Yet, several times when the boys are in the woods, the manga reader sees the ghostly figure of a woman among the trees. She isn't identified, but, by the

---

[61] This compression of words is common in Japanese pop culture. A couple of other examples: the central character in the manga *Gokusen*, which ran from 2000 to 2007 and has inspired both animated and live television versions, is a Yakuza heiress turned boys' high school teacher named Yamaguchi Kumiko; her students compress her name to Yankumi (an allusion to the slang term "yanki", meaning delinquent; and, more rudely, "yank me"). And in Ai Yazawa's highly popular manga *Nana*, which also premiered in 2000, there is a rock band called the Buraku Sutonzu (Black Stones), also known by the compressed name Burasuto (Blast).

time of Akito's surgical crisis, we realize that the ghostly woman is his mother, who died in childbirth. She tells her son to "live, for both of us." We last see her in the operating room, floating up near the ceiling light.

Similarly, the 1998 weekly anime series *Princess Nine* revolves around Ryo Hayakawa, daughter of a once-famous Japanese baseball player and nucleus of the first girl's high school baseball team in Japan. Her father died when she was five years old, but when Ryo requires surgery after rescuing two young children in a flood, under anesthetic her spirit meets her father's spirit. His advice to Ryo is essentially the same as that given to Akito by his mother: keep on trying, believe in tomorrow and in yourself.

It's a message that may seem to ring hollow to some older, more experienced Japanese readers, and especially after the 2011 earthquake and attendant tsunami, but Sana and Akito and Ryo and most of the stars of both stories are not older. They are still of an age where belief is possible, where a better tomorrow is still attainable—the fundamental message of most of the popular culture in Japan.

CHAPTER 19: AT THE MOVIES: SOME CLASSIC POSTWAR JAPANESE GHOST FILMS

The first two postwar decades of Japanese movies are hardly known in the west, except perhaps for the tales of Gojira (a/k/a Godzilla) and its other monster buddies such as Mothra and Rodan. But Japanese studios were able to get back on their feet for a number of reasons, and the popularity of ghost stories is one of those reasons. Three movies made between 1950 and 1965 got to America with impressive "art house" credentials, as well as scares, intact. They're known to serious students of film history as well as those who enjoy a good thrill.

The first of these three movies is barely a ghost story, but it certainly qualifies; its reputation as one of Japan's classic movies tends to overshadow the supernatural action.

Rashomon was filmed in 1950 and directed by Akira Kurosawa (1910-1998), Japan's best-known postwar director. The reason he was best-known is simple: he was a genius whose style evolved according to developments in film technology. Born into a family of samurai ancestors, Kurosawa's father was athletics director at a junior high school. He was also an advocate of the new technology of silent movies, and Akira's older brother Heigo later became a *benshi*, a narrator of silent films that drew on Japan's long storytelling tradition. Akira became an apprentice in 1936 at what would later become Toho Studios.

His influences were broad but also very western, including Shakespeare (*Throne of Blood* was Kurosawa's version of *Macbeth*) and Russian literature, but these were often mixed with Japanese influences such as kabuki theatrical conventions. Similarly, Kurosawa's movies influenced filmmakers around the world. The classic samurai drama *Yojimbo* was supposedly based on the books of hardboiled American mystery writer Dashiell Hammett, but was later remade by Italian director Sergio Leone as the first of the so-called "spaghetti Westerns," *A Fistful of Dollars*. *The Seven Samurai*, supposedly influenced by director John Ford, was remade as the American cowboy classic *The Magnificent Seven*.

xxx

52. Witness from Beyond

Rashomon was based on a pair of short stories by Ryunosuke Akutagawa (1892-1927). Akutagawa's story "Rashomon" serves as bookends for the movie, while the bulk of the film is based on his "In the Grove." In ancient times a young, well-to-do couple traveling through the forest is surprised by a bandit. The husband ends up bound and stabbed to death, the wife ends up raped. The bandit and the wife tell violently different versions of what happened (the bandit said the husband fought like a tiger, while the wife ran away; the wife said the bandit ravaged her, while the husband begged her with his eyes to kill him and then kill herself, which she didn't have the strength to do), and the court hears from a medium who becomes possessed by the ghost of the husband and adds his very different version of events (the bandit raped the wife, who then encouraged the robber to kill the husband; he couldn't do it, especially after the wife ran off; when the robber cut the husband's ropes and ran off, the husband committed suicide).[62]

---

[62]   *Rashomon* has become so well-known in the west that Hollywood has made its "multiple versions of the same events" plot a staple

139

The medium is a *kuchiyose* (literally, "lending a mouth"); in this case, giving a voice to the spirit of the dead man. The story's unique structure offers up different characters telling different versions of the same story, leaving the reader (or movie audience) to try to sort out the truth. Incidentally, a minor character in *Rashomon*, known only as the Policeman, was played by a young actor named Daisuke Kato, who the year before had also appeared in a film version of Japan's archetypal Kabuki ghost play, *Yotsuya Kaidan*. (See chapter 11)

xxx

Three years after *Rashomon*, director Kenji Mizoguchi offered up another classic Japanese ghost story; actually, a pair of stories. *Ugetsu monogatari* (1953) began life in 1776 as a collection of ghost stories with accompanying woodblock prints and commentaries. Written by Ueda Akinari, the title can be translated "Stories Under a Moon in the Rain." Of the nine stories in the collection, director Mizoguchi used two (plus part of a third) in his film of the same name.

The nine original stories actually are quite different from the scare-inducing stories written down by Lafcadio Hearn or the gruesome shock films of today. Ueda's ghost stories are meant to be examples of virtue and moral uplift—even if a couple of the examples are rather extreme. The stories are sometimes pleasant, as in "I Dreamed of a Carp," in which a Buddhist monk from the Heian Era, who was so committed to not killing that he paid fishermen to throw back their catch, has a fever dream in which he lives the life of a carp. "Chrysanthemum Tryst" shows brotherly love to an extreme, as two men—one a poor scholar and the other a warrior nursed back to health by the scholar—swear friendship and vow to

---

in television writing; often for comic effect, but also in an episode of the TV series based on Alan Parker's hit movie *Fame* (in the episode, a medium contacts a student who's comatose rather than dead to investigate a case of school vandalism).

meet again at that year's Chrysanthemum Festival (on the ninth day of the ninth month), after the warrior goes home to help his family. The warrior doesn't return until the night of the Chrysanthemum Festival; in fact, only his ghost returns to the scholar. The soldier was imprisoned when he returned home and could only keep his promise by committing suicide, so that at least his spirit could visit his friend.

At the other end of the scale is "The Blue Hood." This story starts with the obsessive love of an abbot for one of his young students. When the boy dies, the abbot's obsession turns to the most literal way to possess the young student: cannibalism. A more devout priest is able to exorcize the evil spirit of the obsessed abbot.

Mizoguchi's film uses two stories from the *Ugetsu Monogatari* about two married couples, who end up with very different destinies.

53. Welcome Home

In "The House Amid the Thickets," we meet the farmer Katsushiro and his wife Miyagi, trying to make a living on their farm in Shimosa province, on Japan's Pacific coast. Convinced that he can make more money as a silk merchant hundreds of miles away in Kyoto, Katsushiro leaves home one spring day, promising his wife Miyagi that he'll be home by autumn. In fact, he doesn't return for seven years, after bandits steal the money he made in Kyoto and war breaks out in Shimosa. When he finally gets home, Miyagi joyfully greets him. When he wakes up the next morning, he realizes the truth: his wife had died shortly after he set off seven years earlier, and he had spent the night talking with her spirit.

54. Domestic Disturbance

In contrast is "The Lust of the White Serpent." Toyoo, the son of a well-off fisherman, abandons his fiancée and chases after the rich widow Manago. When he agrees to marry her, Manago presents him with a sword which turns out to have been stolen. When the police try to arrest Manago, she disappears with a flash of lightning. Despite this indication that Manago was a demon in human form, she reappears to Toyoo later and asks forgiveness—and he's foolish enough to agree. When an elderly priest exposes Manago as a white serpent demon, Toyoo flees again to his original fiancée. One night, Manago possesses Toyoo's new wife; the serpent is exorcised, but the wife dies.

These two stories from Ueda's anthology were, in a sense, the same story: a cautionary tale from the 18th century that resonated with postwar Japan. *Ugetsu* served, with its stylized ghost stories, to remind its audience to stay close to home, to be faithful to the traditions that kept Japan alive for centuries. Perhaps Mizoguchi already knew the upheavals the rest of the twentieth century would bring.

XXX

One of the oldest English books of Japanese lore focused on ghost stories: Lafcadio Hearn's *Kwaidan* (published in 1904, the year of his death), which also became one of Japan's best-known ghost movies when directed by Masaki Kobayashi, screenplay by Yoko Mizuki (1964).

This film contains four distinct, separate stories. In "Black Hair", a poor samurai, who divorces his true love to marry for money, finds the marriage disastrous and returns to his old wife, only to discover (to put it mildly) something eerie about her. In "The Woman in the Snow" a woodcutter, stranded in a snowstorm, meets an icy spirit in the form of a woman; she spares his life on the condition that he never tell anyone about her. A decade later, in a moment of weakness he forgets his promise. The third story, "Hoichi the Earless", focuses on a blind musician living in a monastery, who sings so well that a ghostly imperial court commands him to perform the epic ballad of their death battle for them. The ghosts of the Heike royalty are draining away his life, and the monks set out to protect him by writing holy scriptures over his body to make him invisible to the ghosts. But, as the title suggests, they've forgotten something . . . Although he pays a large price, in the end Hoichi agrees to play "for the rest of my life so that these sorrowful spirits may rest in peace."

55. Swallowing a Soul

Finally, in "In a Cup of Tea", a writer introduces a fragment of an old story dating from the 17th century. It tells of a man who keep seeing a face reflected in his cup of tea; a face that's not his own. It's the face of a swordsman who threatens to come back and avenge the wrongs done him. However, nobody else can see the ghostly swordsman or his attendants. As for the short-story writer, he has left the tale deliberately unfinished, knowing that the reader's imagination, dealing with the matter of "swallowing a soul" by drinking the reflection in a cup of tea, would be more chilling than anything the writer could make up. The visiting publisher is interrupted by a terrified scream from the writer's servant. She, and then the publisher, run off after seeing the image of the writer reflected in the teapot.

In a sense, this fourth segment is also an inspiration for *Ringu*. Buildings can obviously be haunted, but it's sometimes more horrifying when ghosts are found in common household objects, such as a teacup—or a television set.

Incidentally, there's an anime connection to *Kwaidan*. The blind Hoichi is played by Katsuo Nakamura, a relatively young actor who had already amassed twenty film credits when he made *Kwaidan* at age 25. In 2004 he supplied the voice of Dr. Lloyd Steam, the visionary inventor who harnessed steam power in new ways, and grandfather to James Ray Steam, the title hero of Katsuhiro Otomo's film *Steamboy*. And in 1983 Tatsuya Nakadai, the hapless woodcutter in the "Woman in the Snow" segment, narrated the fifth and final feature film based on Reiji Matsumoto's *Uchu Senkan Yamato* manga (the TV series of which was broadcast in the United

States as *Star Blazers*). Nakadai also appeared in a 1978 live action film based on one of the best-known of Osamu Tezuka's manga, *Hi no Tori* (*The Phoenix*).

xxx

This book has already looked at a number of haunted houses in anime, and there will be others; yet there's one more in a popular Japanese movie that probably wouldn't occur to most ghost hunters.

56. "Hey! Haven't you heard? You're living in a haunted house!"

Animator Hayao Miyazaki went a long way toward establishing his credentials in Japan and around the world—and gave his Studio Ghibli a corporate logo—with his 1988 animated masterpiece *Tonari no Totoro* (*My Neighbor Totoro*). The plot is deceptively simple and at times surprisingly dark, despite the happy, sunny scenes of life in pastoral rural Japan that make up the movie. A college professor and his two daughters, ages four and ten, move to a country house. The girls are greeted with the above declaration by a neighbor boy, Kanta. He may have meant it as a joke or a tease, but supernatural events do indeed begin happening in short order.

Mei, the younger daughter, encounters several totoro (her childish mispronunciation of troll—*tororu* in Japanese). Only she can see them at first; then, the older sister Satsuki sees them too. The girls also encounter the Catbus, which is exactly what its name suggests, and briefly encounter what can only be called sentient soot: called "makkuro kurosuke" by the girls and "susuwatari" by Kanta's granny, these dustballs come closest to "haunting" the house. In fact, they really don't have much of an investment in it; the first night there, as father and daughters play around in the bathtub (a scene which can make some westerners, who see pedophilia in any scene involving parent/child nudity, rather nervous), the "traveling soot" (translation of *susuwatari*) start traveling again. In fact, they ride the wind for more than a decade, reappearing in Miyazaki's 2001 Academy Award-winning masterpiece *Sen to Chihiro no Kamikakushi* (known in the US as *Spirited Away*, a pun which works in both English and Japanese).

This particular house, however, seems to be connected to more high-level spirits. Next door to the property is a road with a torii, a traditional arch used in Shinto to denote the entrance to a shrine or a sacred place. There is no longer a functioning shrine on the property, but the hill behind the house is dominated by a gigantic camphor tree. At the base of the tree are the ruins of an old shrine, while around the tree is stretched a *shimenawa*. This rope, woven of rice straw and covered with paper ribbons, is also Shinto in origin, and has been wrapped around the tree as a mark of respect and, in fact, worship. In addition, the roads around the country house are littered with shrines containing *jizo* statues (see chapter 14 on *Ayakashi* for details) and a shrine to fox spirits is found near the bus stop where they first see the Catbus. Finally, at the film's climax, with Mei missing and Satsuki frantic with worry running down the road with a brilliant sunset in the same frame, we see the highest-order spirit of all: the Shinto sun goddess Amaterasu. The sun isn't depicted as a goddess, because there is no need: a Japanese audience would already recognize the symbolism.[63]

XXX

These films brought Japanese ghosts to the so-called art houses in the west. Starting in 1998, a cinematic explosion of Japanese

---

[63]   A similar scene takes place in Isao Takahata's 1991 anime feature for Studio Ghibli, *Omoide Poroporo* (*Remembering Drop by Drop*), usually referred to in the west as *Only Yesterday*. As part of a vacation with some rural cousins, a big-city Office Lady and her hosts stop harvesting benibana flowers when the clouds part to reveal the sun, and offer up a prayer to Amaterasu.

ghosts possessed the malls and multi-screen cinemas of America, as a host of Japanese ghost movies were given a Hollywood remake: *The Grudge, Dark Water, One Missed Call,* among others. The gateway ghost film, however, was better known by its American remake, which popularized some of the distinctive traits of Japanese ghost stories, while neglecting one of the most important clues.

xxx

Ring versus Ringu

Director Hideo Nakata and screenwriter Hiroshi Takahashi, adapting a novel by Koji Suzuki, redefined the ghost story for Japan and Hollywood, and did it by mixing new technologies with the best aspects of Japanese horror stories. Unfortunately, *Ringu* (1998) was remade as "The Ring" (2002), directed by Gore Verbinski, who's perhaps best known now as director of the *Pirates of the Caribbean* franchise; the screenplay was written from Suzuki's novel by Ehren Kruger.

57. Seven Days

Journalist and single mother Reiko Asakawa is researching an urban legend, interviewing kids about a 'Cursed Video.' When her niece Tomoko dies of "sudden heart failure" with a look of terror on her face, Reiko investigates. She finds out that some of Tomoko's friends who had been on holiday with Tomoko the week before had died on exactly the same night at the exact same time in the exact same way. Reiko goes to the cabin where the teens had stayed and finds an unlabeled video tape. Reiko watches the tape, only to discover it's the cursed videotape. She finds out by a means that is at once mundane and frightening: the phone rings. (This is the "ring" of the title; it doesn't refer to a piece of jewelry.) A voice tells Reiko that she will die in seven days.

Reiko's ex-husband Ryuji helps Reiko try to solve the mystery before the week runs out, and Reiko makes a copy of the tape for him. Things become grimmer when their son Yoichi watches the tape saying his aunt Tomoko (the dead one) had told him to, and the phone rings . . . . Their research takes them to a volcanic resort island where they discover that the video has a connection to Shizuko Yamamura, a psychic who died 30 years ago, and her child Sadako . . .

The resolution of *Ringu* comes as the clock runs toward midnight on Reiko's seventh day. They look under the vacation cabin and realize that it was built over the ruins of the well where Sadako met her death. Reiko searches through the muck at the bottom of the well, and finds Sadako's skull. With literally a minute to go before she stands to die, Reiko is holding the skull of the agency that would kill her. She clutches the skull to her bosom and starts sobbing. As she does, slime oozes from the skull's eye sockets. This scene, which wasn't in the American version, ties *Ringu* to the principal belief, almost an article of faith in Japanese manga and anime: that the purpose of eyes is to cry. Reiko's crying over the skull of the abandoned and murdered Sadako, an expression of compassion for the long-forgotten dead girl, neutralizes the curse for her and her son. Ex-husband Ryuji isn't so lucky, as the ghost of Sadako comes for him by crawling out of the television picture tube . . .

Suzuki's novel has more than a grain of truth to its back-story about Sadako and her mother Shizuko. The character of Shizuko Yamamura is based on a real person, Chizuko Mifune, born in 1886 in Kumamoto Prefecture, who was rumored to have the gift of foresight. After a demonstration in 1910, she was proclaimed a charlatan and committed suicide a year later by jumping into a volcano. (Let the record show, though, that Suzuki's novel was also inspired in part by the Hollywood ghost story *Poltergeist*.)

CHAPTER 20: SPIRIT PHOTOGRAPHY

Two landmarks from modern Japanese ghost cinema have scenes that rely on still photographs for their chills. One interesting scene from *Ringu* shows the heroine looking through photographs of the young people on holiday, a week before they died. Everything looks normal, except in one snapshot: there, the faces of the victims—and only their faces—are blurred beyond recognition, as if deliberately smudged by somebody's thumb. Of course, this kind of botched photo can always be dismissed as a mistake in the developing process. There's surely a perfectly reasonable, logical, and prosaic explanation . . .

A similar scene takes place in *Ju-On* (known in the west as *The Grudge*) after three schoolgirls disappear. They had gone with a friend to a reputedly haunted house; the friend had left early, but was now staying away from school. A few of her other friends offer to take her copies of pictures from the last school trip; when they get them developed, they see that the eyes of the missing girls have all been blacked out. Maybe there isn't always a logical explanation . . .

xxx

Moon Phase

This supernatural romantic comedy, fairly sweet and relatively tame (given that it airs "after hours" on Japan television at 1:45 a.m.), doesn't have a lot to do with ghosts. The heroine is a cute, bossy, juvenile looking and acting vampiress named Hazuki.[64] She bites into a Japanese boy and expects him to become her slave; when that doesn't happen, the lad, Kouhei Morioka, is understood to be in a special category: a Vampire's Lover. Rather than follow Hazuki and Kouhei down the course of true love, however, we should note Kouhei's profession: a freelance magazine photographer. However, he has trouble selling most of his work because of his other inadvertent talent: he's a gifted spirit photographer. So gifted, in fact, that even doing a simple layout in a candy store gets spoiled by the ghosts that appear in his pictures. If his best friend, Hiromi Anzai, wasn't Managing Editor at *Occult Magazine*, he'd probably never sell a single photo.

And then there's . . .

Ai yori Aoshi

This romantic-comedy manga by Ko Fumizuki, which began running in 1998 and was a successful television anime from 2002 to 2004, has a very minor role for some ghosts, but establishes the continuing attraction of ghost stories, even in a technological 21st century, as well as their invasion of that technology.

Kaoru Hanabishi, a college law student, crosses paths with a girl who dresses in old-fashioned kimono and speaks in a formal, stilted manner. She turns out to be the fiancée he hasn't seen in fifteen years. He was "engaged" to Aoi Sakuraba, the heiress to a prominent family, when they were both children. However, Kaoru's mother was sent away from the equally prestigious Hanabishi clan when Kaoru's father died, since his parents had never been married; the clan, however, kept custody of the boy. When his mother died as well, Kaoru ultimately rebelled and left the Hanabishi. Aoi, however, never gave up the dream of her intended fiancée, so, when she turned eighteen, she sought out Kaoru, moving in with him (along with a chaperone assigned by her mother).

She gradually gets to know other facets of Kaoru's life, including his involvement with the college Photography Club. When the club goes on a summer retreat to a mountain inn (in a pair of manga

---

[64] There'll be more about vampires in chapter 29.

episodes from 1999), the club president assigns a task to a new initiate: go into the woods at night and take a picture of a ghost. The newbie does just that—which unnerves the club president, whose own ghost photograph was a fake.

xxx

When Tatsunoko, one of Japan's major animation houses, celebrated its fortieth anniversary in 2004 by producing *Karas*, an OAV about a guardian policing the border between real life and the spirit realm, a press release quoted director Keiichi Sato and his ambivalent opinion on the spirit world:

> "To tell you the truth, I don't really get *youkai* (Japanese [ghosts, spirits, and monsters] causing mysterious, outrageous and sometimes wonderfully life affirming events). I do have a grasp on the fact that they coexist with us and keep the boundary of the human world in balance."

Of course, the whole point of a ghost story is the occasional imbalance, the crossing of a ghost into the human world. This sense of a comfortable reality being violated contributes to the chills one gets from a good ghost story. And this is the context for the Japanese perspective on spirit photography.

xxx

58. Dangerous Crossing

The children of *Gakkou no Kaidan*[65] hear that a woman's ghost has been haunting a rural railroad crossing. Leo gives them all cameras, telling them that "cameras see what humans cannot." Only Momoko, the oldest girl, says that ghosts don't like to be forcibly awoken, so they ought to be left alone. This isn't easy to do, since

---

[65] There's more about the *School Ghosts* in chapter 21.

when Leo develops a picture he took of Momoko, there's a ghostly hand on her shoulder. The next morning, before Leo can show anyone else the picture, Satsuki brings word that Momoko is in the hospital.

Momoko tells her hospital visitors that she just felt a tightness in her chest; this, however, would be a tipoff to anyone Japanese, because the Japanese language has a word for this phenomenon: kanashibari. The word literally means "bound by metal" but carries the assumption that if a sleeping person feels heaviness on the chest, it's the weight of a ghost sitting on them. Momoko may well believe the folklore explanation.

It gets worse. Momoko looks impassively at the ghost photo, then takes off her bed-jacket. This reveals her shoulder; the area touched in the picture by the ghost hand has a large, hand-shaped discoloration. It's the ghost of a woman, Momoko thinks; last night she was at my bedside glaring at me. But I can't tell the doctor or my parents, she goes on.

Satsuki's cat, possessed by a local demon, speculates that the spirit is a jibakurei, tied to that particular place by circumstance. He describes jibakurei as carrying a lot of hostility over the abrupt way they left this world. Leo, meanwhile, tries an amateur exorcism to get the ghost images out of the picture and negatives. Instead, there's an explosion in Leo's darkroom, and a pair of ghostly hands end up around Momoko's neck, trying to choke her to death.

Leo gets to the hospital about the same time as the doctor is telling Momoko's parents that she'll have to be moved into Intensive Care. As the nurses are rolling her down the hall, Leo can actually see the ghost standing next to Momoko. The possessed cat later tells Leo that the jibakurei needs to be approached as the human she once was, to find out what would settle her heart.

Leo brings flowers to the railroad crossing where they first went looking for the ghost, and while there he meets an elderly woman also bringing flowers to the spot. She turns out to be the mother of the dead girl, Shizuko. The mother has an altar set up with incense and other tokens of remembrance, which ought to be enough to dispel the ghost. But Shizuko had been killed in a hit-and-run three years earlier, and no witnesses ever came forward. The real tragedy, according to the mother, was that Shizuko had just gotten engaged. When they found her body, however, her engagement ring was gone.

Leo goes back to the crossing to look for the missing ring. Suddenly he sees Momoko standing on the tracks, with a train approaching. The others try to move her, but the possessed Momoko tosses them aside and runs toward the oncoming train. Leo ultimately drags Momoko off of the tracks, which wakes up Momoko; now she knows where the missing ring is. They go to the local taxi company and find it under the seat of a taxi; the ring was too large and had fallen off Shizuko's finger when the cabdriver tried to help. The driver sees the children poking around his cab and chases them away. However, once again on a rainy night, the driver thinks he sees a woman at the crossing. When she vanishes this time, and reappears in the back seat, she tells the driver that she's found the ring.

The driver screams. The taxi disappears. So does the image of Shizuko from the photograph of Momoko.

xxx

59. Family Snapshots

A two-part episode of the manga by Yoshiyuki Nishi, *Muyo to Rouji*, which premiered in 2005, focuses on spirit photographs, but only as a side-issue. Like so many of the stories in Japanese pop culture, the real point of this tale is human relations.

One of the ghost-hunting firm's former clients returns with a referral—another potential client. This time, it's a high school girl named Nana. She brings in some snapshots, since photography is her hobby. Her friend suspects that some of her photos may contain a spirit; this is a notion that Nana scoffs at. She clearly refuses to believe that spirit photography is anything but fake—even when Muyo tells her that all twenty of the photos she brought contain a spirit in them. He declares that the spirit who appears in all twenty photographs—because there is only one—has violated spirit assault and trespass laws and is to be punished. When he tries, however, the weapons are turned on Muyo instead.

This is a unique safeguard in spirit law enforcement: if the law is misapplied, the mistaken lawyer is punished. Once they realize this, Muyo understands, and tells Nana that the ghost is that of her father. "It must have been very hard for him that his own daughter couldn't notice him. Ghosts usually don't have a clear mind. But they never forget the things that were most important to them." At the end of his life, just before he suddenly died of a heart attack, Nana's father had hit the skids in his photographic career and was taking spirit photographs. Nana argued with her father that he was a charlatan, but still tried otherwise to respect him; she even explains that she participated in his Buddhist funeral, passing his bones among family and friends with chopsticks as a sign of respect, "so that he could go to Heaven peacefully." (see chapter 5) His appearances in her photos were only to accomplish one thing: to tell Nana that he forgave her.

Muyo announces that the father's ghost still broke ghostly law, except that essentially he did no more than commit invasion of privacy. His punishment would be to "ride the boat"; that is, to cross the River Sanzu (see chapter 4) and continue his journey to rebirth.

XXX

Spirit photography goes back to the invention of photography itself, in the middle 19th century. The technology was slow and cumbersome for those early pictures, and involved having subjects pose absolutely still for sixty seconds or longer while the light exposed the chemically treated film. It was always possible to create a double exposure: using the same piece of film to capture two pictures. Usually, this would cancel out both pictures, and any surviving double exposures would be painfully obvious as such. However, by coincidence or other results, some double exposures can seem surprisingly composed, even uncanny in their interpreted meaning.

The first known "spirit photographer" surfaced in Boston in 1861. William Mumler took a self-portrait, noted another figure in the picture beside him, and began running photo-séances. This lasted for about a decade until he was exposed as a fraud; he had an assistant sneak into the picture for ten seconds or so, just long enough to leave a ghostly image.[66]

Of course, it's one thing to find out that ghost photos had been deliberately staged. What happens when an amateur takes pictures, and discovers that what one sees is not always what one gets?

While much of the interest in spirit photography in the West was spurred on by wars (the Civil War, World Wars 1 and 2) and the subsequent desire of families to contact those killed in action, scholar Richard Chalfen suggests that Japan, with centuries of belief that ghosts are no less real than people, plays by different rules:

> photographs made, used and interpreted in Japan may, indeed, carry an alternative epistemological load. These home mode *(sic)* pictures may have a different sense of currency, authority and power than generally accepted in the West. Connections with animistic beliefs may begin to "explain" some of these information issues as well as the tendency to travel with photographs, to reach recently deceased relatives via images, to be comforted by specific pictures, and, indeed, begin to unravel the controversial existence of ghost-snapshots.

> This is a very tricky and controversial area because, theoretically, I do not believe photographs per se contain any information — they do not

---

[66] http://www.ghostvillage.com/legends/spiritphotography.shtml, accessed February 22, 2007.

say anything, and they certainly do not speak to people. People making photographs as well as looking and using photographs create the meaning, the message and significance of what ever might be recognized in an image — people do the speaking and not photographs.[67]

Spirit photography in Japan has moved with the times and technology. For a fee (roughly $3/month), cellular phone users have access to the "Kyofu (Horror) Channel", including a horror role-playing game and accounts of ghost stories from other subscribers as well as spirit photos.[68]

xxx

Spirit photography can be said to be a modern cousin of the legends and artwork from traditional Japan, as well as the ghost stories out of Hollywood and Tokyo studios. These traditional *kaidan* and Hollywood/Tokyo's versions of them meet briefly in another episode of *Akachan to Boku (Baby and Me)*. The toddler Minoru is in preschool; it's autumn, and the teachers tell an old traditional story, titled in the translation of the manga as "The Three Charms and the Mountain Witch." It's also known simply as "The Three Ofuda"[69] and is parodied in part in the Kyoto field trip sequence of the manga *Negima!* by Ken Akamatsu.

An ofuda is a charmed piece of paper on which is written the name of one of the Shinto deities, the name of a temple, or some other significant text. The ofuda is then placed in the home shrine, the kitchen, or some other location to protect the family. (The

---

[67] http://www.richardchalfen.com/wip-jhm.html, accessed February 22, 2007.

[68] http://hudson.co.jp/mobile/eng/jp/imode/horror/index.html, accessed February 22, 2007.

[69] For one English version of the story, see http://web-japan.org/kidsweb/folk/ofuda/ofuda.html, accessed February 9, 2007.

ofuda is often renewed every year, around New Year's Day.) They appear in various anime and manga, usually endowed with very exotic powers. Ofuda are used in *Ghost!* (aka *Eerie Queerie*) to ward off possession by ghosts. They're also part of the arsenal of Sailor Mars in *Sailor Moon*; whether as a Shinto *miko* (temple maiden) or as one of the Sailor Scouts, she hurls ofuda at the enemy, shouting, "Akuryou taisan!" (Spirits of the dead, depart!) They're also used by the Buddhist monk Miroku in *InuYasha* and by Meisuke Nueno, the fifth grade teacher/exorcist in *Jigoku Sensei Nube.*

The Shinto ofuda should not be confused with the Buddhist omamori, although there's a bit of overlap. Omamori are good luck charms or other personal blessings sold at Buddhist temples.

Ai yori Aoshi includes an omamori in one pivotal scene in which Kaoru talks about his childhood. He was brought up within the Hanabishi family, since he was the love-child of the son and heir to the Hanabishi conglomerate and a woman who wasn't of an equivalent social rank. When Kaoru's father died in an auto accident (Kaoru was a child at the time), the Hanabishi clan asked that they bring up Kaoru, and his mother agreed, thinking that at least her son would have a good life. When she died a few years later, the head of the Hanabishi destroyed everything that had to do with Kaoru's mother. He was able to rescue only one thing from the bonfire: an omamori which contained his umbilical cord—the last connection, literally and figuratively, between Kaoru and his mother.

But let's get back to Minoru Enoki, the pre-schooler listening to the story of "The Three Ofuda." Actually, he's also watching it, since the teachers have made hand-drawn illustrations of important scenes in the story. This is a form of manga-style storytelling with a long tradition in Japan, called kami-shibai. The storyteller draws scenes on the spot, or works from a "deck" of already-drawn illustrations, while telling the story, complete with character voices and sound effects.

This particular story is pretty intense for Minoru. It tells of a young and disrespectful student at a shrine, who asks to go to the nearby woods to pick chestnuts which are just ready for harvest. The priest gives the boy three ofuda with which to protect himself, and he ends up needing all three. While he's in the grove, the boy meets an old woman who offers to cook the chestnuts for him at her house. While he's there, he realized that she's an evil witch who is planning to kill him; he sees her sharpening a large knife.

At this point in the story most of the toddlers, not just Minoru, start screaming and crying. Minoru has gone so far as to wet his pants, and has to be taken home.[70] The story leaves Minoru more nervous than usual, especially at night.

For the rest of the manga episode, Minoru is stuck home alone with his brother Takuya while their father goes on a business trip. Minoru asks Takuya to stand guard as he uses the bathroom; he then sees water-spots on the bathroom wall as the glaring eyes of the evil witch.

This all continued the next day, when a friend of Minoru's tripped and fell in school. When she stood up with Minoru's help, her hair was hanging in front of her face, which made her look like Sayako in *Ringu* (or any number of other Japanese female ghosts, including Oiwa in *Yotsuya Kaidan*), which set Minoru off again.

That night, with the wind howling outside, Minoru watches a television program: "The Mystery Horror Hour," one of many supernaturally based TV programs in Japan. This sends Minoru under the bed, and reminds Takuya of the time he had a similar reaction to a televised showing of *A Nightmare on Elm Street*. At the time, Takuya had two parents to comfort him; this night, he's alone with Minoru. Things get "worse" when father comes home, having lost his key and realized that the doorbell isn't working. Knocking on the boys' bedroom window sets Minoru off yet again, but at

---

[70]   Anyone familiar with "The Three Ofuda" recognizes that this is actually an echo of the story. To escape the witch, the boy says that he has to use the witch's bathroom. While there, he takes one of the ofuda, puts it on the wall, and asks it to protect him. When the witch tells the boy to hurry up, the ofuda answers in the boy's voice, which gives the boy a chance to escape. This is one of the scenes parodied in *Negima!*

least they're able to laugh about it afterwards. What finally calms Minoru, however, is Takuya holding his hand as he falls asleep.

The Japanese have a word for this: "skinship." Despite all the media monsters on the Japanese landscape, from legendary ghosts to prehistoric monsters, the most healing phenomenon is through direct touch. Minoru finds this as he holds his brother's hand, as Takuya's parents did the same for him. In this context, it's no accident that Kaoru was desperate to hang onto the umbilical cord that connected him to his mother. And it probably was no accident that, when Japanese citizens who had been kidnapped by North Korea were repatriated after decades away from home, they were not able to loosen up mentally and feel that they were home again until they bathed in a hot springs with family they hadn't seen in years. (WSJ story, spring 2003)

Skinship also is the ultimate reality of a situation, since the skin has been described as the largest sense organ of the human body, including not only the skin itself but the entire neural network of feeling, of temperature and pain. Perhaps it is in this context that spirit photography is especially disturbing. It offers "evidence" of something that can (under the proper conditions) be seen, but not felt (or, in the case of the ghost attacking Momoko in *Gakkou no Kaidan*, something felt but not seen). The notion that something (or someone) can be so physically close, without one being aware of it through any of the senses, certainly generates more anxiety than most fears, especially in a culture which places such a high value on what can be felt.

XXX

60. Preserve the Moment

Yuko Ichihara in *xxxHolic* runs a curio shop in which some of the items are helpful, some are downright dangerous, and some are so mysterious that they seem to transcend the whole notion of good and evil. In one story, however, a customer brings a curious item to the shop.

The customer is a thin, tall, black-haired woman who asks Yuuko's help with something in an envelope—an envelope wrapped in string as if to keep something from escaping. Yuko, whose totem animal is a butterfly, offers a small wrought-metal picture frame that looks like a butterfly, with the implication that it would limit whatever was in the envelope. The woman opens it and takes out a photograph of a woman with light wavy hair in a summer dress, with her back to the camera.

As Yuko's assistant Watanuki watches, the frame begins to melt; not only that, the woman in the picture begins to move. The movement is very slow at first, but gradually she turns to face the viewer and show herself to be a rather pretty woman. She smiles as the customer comes into the picture and stands next to the other woman. They seem to be friends; there is a sudden movement, and the light haired woman drops out of sight below the bottom of the picture. The customer, now alone in the picture, turns so that Watanuki can see the hideous smirk on her face. The customer is talking to herself, accusing the light haired woman of stealing the man who loved her, and saying that the police had decided that the other woman simply slipped on the edge of the cliff.

This was what terrified the customer: letting someone else see the picture, and guess at the truth. She asks Yuko's help in destroying the picture, and Yuko agrees, on one condition: the customer would have to go through life never allowing herself to be photographed again. When the customer agrees, Yuko takes the photograph, which dissolves into the air like sand.

Later, Yuko tells Watanuki that her condition may be impossible for the customer to meet, with surveillance cameras, film crews, and so many other ways in the modern world of having one's picture taken unawares. The customer will have to stay in her house for the rest of her life if she wants to avoid being photographed altogether, and even then, Yuko suggests, there are no guarantees. The episode leaves the unanswered question of which is worse: the customer's fear of what the picture revealed, or what she would have to do to keep it from happening.

xxx

61. A Yukionna

A yukionna figures in one of the episodes of *Gakkou no Kaidan*, as does a photo which drips blood.

In early winter the five children take a train up into the mountains, to a town called Satoyama. They've been invited to an inn run by a distant relative; the inn is a ski resort but is currently closed and the kids can have the run of the place. This perfect arrangement has a few problems, and one is that the daughter of the household, Miyuki, was supposed to meet their train but never did. The kids arrive at the inn with nobody to meet them there, except the younger daughter Yuki. The inn is old and traditional; the lobby contains stuffed animals and paintings, including the figure of a woman they mistake at first for a yukionna. Yuki's clothes are also old and traditional: kimono with snow-boots made of reeds.

As they wait, Yuki takes them to their rooms and tells them the history of the place: that the inn sits on the shore of Bloodstained Lake, whose blue waters turn blood-red when some disaster is about to occur. After lunch, Yuki shows up and tells them that Miyuki is dead. Not only has the lake turned red, but Yuki points to a picture of Miyuki; blood is dripping from the top of the frame.

As Satsuki tries to call the police from the lobby phone, Miyuki appears at the front door. Yuki has the others bar the door to her. When Miyuki goes to the back door, Yuki runs away. Hajime tries to follow her but gets locked in a closet by the yukionna. A heavy blizzard comes up, which almost pushes Miyuki into the lake. Hajime explains, since the closet he was locked in conveniently had a 40 year old newspaper which told of the daughter of a waitress at the inn who fell into the lake and drowned, that child was Yuki. Because she died alone, Yuki's spirit developed a grudge against the living; however, before she can kill anyone and take them with her, the very spell she taught them to ward off a yukionna works against her. As she vanishes, so does the snow, and the lake's color returns to blue.

At the end, the children gather by the lake to pay their respects to Yuki. According to the newspaper, Yuki wasn't merely at the inn: her mother had abandoned her there. Yuki spent a lot of her time waiting by the lake for her mother to return; she also spent a lot of time in the lake before her body was discovered. As she reads the article, Momoko's eyes fill with tears, which should be as clear a signal as the fact that Yuki was capable of running barefoot through the snow. The young yukionna can now rest in peace.

CHAPTER 21: SCHOOL GHOSTS

The so-called "ghosts in school" have made up some well-known old and new anime and manga titles, including *Gakkou no Kaidan, Jigoku Sensei Nube* and *Haunted Junction*. Actually, they're well known but still relative newcomers to Japan's ghost world. (There were no western-style schools in Japan 200 years ago, but many ghost legends had already existed before the Edo era and were simply transferred and updated to the school system.)

xxx

Gakkou no kaidan (*School Ghost Stories*)
This series (more accurately, a series of series) includes books and live-action feature films as well as several weekly anime series, with one of the latter being noteworthy (or notorious) because of the way it was adapted to American audiences.

To begin at the beginning: in 1985 a middle school teacher named Toru Tsunemitsu decided to collect some of the "urban legends" he overheard his students telling each other. As he gathered these stories, he was surprised to find that many of the stories were about ghosts, and that many of these ghosts haunted schools.

The scenario in many *gakkou no kaidan* would have been common in the immediate postwar years: a new concrete school built next to an old and abandoned pre-war wooden school. Rumors about what goes on in the abandoned school after hours are bound to spread. In retrospect, it seems natural that the haunted school would serve Japan the way that the haunted house serves the west; real estate is in such short supply in Japan, and generations live in houses so continuously, that there probably would be more abandoned schools than abandoned houses.[71]

Many of the stories focus on a death at the school in the past, which brings about a continuing ghost problem. A child drowns in the school swimming pool, for example, and other swimmers can sometimes feel the ghost pulling at their legs to drag them underwater.

In 1995 a film appeared which caused a sensation, touching off a wave of school *kaidan* in Japanese movies. There was one difference: *Gakkou no Kaidan (School Ghost Stories)*, directed by Hideyuki Hirayama, was for, and mostly starred, children. The scares were there, since they're the point of any good ghost story, but the overall tone of the film was child-friendly, fun, and wholesome without becoming unbelievable or watered-down.[72] The movie spawned three sequels, with Hirayama directing the second and fourth films as well. The third film was directed by Noriyuki Abe, and the anime series actually starts here.

In 2000 Abe was credited as director and storyboard creator (and, oddly enough, as Music Director) of the anime series *Gakkou no Kaidan*. Co-produced by Fuji Television and Aniplex and animated by Studio Pierrot, the series credits the books by Tsunemitsu as the basis of the series. The scripts' actual author is Hiroshi Hashimoto. It's the story of the Miyanoshita family: widower father and two children, Satsuki (fifth-grader) and Keiichiro (first-grader).

As for the dub . . .

To quote from a company press release by ADV, which adapted the series for western marketing, "ADV's English dub of *Ghost Stories* follows the plot of the original exactly. But in place of a written

---

[71] In movies such as *Ju-On* (known in America as *The Grudge*), a house can be haunted without being deserted.

[72] Another such film, *The Great Youkai War*, was directed by the very edgy Japanese thriller director Takashi Miike, and was set in Sakaiminako, the hometown of Shigeru Mizuki, creator of the long-running spirit-manga *GeGeGe no Kitaro*. Mizuki puts in a cameo appearance, as do his characters.

script, [director Steven] Foster simply blocked out scenes and let the actors go. It's the anime equivalent of [the Home Box Office cable television comedy series] *Curb Your Enthusiasm*, in that the actors have freedom to riff off one another instead of simply following a prewritten script." Foster, the press release goes on, "took a perfectly nice kids' show about modern children who take on supernatural creatures from Japanese folklore and brought in the best voice talent in anime to create a hip, funny action-comedy."

The operative word, it seems, is "hip:" the original series was deemed to be "hipness-challenged," apparently, and ADV decided to fix that. But did they succeed?

When the father drives away from the Amanogawa school after dropping off his children for their first day, in the original he tells his kids "Be sure to pay your respects to the principal." This gets turned into, "Remember, just say 'no' to . . . everything." Not only is this not exactly the world's funniest joke, it's utterly out of character in a Japanese setting, where new students would be expected both to show respect to the adults and to seek out classmates with similar interests. It's even more important here in the family's *furusato* (homeland), since as children the father and his late wife had attended the very same school, where the maternal grandmother was the principal.

Besides, a staple of school anime and manga is the scene where the new kid is introduced to the homeroom and makes a speech about her/himself. This moves the socialization process forward in a culture where social relations are vital. Another Satsuki, the older sister in *My Neighbor Totoro*, is befriended by a girl named Michiko almost as soon as she moves to her new home (and school) in the country. In Hiroyuki Takei's manga *Shaman King*, gang-leader Ryu is defended by one of his gang: "Remember that spring day when I came to a new school with no friends—and you came over and talked to me!?"

The Miyanoshita family has had to move from Tokyo back to their parents' old home town following the death of the kids' mother. As they move into the home that had belonged to the Kamiyamas (the late wife's family), the husband's parents are on hand. Specifically, the paternal grandfather makes an offer that would have been expected out of family feeling and sheer politeness, "You shouldn't have to move into the home of your wife's family. You could move in with us." After an interruption from the children, the old man changes his tune: "I guess this house has more room." He had to recognize, however grudgingly, that he wasn't equipped to take in two grade school kids along with his son.

The English lines for the old man start by putting a negative spin on the entire move: "I don't see why you have to live in your dead wife's house. It's sick! *You're* sick!" Then, referring to the wife standing next to him, he delivers the unbelievable line: "When this bitch kicks (kicks the bucket; i.e., dies), I'm moving to Vegas." This is a reading that says much more about Americans than Japanese, and none of it is flattering.

When Satsuki and her brother first enter the old deserted school to look for Kaya, their odd-eyed black cat, Satsuki originally keeps repeating, "This isn't scary! This isn't scary!" In the dub, what comes out is: "Monsters only attack bad people like Republicans, and we're not even old enough to vote!" All partisanship aside, no fifth-grade girl, in Japan or the United States, would say anything even remotely like this to her kid brother. The key to these school ghost stories, as with all ghost stories, is plausibility. They have to seem as if they could happen in order to be scary.[73] Take away the element of plausibility, make them blatantly impossible, and the stories tip into the realm of comic absurdity, as in the *Haunted Junction* series. That's a completely different sub-genre.

Plus, the line is just not funny, precisely because it tries to be funny. An English line that would have preserved both the sense and the mood of the original Japanese while amusing an American

---

[73]   Plausibility is achieved here in part by bringing in a flock of traditional Japanese ghosts, ancient and modern. In the first episode alone, the group of children at the center of the story encounter a walking Ninomiya statue, Toilet Hanako, a man-faced dog, a headless ghost on a motorcycle, a Teke-Teke (see chapter 27), and much more...

audience would perhaps have had Satsuki say, "I don't believe in spooks! I don't believe in spooks! I don't I don't I don't . . ." For those who absolutely have to have a hip, pop culture reference, this is, of course, an inversion of a line by the Cowardly Lion in *The Wizard of Oz*. But the cast was given general instructions and told to improvise.

In the old school building the two children meet a third, Leo Kakinoki, who calls himself the school's expert on psychic research. This, at least, is plausible. The dub Leo also proclaims that he's Jewish, which in Japan is pretty unlikely.

We also meet a sixth-grade girl named Momoko Koigakubo. Satsuki being in fifth grade, she refers to Momoko as "oneesan"—"big sister". Momoko tells the other kids that "I seem to have a strong sense for detecting spirits." Again, this is a plausible part of many school ghost stories: someone with at least a sense, right or wrong, that he/she has psychic abilities. In the dub, however, she announces that she got this sense after she was "saved." Yes, for no apparent reason, in the English dub, Momoko is a born-again Christian in a country where Christians (born-again or otherwise) are less than one percent of the population.

It is, however, entirely consistent that a Japanese character would attribute qualities to the Christian religion that western Christians would find, to put it mildly, puzzling. Faith was part of the training regimen of the boxer in the manga series *Kamisama wa Sausupo (God is a Southpaw),* which was itself mildly parodied in another manga mixing Christianity and boxing, Rumiko Takahashi's *Ippondo no Fukuin (The One-Pound Gospel).* The Nomura investment house opened its doors on Christmas Day, seeing it as a good omen rather than as a day of rest.

Why go to all this trouble dubbing a kid-oriented anime? Americans have played fast and loose on occasion with dubbing Japanese films (animated or otherwise) for a number of reasons. Sometimes humor is the reason, although it helps if the humor is purposeful as well as funny. Perhaps the best-known example was when Woody Allen and some friends got a 1960s Japanese James Bond-style film, *Kagi no Kagi (The Key to the Key),* and turned it into *What's Up, Tiger Lily?* The jokes were uneven but generally funny, and also mocked the spy-thriller conventions that were the basis of the Bond films. There is, of course, a villain seeking world domination, but the key to this domination is a recipe for the world's tastiest egg salad. (As one character helpfully explains it, "Don't ask me why egg salad; I've got enough aggravation.")

At other times, scripts were changed by dubbing because they had to be. Early American television, like baseball after the 1919 World Series game-fixing scandal and like American comic books after the outcry against crime and horror comics in the 1950s, announced that it would police itself rather than risk Congressional investigation and possible federal legislation. The result was the Television Code of the National Association of Broadcasters, which tried to limit the content of television, from news broadcasts to children's programming. The guidelines for the latter include the following:

Television is responsible for insuring that programs of all sorts which occur during the times of day when children may normally be expected to have the opportunity of viewing television shall exercise care in the following regards:

(*a*) In affording opportunities for cultural growth as well as for wholesome entertainment.

(*b*) In developing programs to foster and promote the commonly accepted moral, social, and ethical ideals characteristic of American life.

(*c*) In reflecting respect for parents, for honorable behavior, and for the constituted authorities of the American community.

(*d*) In eliminating reference to kidnapping of children or threats of kidnapping.

(*e*) In avoiding material which is excessively violent or would create morbid suspense, or other undesirable reactions in children.

This last clause was taken in part to mean that cartoon characters could not refer to death or dying. (Let the record show that the Disney film *Bambi*, made in 1942 and containing a character death necessary to the plot, did not receive its network television premiere until 2005.) When the anime series *Go Lion* was broadcast in the U.S. as *Voltron*, references to dead characters were written out—despite on-screen imagery that would confirm a death to someone with enough experience to decode the symbols (a drop of dew rolling off of a leaf, a sunset, falling blossoms). Even the alien monsters were re-christened "ro-beasts"—implying that they were part animal, part robot, and therefore unlikely to "die" in any meaningful sense.

Occasionally, a Japanese studio would create its own dub into English, with results that could not always be predicted. One famous example (from a Reiji Matsumoto space opera), had an alien utter the immortal line: "This isn't a human; it's a woman!" This would be a literal translation of the Japanese, but a rather strange one to western ears.

Sometimes, the script is so inherently culture-specific, so laden with satiric or serious references to history and puns opaque to all western non-scholars, that liberties have to be taken. This is certainly the case with madcap anime comedies like *Haunted Junction, BoBoBo-Bo Bo-BoBo* or *Excel Saga*. The 1991 series *Kyatto Ninden Teyandee (Cat Bunch Secret History Teyandee)* was a sci-fi parody of life during the Edo period (1600 to 1850), assuming Edo to have been populated by cyborg ninja animals, some of whom ran a pizza delivery service. It was also a satire on contemporary Japanese events and personalities; the references, in any event, were so outside of most Americans' experience or knowledge that the dubbed series was radically altered by creating scripts that stuck to the basics of the visuals and turning it into *Samurai Pizza Cats*. Sometimes a juvenile series is rewritten, leaving the basic story intact but somewhat retold, recognizing the limitations of the intended audience. The conversion of *Ojamajo DoReMi* into *Magical DoReMi* may not have been literal, but at least it was respectful of both its source material and its western viewers (at least, for the one season of episodes broadcast in the United States; the original series, which included Doremi's mother telling her daughter how she once wanted to commit suicide, ran for four seasons). The anime feature *Windaria* was edited for a younger audience by editing out the sex and some of the violence, and renaming it *Once Upon a Time*.

On a more serious subject, the 1954 Japanese science fiction film *Gojira* told of a dinosaur awakened by atomic bomb testing, which proceeded to lay waste to Tokyo and thereby establish a popular movie template copied dozens of times. The original, however, occurred shortly after the H-bomb tests at Bikini Atoll, and scared American government officials with its potential as anti-bomb propaganda. The script even singled out one incident in which a real fishing vessel, the *Lucky Dragon*, had been contaminated by fallout from the blast. Hollywood optioned the movie, showing it only in Japanese-American neighborhood theaters, then in 1958 threw half of the original on the cutting-room floor, and filmed entirely new scenes with narration from a reporter (actually actor Raymond Burr). It would be fifty years before the Japanese original was available on home video in America.

With *Ghost Stories*, though, ADV may have decided to boost sales by fixing something that wasn't really broken. Perhaps they thought that the "perfectly nice children's series" had to appeal to a broader audience that would be too jaded to accept the familiar school ghosts in a post-*Ringu* environment. Unfortunately, they needed to realize that, unlike science-fiction anime set in some distant future or on a faraway planet with social rules built from the ground up, this series was nested so deeply in Japanese culture that attempts to Americanize the story would simply cause it to fall between the two cultures. Fortunately the DVD includes the original Japanese soundtrack, permitting the series, with all apologies due to ADV and *Curb Your Enthusiasm*, to be seen as it was meant to be seen.

The opening shot of the title animation is a portrait of the major characters in the series: Satsuki, her brother, their friends, their father and his parents, the teachers, and (although this isn't clear at first) the children's dead mother. Early in the series they find a notebook she had kept; this turns out to be a detailed guide to the local ghosts, spirits and demons. Not only that, but at times Momoko goes into a trance and apparently channels the spirit of the mother to help the children deal with whatever demon is threatening them (although afterwards Momoko doesn't remember any of it). This not only establishes Momoko as at least a potential itako (spiritual medium), but that the late Mrs. Miyanoshita also had a fair share of psychic powers. This plot device allowed the series to fuse the old beliefs in spirits with the newer ghost stories, and put them all in a modern context.

One more important narrative piece of the puzzle: the land around the town is being developed. This construction activity created a lot of destruction of the forest, including one large camphor tree that was part of an old Shinto shrine. Just the mention of a camphor tree should have set off alarm bells in the anime fan's head; a giant camphor tree marked the shrine in the country next to the house rented by Professor Kusakaba for himself and his daughters in Hayao Miyazaki's signature film *Tonari no Totoro (My Neighbor Totoro)* and a camphor tree was communication channel to Ayako Matsuzaki, the self-proclaimed *miko* in the *Ghost Hunt* series; and there's a large tree on the grounds of the shrine run by the family of Kagome Higurashi in Rumiko Takahashi's *InuYasha*. The second episode of *Gakkou no Kaidan* kicks off the ghostly activity at the school when the viewer learns that, with the destruction of the camphor tree, local spirits imprisoned by it (and by Satsuki and Keiichi's mother in her youth) are loose again, and the rest of the series involves trying to round them up. It's a simple and elegant plot device that allows the original series of books, which was basically a catalogue of ghosts and rumors about ghosts, to be given a dramatic structure.

xxx

When anime and manga examine school ghosts, the number seven comes up, whether there are more or fewer than seven actual ghosts. Each haunted school is declared to have its own "seven wonders of the world," a phrase originally referencing some of the great achievements of ancient western civilization (the great pyramid of Giza, the hanging gardens of Babylon, the lighthouse at Alexandria, etc.)

The anime series *CLAMP Campus Detectives* takes place in a large self-contained world that can hold schools from elementary school through graduate school, plus house students, faculty, their families, and support personnel—ten thousand people in all. Of course, this mega-campus has its own Seven Wonders, which include The Nightwalking Beauty. The story revolves around a picture in the campus art gallery, of a young woman in kimono with a kitten. According to rumor, the painting memorializes a woman and her pet who died in a fire. Still, the ghost reportedly walks by night; hence the name. The ghost turned out to be a rumor, triggered by the sound of stray kittens .

Saito High School has far more than seven resident ghosts, but the principal seven in *Haunted Junction*, based on a manga by Nemu Mukudori, are known as the Seven Wonders. Student Nobuhiro Watanuki, who inherited his family's ability to see spirits, is asked during the manga *xxxHolic* by CLAMP if this gift makes him one of the seven wonders of his school. And in the second anime episode of *Mythic Detective Loki Ragnarok*, one of the deities of the Norse pantheon, trapped in the body of a young boy in Japan, is given a guided tour of his new school's "seven wonders." These tend to be rather lame "wonders" with perfectly normal explanations: a skeleton, for example, that moves by itself is actually just hanging in front of a hole in the wall and is pushed around by a draft. Only the last wonder, a suit of armor inhabited by a spirit, turns out to be very real and very dangerous.

xxx

Ghost Hunt

Ghost Hunt is a ghost manga (art by Shiho Inada, story by Fuyumi Ono based on a series of teen novels she wrote; akin to the *Goosebumps* series in the U.S.) where many of the ghosts are encountered in schools. The manga ran beginning in 1998 in the *shojo manga* (comics aimed at a readership of *shojo*—adolescent girls) magazine *Nakayoshi*. An anime version of the manga premiered in Japan in October 2006 and immediately became one of the Top Twenty anime series in Japan. One odd occurrence: an announcement appeared in *Nakayoshi* that, although the magazine

171

would stop publishing *Ghost Hunt*, the manga would continue to be published in paperback tankobon editions.[74] The eleventh and apparently final volume made it into English late in 2010. In any event, life would continue for this school ghost story that's solidly *shojo*.

Students in a girls' high school are visited by a bishie[75] boy, Kazuya Shibuya, who happens to be the head of Shibuya Psychic Research[76]. He and his eclectic ghost-busting staff begin the series by investigating the goings-on at an abandoned, supposedly haunted high school. Of course, ghosts are only part of the story; Shibuya has a "cute meet" with one of the girls, Mai Taniyama, and they seem to hate each other almost immediately. Of course, this state of affairs doesn't last; after she breaks one of his cameras and sidelines Shibuya's assistant, Mai ends up working for Shibuya (let the love-hate relationship begin). Because of his aloof manner, Mai gives Kazuya a private nickname: "Naru," because she thinks of him as a narcissist. She's not, as it turns out, the only one.

They start by investigating possible psychic activity in the old school next to Mai's. The old school was to be demolished when the new one was built, but demolition could never be finished. Something always happened: workmen were injured; a teacher committed suicide; a truck went out of control, ran onto the schoolyard and killed three students. All of these things could be explained by other than psychic causes, but . . . Joining the Shibuya Psychic Research company in the investigation (at the request of the rather panicky school principal) are a haughty *miko* (a Shinto shrine maiden, although this one isn't associated with a particular shrine), a Buddhist monk on leave from his monastery, a popular television "medium," and an Australian Catholic exorcism student

---

74 Inada Shiho & Ono Fuyumi. 2006. *Ghost Hunt*, vol. 5. New York: Del Rey, p. 151.

75 Short for "bishonen"—literally, beautiful boy; to put it more simply, a hunk.

76 Shibuya is also a very hip neighborhood in Tokyo, a center of commerce, entertainment, hi-tech and youth culture.

named John Brown. He's well-meaning but has a few flaws. For one, he speaks Kansai, the dialect of western Japan, which makes it hard for the Tokyo-bred agency members to take him seriously.[77] Another time, he discusses the funding of Naru's agency; however, the word he uses for "sponsor" is a very different term, one applied to the patron of a prostitute.

Even one of Mai's classmates, a girl who insists that she's receptive to psychic phenomena, gets into the act. In the end, the school's problems are traced to . . . land subsidence. It may be a let-down for that particular ghost story, but it's only the first in a series of psychic investigations.

Mai, by the way, has some sort of psychic ability, although it's hard to determine what it is at first, and it's only "discovered" at the end of the third volume in a roundabout way. Naru administers a test for ESP abilities to Mai: a thousand responses, and she gets all of them wrong. Statistically, this is impossible: she would have gotten a quarter of them right by mere chance. According to Naru, this means that Mai has "latent sensitivity . . . to harmful outside influences." In a way, it's a shame that the story goes off in this direction, attributing Mai's good-hearted compassion to latent psychic powers instead of her intrinsically *yasashii* nature, as would happen in more conventional *shoujo* stories. Still, that nature comes through: in the long story reprinted in volumes 6 and 7 of the manga, Mai enters a trance and makes contact with the spirits of people murdered in a grotesque haunted house. Mai is also the only member of Shibuya Psychic Research to shed a tear for these spirits, and (despite her abilities) she comes to represent the point of view of "Ms. Average."

Haunted Junction

One of the ghost stories told at the very beginning of the *Ghost Hunt* manga recalls Red Mantle, but doesn't quite tell the whole story:

---

[77]   It makes sense, however, to remember that Nagasaki, a center of Christian activity in Japan, would speak Kansai Japanese.

Someone standing outside a public toilet at night (although other locations and times of day come up in other versions of the legend) is asked a question by what seems at first to be a disembodied voice: "The red cloak or the blue cloak?" The only acceptable answer is to run away at top speed, because at least that way you'd stay alive. If you asked for a red cloak, your throat would be slashed from ear to ear, and you'd be left to die in a pool of your own blood (the red cloak). The blue cloak isn't a much better end: death by strangulation, leaving a body with a blue-tinted face.

This time around, however, Red Mantle is a drop-dead *bishounen*, not unlike Tuxedo Mask in *Sailor Moon*. He doesn't kill anyone, nor do the other ghosts in *Haunted Junction,* a "late-night" anime of 12 episodes broadcast in Japan in 1997.

The seven principal ghosts haunting Saito High School are a motley crew, but mostly inspired by school ghost legends. Along with Red Mantle (his sister, Blue Mantle, appears in one episode), there is the Mirror Girl, a child who appears in (and travels through) mirrors, evoking the story "In a Cup of Tea" from Hearn's *Kwaidan.*

On the more modern side, there's the statue of Sontoku Ninomiya[78] which used to stand on the grounds of every Japanese school. Ninomiya (1787-1856) was a prominent agrarian reformer, but was also remembered (and still is today) for setting an example for Japanese youth: the school statues showed a young Ninomiya reading a book while carrying a bundle of firewood on his back. School *kaidan* maintain that the Ninomiya statue can be found running around the school grounds at night; in this case, one member of Saito High's Holy Student Council, a Shinto *miko*, tries to make the ghostly statue her love-slave.

---

[78] In the first episode of *Gakkou no Kaidan,* just before the opening credits, as the ghost attacks a night watchman, the camera jumps to the front of the school; a statue of Ninomiya can be seen to the right of the door. Later in the episode, the statue has apparently moved on its own into the school. Ninomiya definitely got around; according to school ghost stories, so does his statue.

Parallel to this is Kazumi Ryudo, a young Buddhist monk, and his interest in the ghost of Toilet Hanako. Toilet ghosts have a long history in Japan, predating the building of modern schools. The ghost is responsible for toilet stall doors opening and closing by themselves. Calling Hanako's name causes her to appear, as she does in *Gakkou no Kaidan* asking, "Shall we play?"—the rest is often too frightening to tell.[79]

While ghosts in elementary school are all about scaring people, this Toilet Hanako is in Saito High School's boys' bathroom and, with her very revealing schoolgirl uniform, appeals to the sexual side of the male students. She especially appeals to Ryudo, a young Buddhist monk like his father. This teen monk has a thing for Hanako-san, and tries to hook up with her (and any and every other young attractive female toilet ghost in Japan) every chance he gets.[80] Things get in the way, though, including the spirits of various dogs and cats near Saito High; Ryudo is so sensitive to ghosts that he often gets possessed by random passing spirits—even the non-human ones.

Two of the ghosts live in the school science lab. Bones is, as his name suggests, an animated skeleton. Its partner Haruo is also an animated teaching tool; specifically, the "living boy" cutaway statue with removable wooden "organs". Those statues can be creepy enough during daylight hours; it makes sense that the image of this statue, like the Ninomiya statue, moving around a school after dark on its own, would become part of modern ghost lore. These

---

[79] Billy Hammond, "The School Restroom Ghost—Hanako-san", http://tanutech.com/japan/hanako.html, accessed October 25, 2006.

[80] This is part of a long and ribald tradition of making fun of Buddhist monks as oversexed. The young monk Miroku in Rumiko Takahashi's *InuYasha* is another example, since we forever see him caressing some female tush out of reflex and uttering the lamest of come-ons: "Will you bear my children?" He has about as much luck as Ryudo. We'll visit Miroku in a later chapter.

two ghosts, however, are rather lame; their big "scare" in the anime consists of breaking into a Russian folk-dance.

The school gymnasium is haunted by a nameless giant, who's so big that all anyone ever sees of him is his foot.

The Chairman rounds off the list of school spirits; yes, a ghost runs the haunted school, which accounts for most of the ghostly goings-on. He collects occult objects, which brings unwanted spirit phenomena into the school time and again.

While the ghosts often drive the action, with the resident ghosts having either to assist or protect the school and/or each other from outsider ghosts, the story centers on three human high school students. These make up the Holy Student Council, and they're all exorcists out of different traditions, as in *Ghost Hunt*. We've already met Buddhist monk Kazumi Ryudo and Shinto *miko* Asahina Mutsuki; the third member, and often the focus of the series, is Haruto Hojuko. He's a Christian, who sometimes appears in a white variation of Catholic clerical garb—as do both his father and mother. (Perhaps this is part of the joke, that a woman would wear priest's robes, given the Catholic Church's antipathy toward women in the priesthood, as compared to the tradition of Shinto priestesses and Buddhist nuns in Japan.) Unlike John Brown in *Ghost Hunt*, Haruto's exorcist technique isn't orthodox, and is handled almost like a superpower.

Still, throughout the 12 episodes, Haruto bemoans his school, his place on the Holy Student Council, and every eccentric thing in his life. He repeatedly complains that his life isn't *normal*. All he wants is to finish school, get a job, get a girlfriend—all of the mundane things that seem to happen at every other school to every other teenager but never to him. It isn't until the final episode that he gets to see how lucky he is that his life isn't normal (which in this case is defined as dull, gray, and faceless).

XXX

Jigoku Sensei Nube

The title *Jigoku Sensei Nube* (literally, *Nube, the Teacher from Hell*) certainly has more of a flourish than "Meisuke Nueno, Fifth-Grade Teacher at Domori Elementary School." This particular anime, consisting of 48 episodes broadcast from 1996 to 1997, plus three movies and three OAV episodes, was based on a manga with artwork by Takeshi Okano and story by Sho Makura that ran in *Shonen Jump* from 1993 to 1999. Unfortunately, this classic comedy/ supernatural series never traveled outside of Japan.

Meisuke wears a glove on one hand, to cover his *oni no te* (demon hand). As an exorcist, Meisuke had gotten into a battle with a demon, and the only way to defeat it was to take the demon into himself. The hand serves as a weapon against paranormal threats (although Meisuke often botches some of the lesser spells he tries in the school—such as the opening pages of the manga, in which he tries to exorcise a demon from a picture of Beethoven. I suspect that he sometimes loses these contests in part to inspire his fifth graders to keep trying).

He's also married to a *yukionna*, named Yukime, who he rescued from a snowy mountain encounter with a hunter. She left the mountain, moved to the village of Domori, and found a job as an ice skating coach. This is a good example of the tenor of *Jigoku Sensei Nube*: some of the ghosts and demons are truly menacing and threatening, and others are cute or silly. Maybe it's this dual attitude that kept the series from successfully traveling to the west. American ghost stories tend to be either menacing or silly; not both at once.

xxx

Shoujo Kakumei Utena: The Black Rose story-arc

The television series *Shojo Kakumei Utena* (*Revolutionary Girl Utena*), whose creators are collectively known as Be Papas, can be divided into three story-arcs. In the first 13 of the 39 episodes, the viewer learns the basics of Ootori Academy, its odd custom of dueling to "revolutionize the world," and the various characters who make up the cast. For this chapter, we look at episodes 14 through

23, which form its own sub-plot, which happens to be a kind-of ghost story.

62. One Hundred for One

The major incident is shown at the beginning of the arc: a fire which claimed the lives of one hundred students. We never see them as spirits; we do, however, see their silhouettes, like crime scene chalk outlines, in the dueling arena, along with one hundred empty desks. As to why they died . . .

A student named Shouji Mikage introduces Utena (and us) to Nemuro Memorial Hall, where the fire occurred years ago. Mikage has an agenda: searching for "the power of Dios," which he believes to be the key to immortality. At the moment, the power rests in Anthy Himemiya, the Rose Bride, who is "engaged" to Utena. Mikage is convinced that, to get to the power of Dios, Anthy must be destroyed, which means that Anthy's protector Utena must be defeated in a duel. Toward that end, Mikage plays on the fears and doubts of various students, offering to resolve their fears by having them duel Utena. They all lose, of course, and ultimately Mikage has to take up the sword himself and go after Utena.

Before he can do so, we see in flashback what the fire was about. A research professor, named Nemuro, was hired from outside the Academy. He headed up a research team of one hundred students who seem to be searching for the key to immortality. Nemuro didn't really care; cold and detached, he described himself as a robot. This changed, however, when he became fixated on Tokiko Chida, sent by the Board of Governors to inspect the research, and on her sickly younger brother Mamiya. Tempted into believing that time can be stopped, Nemuro's optimism is jolted when he witnesses Tokiko being seduced by Akio, Anthy's brother.[81] The next thing we see

---

[81]   Actually, the Akio who we see seduce Tokiko is only one aspect of Anthy's brother, but that's a topic I discussed in the *Utena* chapter of *Anime Explosion*.

is the building going up in flames; during the flashback we are led to believe that Mamiya set the fire at Nemuro's request. Later, we realize that Nemuro set it himself out of his sense of betrayal.

Although this isn't a traditional Japanese ghost story, there are similarities, notably in the quintessentially Japanese theme that eternal life is a curse, and that ghosts remain miserable after life because they cannot change or grow without assistance.[82] At one point, Mamiya, noting that his sister Tokiko dries flowers to preserve them, wonders "if the flowers themselves are happy, being forced to live so long." Akio also warns the viewer that, as long as anyone stays at Ootori Academy, "a person will never become an adult."

This is taken to another level, becoming more than a metaphor, when we realize that the student Souji Mikage, who has been trying to remove Anthy as the Rose Bride, was actually Professor Nemuro. Having achieved immortality in the shape of a high school student, he can only hang onto it by living a life of illusions, one of which is that Mamiya started the fire and not he, and sending others to fight the duels he only fought as a last resort. Once he is defeated, both he and Nemuro Memorial Hall itself are history.

xxx

Negima: Sayo Aizaka

The tragic nature of a ghost—static and unchanging, bound by the circumstances of its past—even comes into play, although in a surprisingly pleasant form, in *Negima!*, a popular anime based on an equally popular manga by Ken Akamatsu. Mingling aspects of Akamatsu's successful "harem romance" manga *Love Hina* with bits of the Harry Potter story, *Negima!* tells of a ten year old British wizard, Negi Springfield, who must complete his training by going to Mahora Academy, an all-girl school in Japan, to teach junior-high

---

[82]   This also parallels the Japanese "take" on vampires; see chapter 29.

English. In addition to the overabundance of "fan service,"[83] most of Negi's students are also magical, and range from a robot to a ninja, a sorceress disguised as a vampire, and a ghost: Sayo Aizaka.

63. A Ghost in the Garden

There's never been an adequate explanation at Mahora Academy of why Sayo Aizaka should be on the rolls for second year of middle school, but never shows up for class. Some say she was a transfer student who never left her old school. Others call her "Typo Girl" believing that a printing error keeps her name on the roster year after year.

The first hint of Sayo's true condition is when we first "see" her in the manga: in the roster of Negi's homeroom students, complete with photos. While all the other girls were photographed wearing the modern girls' school uniform of white shirt, tie, and blazer, Sayo is the only one wearing an old-fashioned middie blouse. Under her picture is the cryptic statement: "1940—Don't change her seating." Things are different in the anime: from the first episode we see Sayo in crowd scenes, but she speaks to nobody and nobody speaks to her. It's all a tease (and a tip of the hat to M. Night Shyamalan) that doesn't get explained until much later.

We find out that 1940 was when she died, at age 15. According to her back story in the nineteenth episode of the anime (which isn't shown in the manga), Sayo's younger sister had planted a flower garden at Mahora Academy; she believed that their mother would come back to them if she planted a bed of yellow tsuwabuki flowers. However, as the "rising sun" flags and planes flying overhead remind the viewer, this flashback took place during World War 2.

---

83   Fan service, the gratuitous display of breasts, butts, and underpants, was a hallmark of *Love Hina*, in which a college-bound boy lives in a rooming house with 5 girls and a hot spring in the back yard. In *Negima!*, there are 30 girls in Negi's homeroom class, multiplying the possibilities accordingly.

It wasn't likely that either of their parents would come back from the war. Sayo, however, tried to protect the flowers during a violent thunderstorm and died.

Since then she's been a *jibakurei*—a ghost who is attached to a particular place because of sudden or violent death. Still, she doesn't exactly haunt the school; most students and faculty don't even know she's there, because she doesn't possess the power to manifest. When we see her, six decades have taken their toll, and she's completely forgotten why she became a *jibakurei*. Still, she seems quite happy just to watch the life of the schoolgirls around her.

At first only three students can see Sayo, and one of them does so as part of figuring out the mystery of her identity. Kazumi Asakura writes for the Mahora school newspaper and traces Sayo's picture back to the years when she was alive. In the anime, the mention of a bed of tsuwabuki flowers triggers a memory, and Asakura dashes across campus to the ruins of an old chapel. There, instead of a bed of flowers, she and Sayo find that the tsuwabuki flowers have grown all over the courtyard. But Sayo finds something else. Her little sister had left a message in the flowerbed asking that their mother return to them. For the first time, Sayo reads that the message was amended to ask that "big sister" also be returned. Faced with this reminder of her death, she loses her composure and breaks down sobbing among the flowers. In doing so, she becomes visible to Asakura, who's tempted to photograph the ghost. However, she stops herself, saying "it wouldn't be right." Evangeline McDowell, a sorceress posing as a vampire who, on top of everything else, has a long-standing grudge against Negi's father for imprisoning her in a child's body, makes Sayo visible to the rest of the class. Rather than be frightened, the entire class rushes to befriend her. She was even able to lose her attachment to the school grounds and accompany the class in the anime on their field-trip to Kyoto—very unusual behavior for a *jibakurei*.

The third person who sees Sayo is Mana Tatsumiya, a *miko* (Shinto temple maiden) who almost exorcises Sayo. Thus each of these three have their own reasons that would allow them to perceive Sayo before she became generally visible.

The anime also establishes that Mahora Academy's elderly Headmaster (and grandfather of one of Negi's students), Konoe Konoemon, not only knew Sayo when she was alive but in his youth had a crush on her. We know this because he keeps tsuwabuki flowers in a vase on his desk.

Sayo's manga persona at first is that of a lonely ghost, unseen by virtually everyone. She appears to Negi during a project on haunted houses, and is almost exorcised, except for the timely intervention of Negi and Kazumi. After that, when she is not only rescued but befriended, she in turn becomes much more friendly.

xxx

Shaman King—Helpful School Ghosts

The hero of Hiroyuki Takei's successful *Shonen Jump* manga series (and its animated version), Yoh Asakura, is a student in his first year of middle school (the American seventh grade). Actually, he's not much of a student, and gives the appearance of being a total slacker. However, because he has the family talent of communing with ghosts, he has cultivated a stable of school spirits to do the work for him.

The first ghost is Suzuki, who claims that the only skill he had was in taking tests. Described as the smartest kid in class, Suzuki nevertheless committed suicide five years earlier to escape *ijime*.

The word is translated as "bullying" and sometimes as "hazing," but takes on a very different meaning in Japan. A western bully would typically be an overbearing kid with one or two hangers-on, threatening physically weaker kids for money or favors. Harry Potter's nemesis cousin Dudley Dursley fits this pattern, especially in *Harry Potter and the Order of the Phoenix*, which gives him a mini-gang.

In Japanese schools, the size of the bullying group is larger, sometimes pitting one student against the rest of the class; the schools (trying to save face) usually choose not to notice even when the bullying gets to be too extreme; and (in a perverse endorsement of the images of heroes in manga and anime) those who are bullied are expected to grow out of it or fight back as a part of growing up.[84]

Some students cannot and do not fight back, and a few *ijime*-related suicides hit the newspapers every year.[85] T. R. Reid, whose family lived in Tokyo for years while he was the Asian Bureau chief for the Washington *Post*, noted a ripple effect connected with these suicides:

> There have been about a dozen such suicides annually. Many of the victims leave behind farewell letters or diaries; they are painful, indeed shattering, to read, filled with details about the fear, shame, and despair the child felt after being branded the outsider. To make things worse . . . a case of teen suicide is frequently followed, a day or two later, by another suicide by another victim of *ijime*, often way off in a different corner of the country. It's as if these poor children, feeling hopeless because they are outside the group, suddenly find a group they can be admitted to—the group of suicide victims.[86]

---

[84] Bullying in anime/manga covers a wide spectrum, from physical to psychological abuse. In *Hikaru no Go*, Akira Toya, a prodigy at the game of go, joins his junior high school go club as a first-year student; the intimidated older students try to put him in his place by ordering him to play two games simultaneously—without looking at the boards. An extremely unrealistic example of *ijime* occurs in the romantic-comedy manga *Hana Yori Dango* (a complicated pun) by Yoko Kamio, in which the hazing at an elite high school ranges from pelting students with garbage to (apparently) attempted rape. When the heroine of the series stands up to the bullies, not only do they start to back down, but one of them falls in love with her!

[85] http://www.sunfield.ne.jp/~mike/essays/ijime.htm, accessed November 4, 2006.

[86] Reid, T. R. *Confucius Lives Next Door: What Living in the East Teaches Us about Living in the West.* 1999. New York: Vintage, pp.

Yoh is at least respectful toward Suzuki's ghost, even if he does seem to exploit him.

For physical education, Yoh lets himself be possessed by the ghost of Kobayashi, the former captain of the track team. Unfortunately, Kobayashi was hit by a motorcycle during a race.

Neither brains nor athletics would help in the arts, and two ghosts aid Yoh in this area. Ashida was a member of the Visual Arts Club and an aspiring manga artist; unfortunately, he was so into manga that he stayed up for two weeks with no sleep working on one of his creations, and died of exhaustion. Finally there's the pianist known only as Noriko (unlike her ghostly male counterparts, she doesn't even rate a last name in a society that places the family name first; thus is male chauvinism taught at an early age in Japan). She grew ill and died just before she was supposed to give a concert.

All four are thus the kind of ghosts that legend would expect to haunt a school. Suzuki fits the image of the suicide escaping this world for the next, while still full of regrets and unfulfilled plans. The others were actually cut down in the middle of what they loved doing, and are classic cases of ghosts with unfinished business. Once they do what they wanted to do (run in a track meet, complete a manga, play a recital), they ought to have found peace and Become One with the Cosmos. However, it doesn't always work that way, as the next example shows.

xxx

Here is Greenwood, episode 4: "Mitsuru and the Ghost: The Phantom of Greenwood"

This 1992 entry, the fourth in a series of six OAVs, may be ghostly, but also continues in the comedic vein of the series, based on a manga by Yukie Nasu serialized in the *shojo* manga magazine *Hana to Yume*. It's the tale of Kazuya Hasukawa, a hapless teen who has a deep crush on a young woman; when that woman gets married to Kazuya's older brother, he decides that he can't live in the same

130-131.

house with his brother's new bride, and heads off to Ryoukuto High School, his brother's prestigious alma mater, where the older brother is employed, and which has a dormitory known as Greenwood. Here he meets the requisite group of wacky characters, including a student so in love with his motorcycle that he carries it up and down the stairs to his room rather than leave it outside, a baleful Christian evangelist, Kazuya's roommate Shun who wears his hair long and acts like a girl, Student Council President Shinobu Tezuka, and Shinobu's roommate and Greenwood dorm leader Mitsuru Ikeda.[87] Although the manga and its anime focus on Kazuya, in one episode Mitsuru ends up being haunted.

64. One Last Thing to Do

During a thunderstorm, the Greenwood dorm momentarily loses electricity. When the lights come on, the residents of Greenwood see the classic glowing demonic *yuurei* ghost-woman. But that's not the real Misako, who turns out to be a pleasant little blonde female "wandering ghost" in a high school uniform, age 16 at the time of her death. Unlike the vengeful woman spirits like Oiwa (which she disguised herself as because she thought that's what was expected), she claims she has no idea why she's still on earth: "I cannot rest until my soul is cleared of all hatred and regrets. I'm not sure when that's gonna be . . .". Still, she announces her intention to haunt Mitsuru.

Everyone else in the dorm think it's cool that they get a young and pretty girl ghost; Mitsuru and Shinobu, of course, think otherwise.[88] The older woman who supervises the dorm seems to

---

[87] It's no coincidence that the two sempai (upperclassmen) are named after prominent manga artists: Osamu Tezuka, creator of *Astroboy* and countless other titles, and Ryoko Ikeda, creator of *The Rose of Versailles*. It's a deliberate in-joke and tribute.

[88] Shinobu doesn't want any part of trying to exorcise Misako, saying he's not a "youkai-basutaa"—a Japanese-English combination

take it in stride: "I've seen lots of ghosts here but I've yet to see one this lively." This is our first real indication of psychic activity at Greenwood Dorm; other examples come quickly. Misako gets upset and cries when Mitsuru yells at her (which he does a lot) and the results are akin to an earthquake.

Rumors fly about Misako: she was a suicide, she had an affair in middle school with Mitsuru, she carried his unborn child, she was his sister . . . Misako finally tells the truth to the matron: she'd been in girls' schools all her life, she fantasized about having a boyfriend, and then she got hit by a truck. She wanted to act out her romantic fantasy, and picked Mitsuru at random because of his good looks. That's all. Playing house (or "dorm") with Mitsuru isn't enough to satisfy her; she wants to kiss him, but has to possess someone else's body to do it. Of course, none of the boys in the dorm want to lend themselves out so that she can kiss Mitsuru. Misako ends up possessing a stray cat, kissing Mitsuru, and leaving.

Usually, that would be the end of the story: the ghost has satisfied her earthly curiosity, achieved what she wanted to do, and departed to Become One with the Cosmos. Not Misako: she returns declaring that "Once I kissed Ikeda-san, I became even more reluctant to leave this world." She even brings other wandering teenaged girl ghosts to Greenwood, all of whom want to experience boys, and end up choosing them at random.

XXX

The episode starts with a girl in a high school uniform hovering yards in the air above Greenwood. This convention in anime and manga usually means one of three things: that the person is (a) an alien, (b) an esper (someone possessing psychic powers), or (c) a spirit. The title tells the viewer up-front which one she is.

This is one of the rare cases of Japanese ghosts that take place in the winter but does not involve a *yukionna*. (Many Japanese ghost stories, as we've seen, look to a different part of the calendar:

---

word meaning "ghost-buster."

summer.) We realize it's winter when we see Kazuya and Shun reading under a kotatsu: the short, padded table with a heating element underneath that is unlike any kind of western furniture, simultaneously providing a heat source (while conserving resources) and fostering camaraderie. As time passes, the branches of the trees near the dorm grow bare. In the end we actually see it snow.

xxx

65. School Spirit

There are two reasons why "The Never-Ending Story," one installment of the anime OAV *Sentimental Journey,* is unique among other ghostly anime: it has a non-human narrator, and it's based not on a novel or a manga, but on a dating simulation computer game.

The dating sim, titled *Sentimental Graffiti,* appeared in 1998, inspired by the success of another such computer game, *Tokimeki Memorial.*[89] That same year, the Sunrise anime studio brought out a twelve-episode series of romantic short stories: each one unrelated to the others, telling of, as the title says, "twelve girls in twelve cities." They range in type from a guitarist in a rock band who refuses to write love songs, to the daughter of a kimono-maker who's expected to inherit the family business. The tenth installment, "The Never-Ending Journey," features Emiru Nagakura, who lives in Sendai, in Miyagi Prefecture, north of Tokyo.

The anime begins with the ruins of an old school. A new school has been built next door and demolition of the old building is underway. Yet the viewer hears a voice: "So, I wonder how many years I've been like this? But, since I'm already a part of the never ending story, I've accepted it as my destiny." The camera travels through the dilapidated ruins of the old school, and the viewer imagines that the school itself is doing the talking. We then hear that "she is coming."

---

[89] This title is wickedly parodied in Bisco Hatori's *Ouran High School Host Club.*

She is Emiru Nagakura, who has come repeatedly to visit the ruins of the old school—because it was her old school.

Emiru makes her way onto the grounds of the school, where a bulldozer waits to clear everything away. Her only concern at this point is in rescuing a soda bottle, which she says holds "my past and my future." At this point, however, strange things start to happen: a crow appears on the school roof, then dozens more crows. Some objects, she remembers, have their own spirits, which can survive even centuries after they were built—a very Shinto notion. The word "tsukumogami" is invoked at this point: a reference to tools that have either "grown" awareness by being very old, or grown a bitter soul because they've been brusquely thrown away. She narrowly misses being flattened by a door that falls off its hinges, and the deck of Tarot cards she carries forecasts destruction by showing The Tower upside-down. Clouds appear in the sky and she has to take shelter in the school, where a disembodied voice tells her menacingly, "I won't let you go until you let go of yourself." It's then she notices that her clothes are dry, the crows are gone, and the sun is shining outside as if it hadn't rained at all.

We find out that this sort of happening isn't unusual for Emiru. Since childhood she's believed in all sorts of unconventional things, from UFOs in the sky to fairies in the flower garden. As a result, most of her peers want nothing to do with her, dismissing her as a liar or, at best, creepy. She finally met one kindred spirit, a boy who transferred from another school . . .

Back in the ruined school, Emiru almost gets hit by a falling light fixture. The ghostly voice of the school tells her that it will never let the place become a park. The illusions begin to pile up, ranging from prosaic objects like book bags and sneakers to a shower, but this time of blood. Emiru finally stumbles into a classroom where her friend had drawn a magic circle on the floor; he promised that its magic would protect her, whether he was there or not.

As she sleeps, she remembers a time when the two of them, investigating a hole in the floor of a classroom, find an old (circa 1919) soda bottle. Soon thereafter, the boy has to move away. They wash out the bottle and put a note in it, promising to meet again when they grow up. At this point, we realize that the "narrator" of this story has been the spirit of the bottle.

The bottle-spirit, realizing that the school is inhabited by a tsukumogami, creates a vision of Emiru's boyfriend (who's known in the story only as "Darling"). Instead of leading her to safety, he leads Emiru up to the attic where the clockworks are housed. It seems Darling's spirit was created by the school, not by the bottle. Emiru challenges the school as to why it's putting her through all this; the bottle spirit responds that the school has a lingering attachment to this world, and tries to tell Emiru to throw away such attachments in herself. "If you lose something and nobody remembers it, then it's nothing forever," the school spirit tells her. Rather than go into oblivion when the school is destroyed, the spirit wants to live on—through Emiru. She allows the school to possess her; suddenly, she's floating above the landscape when the school was built in 1919. All she sees is farmland, which makes her realize that she was wrong to think that she had to keep the school's memory alive. "Memories aren't lost. Even if the school building doesn't stay, the building will exist forever in my memory. And, even if I die, my memory will live forever."

This perception quiets the spirit of the school, and allows Emiru to search for the soda bottle. We see her find it; we see her leaving the school. She stops and says good-bye to the soda bottle. The last we see of it officially is a few months later, with the school gone and the ground being prepared for construction; the bottle, still undisturbed, is shown just below the surface of the ground, the green glass of the bottle reflecting the sun and clouds passing by overhead. Actually, this is one of only two of the twelve episodes with additional footage: as the credits end, we see the soda bottle, washed off, given a proud place on one of the bulldozers at the construction site.

CHAPTER 22: THE SCHOOL

BOARD—KOKKURI-SAN

Several Japanese stories of the supernatural turn on something that resembles the western Ouija board. The notion of providing some way for the dead or other spirits to communicate with the living is old and widespread; the Chinese had something like it about 1200 B.C.E., called fuji. Greece in the sixth century B.C.E. also had such a device. Although the so-called Ouija board as we know it was patented in 1891, it's been around a lot longer, and first surfaced in Japan around the beginning of the Meiji era.[90]

In Japan the board known as kokkuri-san[91] is drawn on paper each time it is used. At the center is a grid of the letters of the

---

[90] Much of the following is thanks to Michael Dylan Foster's "Strange Games and Enchanted Science: The Mystery of Kokkuri" in *The Journal of Asian Studies*, volume 65 number 2 (May 2006), pp. 251-275.

[91] Kokkuri-san or –sama is a multi-layered pun. The phonetic readings of the Chinese characters in the name Kokkuri mean "fox" (ko), "dog" (ku) and "tanuki" (ri). (For the special history of the tanuki, an animal often mistranslated into English as "raccoon" or "raccoon-hound," please see my book *Anime Explosion: The What? Why? And Wow! Of Japanese Animation*.) In this case, "ku" refers not to a literal everyday dog but the *tengu* or heavenly dog, a nature spirit sometimes described as having crow-like features, and is also pictured as human but with a very long nose. The verb kokkuri

alphabet (in Japanese, this means 46 letters instead of the 26 characters of the Anglo-American alphabet); the words "yes" and "no" are also written, sometimes the numbers 1 through 10 or 0 through 9, and some have a drawing of a Shinto torii arch. While some versions use the western spade-shaped miniature table, called a planchette, which is supposedly moved across the Ouija board by an otherworldly spirit, in Japan usually the players either touch a finger to a small coin (a ten-yen piece, one of Japan's smallest coins) or they hold onto a pen or pencil as the point moves from letter to letter. Sometimes, when Japanese use a planchette, there's a piece of paper in each leg with one of the three characters of the name kokkuri.

A benign use of this divination method appears in the *Shaman King* manga. Episode 49 introduces the reader to Tamao, an eleven-year-old girl and apprentice fortune-teller who has been studying for years with the father of the main character, Yoh Asakura. She also has a very deep crush on Yoh. Between her waiflike appearance, her position in the Asakura household and her adoration of Yoh, we know her motives to be pure and her powers to be untainted.

This can't be said of everyone who uses kokkuri-san, however, and this is where the trouble starts. The Korean film *Bunshinsaba* (2004), which features kokkuri-san and is heavily influenced by Japanese films in the same genre, focuses on three girls who turn to kokkuri-san to get back at a school bully. In the process, they unleash the vengeful ghost of another student, who had committed suicide 30 years earlier. This is a good example of the pattern such stories take.

These next examples illustrate the same lesson: that having impure motives when dealing with kokkuri-san can lead to the summoning of very unhelpful spirits. Putting motives aside, another lesson offered in these stories is that, if you insist on dealing with

---

means to tilt or to nod, and refers to the kokkuri-san's planchette tipping one leg up when answering a question. Thus, the name kokkuri-san could be rendered in English as "Mister Wobbles."

the spirit world without a professional medium, you do so at your own risk.

66. "I'm not a dog!"

Shibuya Psychic Research, the team of youthful exorcists of the *Ghost Hunt* manga, is hired by the head of the Student Council at Ryokuryou High School to investigate supernatural activity. There have been cases of food poisoning, spontaneous fires, at least one suicide, and students being attacked by a phantom dog. While the principal is skeptical and one teacher, Hideaki Matsuyama, is openly hostile toward the members of Shibuya Psychic Research, the students have been playing kokkuri-san. Most of the time the same thing happens: nothing. Yuko the witch of *xxxHolic* explains: "Normally occult practices done by amateurs aren't successful. So they try and try and the only thing they get is empty effort." (vol. 3, p. 70) In this case, however, the high school was built over a burial ground dating back to the Nara period (C.E. 710-794). Spirits were not only being raised, but sticking around and attacking the school, its occupants, and each other. In a kind of paranormal Darwinism, the spirits started consuming each other, with the strongest survivor threatening to unleash some serious evil, unless SPR could do something about it. This would include the main object of much of the kokkuri-san: the hoped-for spirit murder of the teacher Matsuyama, whose incessant bullying drove one student to suicide, leaving behind the one-line suicide note: "I'm not a dog."

In the end the curse is nullified by transferring it back onto the students who caused it; specifically, onto hitogata dolls in place of the students themselves. Many of the dolls are broken so violently that it makes you wonder what would have happened if the curse had bounced back onto the students themselves instead of their dolls.

67. "Didn't I say you'd be cursed?"

Another high school has been dabbling in kokkuri-san in the *xxxHolic* manga by CLAMP, with the result that "something really bad" seems to be happening at the school. This occurs despite the "precaution" of the game being renamed "angel-san", in hope that this would lessen any threat. No such luck.

Yuko the witch sends her hapless student worker Watanuki to investigate. It's bad enough that he has to be accompanied by another high school student, Domeki, his rival for the attentions of the pretty student Himawari. Even worse, he's made to look foolish by having to communicate with Yuko by wearing a pair of cones over his ears that look like the "ears" on Chi the computer in another CLAMP manga, *Chobits*. Watanuki, who's more than a bit of a whiner, is convinced that Yuko did this just to embarrass him.

The evening Watanuki and Domeki arrive at the empty, supposedly haunted high school, Watanuki sees thick black smoke surrounding the school building, and picks up a sickening smell inside the building; Domeki isn't aware of any of that. It seems to be worst on the roof of the school. When they get there, Watanuki hears the sound of girls crying, and finds three girls working a kokkuri-san. One girl is standing off to the side, while the other two are grasping a pen over the piece of paper, which is almost obscured by the repeated drawing of the Japanese command: die. When Watanuki tells the girls to let go of the pen, the girls tearfully say that the kokkuri-san won't let them; it told them "I won't let go until you are dead. If the hands separate, you will be cursed." When Watanuki forces the girls to let go of the pen, the three crying students suddenly change. With evil grins, they say, "Didn't I say, if the hands separate, you'd be cursed" as they push Watanuki off the roof.

From Domeki's point of view, Watanuki has been running around the school roof talking to himself; when he goes over the edge, Domeki saves him from falling. But the spirits at the high school aren't through. One monstrous shape attacks Domeki even as he's trying to pull Watanuki back onto the roof; as this happens, the column of black smoke surrounding the school turns into a gigantic serpent that first swallows the monster attacking Domeki, then swallows the earpieces. When the snake goes away, the atmosphere changes to normal.

We've already read Yuko's explanation of the results of an amateur attempt to contact the spirit-world. But she went on: the boredom of repeated non-results "leads to quite a number of students who start thinking that it would be better if scary things appeared, better if weird things appeared, better if someone happened to die. That would be interesting." The kokkuri-san responsible for the curse in *Ghost Hunt* was a conscious attempt to kill an abusive teacher, to avenge a student driven by his abuse to suicide. In this case, however, the evil wishes of the students are motivated more by boredom and a sense of thrill-seeking. The illusion of the girls on the roof, and the monster that attacked Domeki, were "the dregs of 'innocent curses' of the students."

The giant serpent, on the other hand, was the protecting spirit of the area, a concept that fits into Shinto belief that kami are everywhere and exist for every contingency. It circled the building, keeping the spirits raised by the kokkuri-san from escaping. When it devoured the spirits, it also took the earpieces as an offering; we hear (more accurately, in the manga we read) Yuko telling the snake spirit through the earpieces, "To those who have inhabited this land from long ago, we present this sacrifice to your brave and honorable selves." Yet, when Watanuki asks Yuko if the serpent was a good spirit, her answer rejects such a simple question: it wasn't a bad spirit "for you two at that particular time. Good and evil are concepts that humans decide. Those concepts don't apply to non-humans."

68. The Coin and the Angel

As some fifth graders find out in a 1994 episode of the manga *Jigoku Sensei Nube*, calling kokkuri-san "Angel-sama" doesn't automatically make it more benign. Nor does arranging the letters and numbers in the shape of a heart.

Fifth grader Miki Hosokawa has organized a session of "angel-sama" at the school, which quickly falls into slapstick involving the ten-yen coin. The demon-possessed teacher Nueno puts a stop to it, telling the students to reconsider what they're doing (while telling them the history mentioned above of kokkuri-san in the Meiji era). Miki tears up the paper with the board and uses the ten-yen coin to make a prank call, but the damage has been done. A ghostly voice tells her over the phone, "You are going to die."

When the phone returns the ten-yen coin, Miki takes it to a video arcade; however, when she drops it into a game machine, the machine tells her "You are going to die" and gives back the coin. She even puts the coin into the offering box of a man soliciting charitable donations on the street; that night, a crow bursts through Miki's bedroom window and drops the ten-yen coin from its beak.

Nueno tries to exorcise the coin, which at first brings out a lot of poltergeist activity, followed by the appearance of Angel-sama: a handsome, winged boy. However, he reveals his fangs and his true intent: Miki's summoning him was a sin, punishable by death. Fortunately, Nueno is able to subdue the spirit with the power of his demon claw.

69. The Devil's Spell

One girl tries reading a kokkuri-san-like game in the old school alone at night in an episode of *Gakkou no Kaidan*. The bad news for the girl is that she's alone; for precautions, she's set up four candles, one lit at each of the four corners. Yuko and company set up the same precaution during the hyaku monogatari in *xxxHolic*. It didn't work too well for them, either, although they had the good sense to stay within the protection of the candles.

Next we see three other schoolgirls talking about experimenting with spells. Actually, that's a pretty strong word for what they're interested in. For example, they've heard that a boy will talk to you if you write his name on an eraser. One girl, Shinobu, seems more knowledgeable about this magic than the others.

Even Satsuki succumbs to the fad, from buying a lucky keychain to a lucky hair-ribbon for an upcoming exam to getting a special manicure to help lose weight. When she gets to school, though, Satsuki sees Shinobu and the other three with a kokkuri-san chart, which they hurriedly hide.

They gather again in the classroom after school; Satsuki arrives, and they pretty much have to let her stay. Shinobu intones a spell that will grant their wishes within a week. If they speak of the ceremony before then, they will be cursed. Shinobu also reminds them that there is an "escape clause," but doesn't tell them what it is.

That night Satsuki wakes up to find she can't move; she knows about "sleep paralysis," although that doesn't explain the bloody tracks left on her bedroom floor. Worse news comes the next morning, when the teacher calls the roll. He neglects to call one of the girls from the previous night's kokkuri-san, a Miss Etou;[92] he tells Satsuki that the class has never had a girl by that name.

The others try to get out of the contract, but Shinobu simply reminds them that she's at risk, too.

That night, Shinobu—now revealed to be a spirit named Yamime—comes after Satsuki, who gets help from the other three girls and the demon-cat Amanojaku. Once the other three girls tell Satsuki the demon's real name, she subdues it with red string (in this case, lipstick lines on a mirror) and sunlight (a camera flash). She then finds out that Shinobu was the name of a student who went missing 28 years earlier.

---

[92] I like to think of this as an in-joke; "ee tou" is one of those phrases Japanese say while thinking, as in, "Let's see, what was her name again?"

CHAPTER 23: GHOSTS AND SEX

Love and death are supposed to be mutually exclusive. "The grave's a fine and private place," according to poet Andrew Marvell, "but none, I think, do there embrace."

Japan, however, has traditionally taken the most powerful passions into account. Ghosts who are driven by a single-minded pursuit sometimes find a way to get involved in amorous matters, one way or another, even after death. Traditional legends of people who commit all sorts of debauchery while possessed by a spirit are many and intriguing. Their modern anime and manga counterparts are the same.

One traditional tale was recounted by Lafcadio Hearn in his collection *In Ghostly Japan*. As will be seen, this isn't a ghost story for children:

70. "I have the twin cherry blossoms!"

The year, they say, was 1829 by the western calendar; it was spring, and the cherry trees were in bloom. The wife of a certain daimyo had been ill for three years, gradually getting worse and worse, until everyone knew that she was near the end of her days. She thought of many things: her husband, the children she had borne him. And she thought of her husband's favorite concubine, Yukiko, age nineteen. She asked her husband to summon Yukiko, who quickly came and knelt down beside the couch where the daimyo's wife was lying.

"Yukiko, I am going to die. I hope you will be faithful to our lord in all things, for I want you to take my place when I am gone." Yukiko started to protest these words, but the wife cut her off. "This is not a time for ceremonial words; let us only speak truth to one another. Yukiko, there is one thing I want you to do for me. In the garden there is a yae-zakura[93], which was brought here last year from Mount Yoshino. I have never seen it in full bloom, and I must see it before I die. Carry me into the garden so that I may see it; take me upon your back."

The kneeling Yukiko, with the daimyo looking on, turned her back to the dying woman, so that she might hold onto Yukiko's shoulders and be lifted up. "My lady, please tell me how best I can help you."

"This way." The old woman seized Yukiko's shoulders and lifted herself to her feet. But suddenly, she pushed her hands inside Yukiko's kimono and grabbed the girl's breasts.

"I have my wish!" the old woman shouted, laughing wickedly. "I have the twin cherry blossoms! I could not die until I got my wish. Now I have them! Ah, such delight!"

With those words, she fell forward upon the crouching Yukiko, and instantly died.

But this was not the end of the story; only the beginning.

In some strange way, the old woman's cold dead hands had attached themselves to Yukiko's breasts. Any attempt to remove them drew blood. A Dutch physician[94] was summoned, who confirmed that the dead hands did not merely clutch at the live girl's body; the skin of the fingers had actually fused and become one with the skin

---

[93] A variety of cherry tree that bears twin blossoms.

[94] This was still during the Tokugawa or Edo period of Japanese history, when the country isolated itself from western science and technology, including medicine. Because the Netherlands were among the few countries willing to trade with Japan on its terms, interest in anything western came to be known as "Dutch studies." In this case, a Dutch physician may refer to the doctor's nationality, but definitely is a euphemism for a doctor of western medicine.

of Yukiko's breasts. For the time being, the only thing to do was to cut the hands off at the wrist. This was done, and the hands soon shriveled and darkened like the hands of a mummy.

However, there were times that the hands would stir, moving of their own accord. And nightly, at the Hour of the Ox, the dead hands would squeeze painfully, torturing Yukiko. They would only stop at the Hour of the Tiger.[95]

Shortly thereafter, Yukiko became a Buddhist nun, shaving her head, and making daily offerings so that the jealous spirit of the hands could find rest. However, the tormenting hands were still attached to her the last time anybody spoke to her, which was seventeen years after the death of the daimyo's wife. After that, nothing more was ever heard of her.

xxx

The point of the story is clear in Hearn's title: *Ingwa-banashi*, "A Story about Ingwa." Ingwa is a Japanese Buddhist term referring to bad karma, to the evil consequences of misdeeds committed in the past, or even in a previous incarnation. But the concept is a bit more complicated than simple cause and effect; Hearn writes that "the dead have power to injure the living only in consequence of evil actions committed by their victims in some former life." So, while there was fault on the part of the daimyo's wife and her anger at the girl who had usurped her place (an anger which she kept hidden but was still very real), Yukiko shared some of the blame, whether in this life, by alienating the daimyo from his wife, or by something done in another life. Needless to say, these questions are never easy to solve.

---

[95] The cycle of twelve animals in the Chinese calendar doesn't just apply to years. The day is divided into twelve two-hour periods, governed by the same cycle. The Hour of the Ox (2 to 4 a.m.) is especially regarded as the time when ghosts have control. Their power diminishes at the Hour of the Tiger (4 to 6 a.m.)

xxx

Hearn tells a more hopeful story in *Kwaidan*, his 1904 collection of ghost stories. Again, the mood is that of a Buddhist moral lesson. The story takes place in Niigata prefecture, in the northwest of the main island of Honshu, which is a popular resort for skiing in the Japanese Alps and vacationing in the local volcanic hot springs. Niigata has been home to many prominent Japanese, including two major pop culture names: manga artist Rumiko Takahashi and the late Yoshifumi Kondo, lead animator for Studio Ghibli.

71. O-tei Returns

Long ago, a man named Nagao Chousei lived in Niigata. His father was a physician, and Nagao was trained in medicine. When he was still young he became engaged to O-tei, the daughter of a friend of his father. The two were very much in love, but they agreed to wait until Nagao had finished his medical studies. Unfortunately, O-tei's failing health would not let them wait. When she was fifteen years old and he was nineteen, they both realized that the end was near for her.

"Surely the gods know what is for the best," she told Nagao. "I would wish to live even a bit longer, but my strength is failing and would only cause pain to me and be a burden to you. My hope is that we will meet again."

"Surely we will," Nagao answered, "in the paradise of the Pure Land."

"No, my love; here on this earth. Although I will be buried tomorrow, we will meet again, if you wish. But you must be patient, my beloved, for I must be born again, and grow to be fifteen years old again."

"Do not worry," Nagao answered. "Waiting will be a joy as well as a duty."

"And you do not doubt at all?"

"Dear one, I wonder only how I will know you in another body."

"Alas, only the Buddha and the Heavenly Gods know how and when and where we shall meet again. But, if you are willing to wait for me, I know that I shall find you once again. Remember my words . . ."

And, with that, O-tei closed her eyes and breathed her last.

Every day after that, Nagao made offerings to heaven in front of a memorial tombstone he had made. The memorial stone bore O-tei's earthly name, instead of the heavenly name given to her by the Buddhist clergy as part of the funeral rites, as well as his promise to marry her if she returns to him.

Still, Nagao was the only son of his parents, and eventually they pressured him to take a wife. Even though he did so, he made daily offerings to his memorial to O-tei. In time, both of Nagao's parents died; so did his wife; so did their only child. Alone and sorrowful, Nagao set out on a long pilgrimage.

One day he stopped at a mountain village famous for its volcanic hot springs, and he stopped in amazement. The young girl who came to wait upon him looked so much like O-tei that he had to pinch himself to make sure he was awake. Everything she said and did for him was an uncanny reminder of the young girl to whom he had been engaged so many years ago. Finally he spoke to her: "Forgive me, but you strongly resemble someone I used to know. Please tell me your name, and where is your home."

With that, the girl immediately answered, "I am O-tei, and you are my beloved Nagao Chousei, to whom I am engaged. I died in Niigata seventeen years ago, and you wrote a promise to marry me if I returned to earth in the body of a woman. You carry that promise now, sealed in a memorial stone."

And, before she could say anything else, she fainted dead away.

So they were married, and lived happily together. But, oddly enough, she could never remember what she told Nagao on that day when they were reunited.

XXX

Ghost talker's daydream

This 2004 anime is based on a manga published in *Shonen Ace*, and suffers from some of the problems of any long-manga-turned-anime: more than a few questions come up during the course of the 4-part OAV that wouldn't bother anyone with access to the manga. The American manga market, however, is geared currently toward the teen and even pre-teen age group, so this particular manga (artwork by Sankichi Meguro, story by Saki Okuse), would seem unlikely to be translated and published; however, it has been published in translation by Dark Horse comics. (The title is translated literally as "Vulgar Ghost Daydreams"—the first two words are the kanji "teizoku rei", with "daydreams" written out in the Roman alphabet.)

Misaki Sakai is a ghost-hunter, like her counterparts in *Ghost Sweeper Mikami* and *Phantom Quest Corp.*, and, like her counterparts, she finds that spiritualism doesn't pay the bills. However, her choice of a second job is unusual: a dominatrix in a sex club. The anime shows her on the job only once, and the sight of her whipping a bound, gagged and blindfolded man (identified in the manga only as "a famous Japanese athlete") tends to leave one feeling more squeamish than aroused. It's pretty hardcore, and a radical departure from the rest of the series' dealings with her sexual line of work. Most of the other references involve slapstick pratfalls exposing her panties, a good deal of nudity, and jokes about used underwear and the refusal of her pubic hair to grow in; it's all rather light-hearted compared to the whipping scene. If nothing else, that scene is the context for her constant complaints that she needs a different job.

But other questions arise as we watch her solve the supernatural dilemma of a schoolgirl named Ai who then becomes Misaki's informal apprentice (since she, too, can see ghosts) while a male classmate of Ai's constantly stalks Misaki to photograph her. Questions come up, like: what happened to Misaki's parents that caused her to be raised by her old-fashioned grandparents? Did that have anything to do with her ability to converse with the dead? And what is Kinue, the rope she carries that seems to have a consciousness, and obeys Misaki's commands like Wonder Woman's lasso? The manga would be helpful here.

We would find out from the manga, among other things, that Masaki is only 19 years old, and therefore technically still a minor[96]. However strange the notion of a dominatrix who's a minor may be, it's even stranger to find out that she's a virgin. The manga at one point flashes back to a time when Masaki was in high school, and she and her boyfriend decided they wanted to sleep together. Unfortunately, they never went the distance, since the boy told Misaki that her hairless state was a bit of a turn-off; it reminded him of his kid sister.

Why would the manga creators offer us a heroine in this position—an underage virgin dominatrix? I think it is so that readers will see that, despite the tawdry nature of her job, she still has a shojo nature, meaning that her innate compassion, although masked by a shell of cynicism, allows her to converse with the dead in the first place. Misaki mirrors Ai in the series, and becomes a reluctant Big Sister to the apprentice Ghost Talker. This would be less likely to happen if Misaki really was as jaded and cynical as she appears.

There's another reason Misaki is shown as so young: youth is tied to her ability to converse with ghosts, as it is with Ai. This is ratified in a manga scene, an exchange between Misaki and another woman she meets at a hot springs in Hakone, one of many resorts near the base of Mount Fuji. This woman tells Misaki that she, too, used to work with the Tokyo police paranormal unit. Then she got married, and gradually the business of this world overwhelmed her connection with the next world.

---

[96] In Japan, one is not considered legally an adult until the year in which one turns twenty. This is usually commemorated on January 15 of that year in the Coming-of-Age Day (Seijin no Hi) ceremony.

72. They probably don't even know

We may not get all the answers in the anime, but we get ghosts, and many of them are children. While the first two episodes of the OAV are based on chapters of the manga, parts 3 and 4 are essentially one long original episode in two parts, and include acts of chaos and destruction caused by the ghosts of dozens of children whose bones were unearthed at a construction site near Hakone. These ghostly children end up killing and injuring people, but Misaki excuses them: "They were just playing. They probably don't even know they're dead yet." The same sort of situation comes up in the *Ghost Hunt* series, when a school field trip is interrupted by a landslide, killing the children and their teacher. The class, having become Hungry Ghosts, kidnap the living, not out of malice but because they don't know how to change their situation. Mai convinces the teacher and students to allow the living to return to the world.

The children, it turns out, were murdered by a deranged person named Ichinose. Despite this typically masculine name, Ichinose was a girl who was sexually molested by her uncle; after his death in a boating accident, she assumed a male persona and, even in death, killed children to "save them" from the molestation she suffered.

Child molestation is virtually a theme that runs through the 4-part anime, and it's courageous for director Osamu Sekita to tackle it. But other ghosts appear as well. The spirit of a dead soldier haunts his old family home until Misaki tells him that his parents, too, are dead and that he must join their spirits. Ai is almost killed when she tries to converse with what seemed to be the ghost of a suicide. Instead, the ghost turns into a wrathful woman who almost kills Ai, lamenting that the world shunned her in life because of her "difference." True, her face is grotesque as a ghost, but does it reflect her looks in life? Was that her "difference"? The anime isn't too clear here.

As for Kinue, the rope that moves on its own, apparently it's a "hungry ghost". In volume 1 of the manga, Misaki tells the rope "you can feed" on the dying man who accidentally killed a toddler. When it's through, there's hardly any body left.

xxx

Eerie Queerie
Shuri Shiozu's 1999 manga was printed in Japan in *South* magazine and known simply as "Ghost!" The new English title was reportedly required for "copyright related reasons"[97] perhaps applied by Tokyopop Publishing to tip off western readers that the supernatural is mixed with *shonen ai* (Boy Love), although both the scares and the same-sex romance are downplayed at first.

Mitsuo, a student at a boys' high school who's also something of a loner, sees dead people. These ghosts have unfinished business, they're female (at first, anyway), and they're definitely not out for vengeance. In fact, they possess Mitsuo and use his body to act in ways that cause Mitsuo to be labeled as gay. Most of this labeling by his classmates is more humorous than stigmatizing; one student's comment that "This is the first time I've ever seen a real gay guy", which is echoed by many of his classmates, reflect the reality that Japanese homosexuals are still very much "in the closet." Mitsuo, after all, would not do things like ask another boy out on a date if he weren't being possessed.

73. An unspoken crush

His first ghost, Kiyomi Suzaka, has only been dead for a week; in life she was a student at a girls' high school who was hit by a car. Her unfinished business includes trying to get next to Hasunuma, a classmate of Mitsuo at a boys' high school. He's taller and

---

97 Anime News Network press release of Jan. 7, 2004 (www.animenewsnetwork.com/article.php?id=4492); perhaps there's a *manga* out there based on the movie starring Patrick Swayze, Demi Moore and Whoopi Goldberg.

darker than Mitsuo and looks decidedly *bishonen*, while Mitsuo is younger, shorter, and looks almost feminine (which is convenient when a female ghost is talking through him). Hasunuma seems to return Mitsuo's attentions (which are really Kiyomi's attentions). At one point, Hasunuma whips open his high-school tunic to reveal . . . more than a dozen ofuda. "I figured you were either schizophrenic or possessed," he tells Mitsuo.

Mitsuo had earlier submitted to a Shinto exorcism, but the priest was old and clueless; he assumed Mitsuo was possessed either by a fox or a tanuki, the two classic shape-shifter animals of Japanese legend. The fact that Hasunuma's ofuda work when the priest's exorcism failed seems to validate a belief in Shinto for the reader while giving it a young person's perspective. Spirituality, like technology and popular culture, must keep up with the times.

For three days after the amateur exorcism Kiyomi's spirit is gone; then, Mitsuo hunts for her and finds her where he found her in the first place, at the site of her death. He goes looking for her because, despite her being such a nuisance, he was lonely and missed her. He allows Kiyomi to possess him again; she tells Hasunuma about her crush on him, and it turns out that he too had an unspoken crush on her. This resolution gives Kiyomi the chance to Become One with the Cosmos, and conveniently demonstrates that Hasunuma is heterosexual. When he and Mitsuo decide that they're now friends after all this, there's no suspicion that it's anything but platonic.

74. For a soccer ball

Mitsuo moves from a schoolgirl to an adult woman in his next ghost. Natsuko Shiiba had a set routine when she was hit by a truck at age 22: as she walked to work, she would see a young boy, Ichi Shirai, practicing with a soccer ball, and sometimes stopped to encourage him. One day, she chased the ball as it went into the street . . .

She spent the next six years hating and haunting Ichi, even though he couldn't see or hear her. But, like Kiyomi, she is no longer vengeful. She came to realize that "blaming Ichi was easier than blaming myself," and that there were a number of variables involved in her death. Most importantly, even though the young Ichi left the ball in the street that day, to have an excuse to talk to the beautiful lady, Natsuko no longer regrets chasing the ball, nor does she blame Ichi for her death. As Mitsuo (possessed by Natsuko) tells Ichi (who turns out to be a classmate of Mitsuo), "I decided to pick up that ball of my own free will. I'm responsible for the life I chose." Ichi had meanwhile spent six years blaming himself for her death, and refusing to ever play soccer again; after telling Ichi to forgive himself and "cherish every moment of your precious life," she too drifts off to Become One with the Cosmos.

This ghost story is barely about the ghosts in it at all, except for the ways they are expected to conform to the behavioral ideals of the living. The female ghosts cannot become reborn until they become *yasashii*. Kiyomi, who was only dead six days, couldn't work up the courage to talk to Hasunuma in life: "I hated myself for being such a coward. I kept saying I'd change eventually." She got over her self-hatred by possessing Mitsuo and doing what she needed to do in life. Natsuko began her career as a ghost by hating Ichi, but later realized that his role in her death was just part of a larger, more complicated picture. In both cases, compassion leads these women to forgive and move on, and, perhaps not so ironically in a society still largely driven by male privilege, they could not exercise their compassion without the help of a male. A different *mangaka* might have had these ghosts encounter a *miko*, but, since the objects of their quests were both students at a boys' high school (which becomes symbolic of the demarcation of adolescent sexual roles in Japan), it would have been much more difficult for another female to act on their behalf.

So, does *Eerie Queerie* exist to teach attitudes to males or to females? Probably both, since *Ghost!* ran in a *manga* magazine that focused on *bishonen*. Humor and sentimentality balance each other out. In any event, any sexual paradigm exists to teach both genders what is expected of them, while in this case also teasing the reader with hints of "the love that dare not speak its name." Neither males nor females live their lives in a vacuum, and behavioral instructions to one gender must always occur, overtly or implicitly, in context to the other.

xxx

But let's get back to the bishonen boys of *Eerie Queerie*. Ichi now hangs out with Mitsuo and Hasunuma, even though things begin looking like a romantic triangle. In the four-part story "I Miss You," the geometry expands to a romantic pentagram—one which incorporates both the quick and the dead.

75. I miss you

Mitsuo feels as if he's being followed. Despite the diligence of Ishi and Hasunuma, the ghost of a boy in a school uniform appears to Mitsuo, and arranges to meet him in the Drama Club room after school. Once there, the ghost, named Kanau, tries to push Mitsuo out the window. Hasunuma grabs for Mitsuo, and they fall out together. They live, but Hasunuma is in a coma; as a Shinto priest (young and bishonen, of course) explains, his spirit is detached from his body. This priest, named Mikuni, has a taste for guys as well as for "playing games"—first with Hasunuma's spirit, then with Kanau's.

The *Eerie Queerie* series ran long enough to be printed in four paperback volumes, but Shiozu got sidetracked; in the middle of the story he was commissioned to create a manga for *Dear T*, which he described as "the main publication for boys' love series."

xxx

In the manga/anime *Yuyu Hakusho*, the teen punk named Yusuke finds out that he has died from a cute young girl in traditional kimono, riding the oar of a boat. Her name is Botan, which in this case is a loaded name. Botan is a popular brand of Japanese rice, as well as a popular brand of candy. But botan (Japanese for peony) calls up its most supernatural association with another of the classic ghost stories: the *Kaidan Botan Doro* (Ghost Story of the Peony Lantern).

76. The Peony Lantern

This particular tale came over in the early 1600s from China, in a series of stories that were Buddhist morality lessons told as ghost tales, like the *Ugetsu Monogatari*. In 1666 Asai Ryoi adapted this story, among others, into a collection titled *Otogi Boki* (Hand Puppets), changing the Chinese locales to Japanese ones. The story took on new life in 1884 when it was adapted into a rakugo, a kind of stylized monologue. In 1892 *Kaidan Botan Doro* was further adapted as a kabuki play, and a prose version of the stage version appears in Lafcadio Hearn's *In Ghostly Japan*. The story's also been adapted to the modern stage; the kabuki version's been filmed.

In the original, the story begins appropriately on the first night of Obon. Appropriately, since this is a love story between the living and the dead. A samurai widower named Shinnojo Ogiwara sees two figures walking down the road in front of his home. As they draw closer, he sees that they are a woman with a servant-girl who's holding a peony lantern. The lady is quite beautiful, so he stops them and engages in conversation. After learning that the lady's name is O-Tsuyu (which has been Romanized several different ways), they vow eternal love. For the next few evenings, the woman and her servant come to the home of the samurai at dusk, always leaving before dawn. An elderly neighbor, however, becomes suspicious, looks in on the samurai one night, and sees him in bed embracing a skeleton. In the morning he tells Ogiwara about his beloved; the shaken samurai consults a Buddhist priest, who tells him to place a protective charm around his house to keep the ghost away. The charm prevents O-Tsuyu from entering his house that night, so she calls to the samurai to come out; unable to resist, he leaves the house to go to her place. "Her place" is a newly-dug grave on the grounds of a temple, but he doesn't care. In the morning, Ogiwara's body is found in the grave embracing a skeleton.

xxx

77. Let's Spend the Night Together

The resident ghosts of Saito High School, in the *Haunted Junction* anime series, are usually more than a handful for the Holy Student Council: three teen clerics (a Buddhist monk, a Shinto miko, and a Christian exorcist) who are generally excused from the more mundane aspects of high school. The haunted high school, however, attracts other ghosts, with some posing bigger challenges than others.

Episode 3, "Love to the point of possession", begins with a pretty young girl uttering her "final prayer." We meet the girl in the next scene, when Ryudo the Buddhist student monk and Haruto the Christian student exorcist meet her outside the school gate. The girl asks the monk to lend her his body. No, not like that.

In life, she was a waitress at a coffee-house where she met Toshi, a musician with an up-and-coming group. She said it was "love at first sight," but they hadn't even had a month together when she was killed in a traffic accident. She wanted to see Toshi again, but he couldn't see her, unless she inhabited a living body. She was a ghost with unfinished business, since Toshi had asked her to spend a night with him before she died.

This put things in a different light for Ryudo; he wasn't about to let her inhabit his body so that another guy could have sex with it. He was just too much of a skirt-chaser, especially of the school's Toilet Hanako ghost. Mutsuki, the miko on the Holy Student Council, gets into a spiritual battle royal with Ryudo, trying to force him to let the girl possess him, but the girl calls a halt, not wanting such a bother for her sake and apologizing for not realizing Ryudo's feelings. After she leaves, the principal (a ghost himself) reveals that her spirit is now too weak to sustain itself past midnight, so the girl

210

(whose name, we finally learn, is also Hanako) has one chance left at her unfinished business.

We also learn another reason why Hanako couldn't approach Toshi: some of his other fans were complaining that Toshi had stopped singing since Hanako died. She also explains what a night together would involve; no, not that. Toshi had written a song for her, and called Hanako to ask if he could spend an entire night singing his song to her, an audience of one. However, she died the next day.

Ryudo has an immediate change of heart, since no other body parts are involved. Toshi and his female fans go directly to Saito High School, where Toshi was once a student. He's used to the school's ghostly activity, but the other girls flee in terror. Up on the roof, Toshi can not only see Hanako, without her possessing anyone, but can embrace her; the principal chalks it up to the school's "special powers." Toshi serenades her, and she Becomes One with the Cosmos, thanking Toshi and the Holy Student Council.

Despite being aired "after hours" in Japan and having a few ribald bits (the principal, for example, wants to prepare Ryudo for his date with Toshi by castrating him with a pair of garden shears), typically episodes of *Haunted Junction* ended like this: sweet and sentimental, or with a dose of crazy slapstick. The tease of Ryudo dating another guy was just that: a tease. *Eerie Queerie* is a mild example of Boy Love, and broadcast anime seldom goes any farther.

XXX

78. Babysitter

An apparent *yukionna* puts in an interesting appearance in the episode of *InuYasha* titled "The Snow of Seven Winters Past." During a summer snowstorm, Miroku the young, lecherous monk encounters Koyuki, whose name and pallid complexion should have been a giveaway. She enlists Miroku's aid, not to feed off of him (as she almost did years ago, when he was a child lost in a snowstorm), but to take care of dozens of infants in her keeping. Actually, these are all spirits of children abandoned or orphaned by war, whom Koyuki sought to care for. Yet she claims that she was the mother of all these children, and Miroku was the father!

Was she a snow ghost? Not in the classic sense. She too was a victim of war (the *InuYasha* series allowed Rumiko Takahashi, for truly the first time in her career, to deliver a clear antiwar message). The real villain here, and even this is not necessarily evil, was a lion-like ice demon who killed the victims lured by Koyuki, feeding their souls to her.

Did Koyuki also have some goodness in her? Of course, since she sought help from the living to care for the children, even though they were spirits. Miroku recognizes this, and at the end of the episode erected a shrine to Koyuki and is seen praying for her soul. Japanese cartoons are seldom simple, and Miroku's leading role in this episode reinforces a Buddhist article of faith illustrated here: that all sentient beings, presumably including snow-ghosts, are capable of enlightenment.

From a perspective based on western feminism, Japan's history has never given women parity with men. Modern times have seen attempts to level the social field (less during the militant, conservative era from the Taisho emperor to the 1945 surrender), but little has changed by western standards. Of course, the problem is largely a matter of perspective: the western standards used to evaluate feminism in Japan have little to do with centuries of Japanese culture.

And what of Miroku? This teenaged Buddhist priest is caught between his vow of celibacy and his hormonal attraction to any and every female he meets; yet, his come-ons are so inept that the reader/viewer can come to only one conclusion: Miroku is still a virgin. So how could he accept the yukionna's claim that he sired all of her babies? Surely he would have remembered something like that. Why doesn't he protest his lack of paternity, instead turning with alacrity to care for the children?

The answer may lie in a famous old Zen Buddhist "joke," one of many teaching stories told about the faith and its practitioners.

In this story, a young unmarried girl conceives and bears a child. When her father repeatedly demands that she name the father, the girl finally names the priest at the local Buddhist temple. The girl's father angrily takes the infant to the temple and thrusts it at the priest, telling him to take care of his own child. The priest didn't protest his innocence or deny fathering the child. Instead, he spoke only one sentence: "Sou desu ka?"—Is it so?

Six months passed, during which the priest, totally unaccustomed to bringing up a baby, nevertheless tried his best. At the end of that time, the young girl finally broke down and confessed that the baby's father was really a young man from a neighboring village. Her father immediately rushed to the temple and apologized profusely to the priest. As he handed back the baby, the priest spoke only one sentence: "Sou desu ka?"

This brief story contains a number of object lessons—accepting responsibility, whether it's fair or not, while not growing attached to the things of this world, taking all circumstances equally, and sometimes living as if truth is irrelevant. There is also the object-lesson of Buddhism's belief that all people are capable of receiving enlightenment: in this case, the man whose daughter finally stops lying to him. Perhaps most important, though, is simply the belief that compassion must be shown to all sentient beings without discrimination. This certainly applies to Miroku when a roomful of bawling infants is forced upon him. Even if he had not sired any of them, they all need help now, and he is in a position to give it. To walk away from that responsibility would be to abandon a core teaching of his faith. Miroku does not regret having to play with, feed, and diaper a few dozen babies who are not his own; yet he also feels no regret when that responsibility is taken from him as suddenly as it arrived. Given that Miroku often comes onstage in *InuYasha* either to battle demons or to serve as comic relief, this encounter with a sort-of *yukionna* may be his finest hour.

XXX

Finally, we can cut out the references to compassion, sincerity, and all of that, and turn to a bit of comedic ghost porn. The F^3 series of hentai (literally "perverted,", the word generally means "sexual") anime created in 1994 center on a woman who can't reach orgasm, no matter who does what to her. The third installment shows our heroine and a houseful of other women invaded by a wandering, lecherous ghost. At first it possesses one of the women (possession also causing her to grow a penis); it's then exorcised into several of the sex toys in the house. It finally ends up in an inflatable human love-doll[98]; the women throw away the doll, which proceeds to molest the garbagemen who find it . . .

XXX

79. Chaperone from beyond?

Volume two of the *Ghost Hunt* manga has a side-story that, while more benign than the main ghost story, is also more classically Japanese in its presentation of the ghost; it's almost a young people's version of the *Yotsuya Kaidan* as it pokes some gentle fun at the image of the female ghost out for revenge. Celebrity itako (medium) Masako Hara tells her colleagues at Shibuya Psychic Research that a television crew has been trying to film in a Tokyo park, but shooting has been interrupted by water mysteriously falling on the cast; research indicates that this phenomenon has also afflicted others in the past six months. In addition, the mysterious downpour only affects romantic couples (or actors pretending to be a couple).

---

[98] The most potentially offensive thing about this movie is that the doll's features are modeled on a cartoon-y version of a Negro; still, as the entire movie is based on sexual humor rather than the possibility of ghosts, the racial caricature probably should not be taken too seriously.

The mystery is cleared up when Masako becomes possessed by the troublesome spirit: that of a young woman who attempted suicide in the park six months before. She had met a young man there, and the two of them had dated, but one day she saw him with another woman. She confronted her boyfriend, who poured a bottle of water on her. She wanted to commit suicide in the park, but, after some failed attempts, she died in a most tragi-comic manner: she tripped over a cat, banged her head on a curb, and died.[99]

Since then, she tried to appear as a ghost to her unfaithful boyfriend, but he was too insensitive to even notice her. In frustration, the ghost decided to disrupt other couples' happiness, delighting in their misfortune. Mai and the monk point out to the ghost that revenge born of envy isn't really making her happy; the ghost agrees, thanks them for listening to her story, and allows herself to be exorcised. The last picture of her is as she was at the time of her death, with half of her face bloodied by the head wound. This parallels her to Oiwa of *Yotsuya Kaidan*, not only recalling the facial distortion caused by the medicine, but also the general theme of a woman betrayed through no fault of her own.

Although the manga does not name the park, a Japanese reader would probably assume the location is a place where couples may run into ghostly trouble: Tokyo's Inokashira Park.[100] The park's current reputation is as one of the most hostile places for a date. The cause of the problem? One of the Seven Chinese Good Luck Gods,

---

[99] This parallels a gag in Satoshi Kon's 2003 movie *Tokyo Godfathers*, an anime parody in many respects of the classic John Ford western *Three Godfathers*, complete with Christmas symbolism. In this case, one of the three misfits who find an abandoned baby on Christmas Eve is Hana, a middle-aged drag queen. At one point, he returns to the drag bar where he used to work, and tells the "mama-san" that he's now homeless because his lover is dead. Mama-san asks the dramatic question: "AIDS?" Hana shakes his head: "He slipped on a bar of soap."

[100] The following is from Benj Vardigan, "The Thrill of the Haunt", in *Shojo Beat,* vol. 3 #2 (January 2007), p. 184.

the goddess Benzaiten, is believed to reside in Inokashira Park. She's also believed to be so sensitive and so jealous that any display of affection by human couples puts her into a rage. Relationships are endangered simply by holding hands or kissing, or even by riding one of the paddleboats on the lake. Couples are advised to either stage an argument or pretend that they're strangers to each other, to avoid the wrath of Benzaiten.

Does this really hold in the 21st century—worrying about interference from a Chinese ghost? The shrine to Benzaiten has been there for centuries; the artist Hiroshige created a beautiful woodprint, *The Benzaiten Shrine at Inokashira in the Snow*, in the 1760s.[101] The park was officially created in 1918. There's no way of knowing how far back rumors of Benzaiten's influence goes, but certainly the most dramatic end of a love affair in Inokashira Park took place in 1948, when renowned novelist Osamu Dazai and his lover committed suicide in the park.[102]

Still, the park attracts all sorts of visitors, because of its ponds, its cherry trees, its musical performances, and, near one end of the park, the Ghibli Museum, commemorating the work of Hayao Miyazaki and Isao Takahata, creators of some of Japan's finest anime.

xxx

"Monk-san" answers one question that Mai asks and certainly one that some readers will have pondered: is there justice in letting the spirit of the dead girl Become One with the Cosmos when her creep boyfriend is never held to account for the shabby way he treated her?[103] At least Yusuke in *YuYu Hakusho* reached out and

---

[101] http://commons.wikimedia.org/wiki/Image:Hiroshige_Benzaiten_Shrine_at_Inokashira_in_Snow.jpg, accessed January 19, 2007.

[102] http://www.jref.com/practical/kichijouji.shtml, accessed January 19, 2007.

[103] Spoiler alert: he is held to account in the anime version.

punished the guy who disrespected his girlfriend, after she'd spent months as a *jibakurei*.

The monk's response is simply a statement of faith that karma eventually will catch up to the creep. This belief that a kind of supra-natural justice, handed down by Fate or The Universe, will ultimately rectify everything may seem too passive for the action-oriented west, but Buddhism is about taking the long view. This confidence that everything happens for a larger purpose and that justice will ultimately be served helps to explain why Japan is one of the least litigious nations on earth.

CHAPTER 24: GHOSTBUSTERS

Not all spirits are benign, but exorcising the ones that need to rest in peace, because of the problems they're causing in the human world, often requires a specialist. Fortunately, there's no shortage of these, whether in the world of anime/manga or the real world.

Old-school manga titles about ghostbusters include:

GS Mikami

One of the best-known and longest-running comic manga based on a psychic (although it has yet to be translated for American readers), *GS* (for *Ghost Sweeper) Mikami: Gokuraku Daisakusen!!* (*GS Mikami: Big Paradise Battle!!*) was created for *Shonen Sunday* in 1991 by Takashi Shiina; it ran until 1999 and spun off into a year's worth of weekly anime and a one-hour movie.

The story is simple: Reiko Mikami (the kanji of her name means "beautiful goddess") is a voluptuous redhead who's also a gifted psychic. She's in it for the money; she charges outrageous fees for her services, and is capable of attacking her clients if they don't pay their bills. She saves money by hiring as an assistant a high school student named Tadao Yokoshima. She pays him ¥250 per hour (about $2.65), and he goes along with it for one reason: his boss is a voluptuous redhead, and he hangs around hoping to peek in on Mikami in the bath, a hot springs, or somewhere else requiring skimpy attire.

Yokoshima has a few latent psychic abilities, but he's only one of several assistants to Mikami. These include an exorcist named Father Karas (yes, named after the priest in *The Exorcist*), and Meiko Rokudo, a soft-spoken young girl who has a dozen shikigami spirits within her. They appear when Meiko loses her composure—which she does quite a lot.

80. A Ghost Sweeper's Apprentice

However, Mikami's most valuable apprentice appears in the first episode of the manga series: a onetime miko named Kinu Himuro, generally called Okinu. She's sweet, compassionate, but sometimes a bit dense.

Their association started when Mikami and Yokoshima went up into the Japanese Alps to exorcise a ghost that was bothering the clients of a volcanic hot springs resort. As Mikami and Yokoshima were walking down the road, they were watched by a ghostly woman. Deciding that Yokoshima is good for her plans, she approaches him, asking him to fetch some medicine for her; when he tries to fetch the medicine, from a death-trap stage that would have fooled nobody, he's almost crushed by a boulder. The woman is in fact trying to kill Yokoshima.

Once they get to the resort, Mikami and Yokoshima go hunting for the ghost, and in short order they find him: a mountaineer who got lost during a climb and died. He asks Mikami to rescue his body; she indirectly agrees, sending Yokoshima into the snowy night up the mountain with the ghost while she stays warm and comfortable at the inn.

Yokoshima, slogging through the snow, encounters the woman who's still trying to kill him. The mountaineer, meanwhile, wants to show Yokoshima how manly mountaineers keep warm in a snowstorm, which is not Yokoshima's idea of fun. Yokoshima instead chases the woman, even as he's chased by the mountaineer's ghost; they all run right down the mountain and into Mikami's hot springs.

Okinu, the woman, explains that she died some three hundred years ago, when she was sacrificed to the volcano god. However, she never actually crossed over to become a mountain spirit. With Mikami's help, the mountaineer's spirit becomes god of the mountain; as for Okinu, she was supposed to let go of her life on the mountain and Become One with the Cosmos—except that she forgot how to do that. Mikami takes Okinu on as an assistant, for 30 yen per day.

81. Beware of Cat

Another early episode highlights both Mikami's flexible attitude towards the ghosts she's paid to exorcise and her major concern: money. The episode titled "Ookamitachi no Shigo" (Post-Mortem for the Wolves) deals, despite the title, with bank robbers.

The first scene takes place outside the Kanegura Bank, as two would-be hold-up men drive toward their target. However, a cat wanders into the road, the driver swerves to avoid it, and runs into a lamppost. We next see a bouquet of flowers laid at the lamppost; an indication that the robbers died in the crash. However, we also see their ghosts out on the sidewalk in front of the bank, looking through the window as Mikami meets with the bank manager. The ghosts can't rest in peace while they have unfinished business on earth; in this case, robbing the bank. Putting up anti-ghost protective charms around the bank would keep away the ghosts, but also drive away customers. Mikami wants to charge the bank ¥100 million to banish the ghosts; the bank manager refuses to pay more than ¥10 million.

Mikami decides to play both ends against the middle. She talks the bank into letting her take part in a robbery prevention drill. Meanwhile, she arranges with the ghosts to help them rob the bank. By carrying out their unfinished business, they can rest in peace; and, because they can't take the money with them to the afterlife, Mikami would be happy to take it off their hands.

Mikami and company pull off the robbery, taking about ¥300 million in 30 seconds. As the ghosts happily Become One with the Cosmos, Mikami and Yokoshima are chased, and caught, by the bank's tellers, acting as their own police force. At first, Mikami seems broken up about having to give back the money. All is not lost: back at the bank, Okinu-chan is using one of the computers to transfer ¥1 billion to a Swiss bank account.

The percentage of manga that have been translated into English is relatively small. *GS Mikami* is one of the titles that hasn't come over, and it should. Even though it dates from the Nineties, is long (running to some thirty-plus volumes), and may be considered "Old School," it's imaginative, well-drawn and, most important, funny.

Jigoku Sensei Nube

This series started appearing in *Shonen Jump* magazine in 1993, and ran for 6 years as part of the interest in school ghost stories. Artist Takeshi Okano and writer Shou Makura sets the action in the fifth grade of a modern school; the teacher, Meisuke Nueno, is an exorcist and comes from a long line of exorcists. His father got into trouble with one exorcism, and Meisuke saw no choice but to take the demon into himself. This is why he keeps his left hand gloved: his left hand is now a demon's claw, which he uses to perform magical feats. Apparently, in his school, there's often a need for magic.

Nueno has run up against most of the standard psychic threats, from spirits raised by kokkuri-san to walking anatomy statues. He's also had to deal with evil people and mythical beasts; in one early episode, a student is harassed by a kappa, a half-human half-turtle spirit, who was actually only trying to warn the school that it had been built over an unexploded bomb from World War 2.

Yugen Kaisha

I think of this series as "GS Mikami Lite". It has many of the same ingredients as the manga by Takashi Shiina: the psychic detective agency is run by Ayaka Kisaragi, a vivacious redhead who sees ghostbusting as a relatively cheap and easy way to make money. She has a small stable of assistants, some of whom are children. And, contrary to expectations, the business never seems to turn a profit.

The name translates as Phantom Quest Corporation (but the pronunciation of the kanji is the same as for the more mundane "Limited Corporation"). Four OAV anime episodes were created, and a supplemental episode (known as Part Zero) featured the origins of the series. Beyond dealing with Dracula and an extreme sect of Buddhist monks, the company really only has to deal with one ghost—and he turns out to be one of the good guys.

82. Love Among the Mummies

The episode starts with a night watchman at a museum where an exhibit of artifacts from ancient Egypt is about to open—complete, it seems, with ghost.

We jump to the head of Phantom Quest Corp. meeting with the young and handsome head of the Nakasugi Corporation, underwriters of the exhibition. They then meet separately with Natsuki Ogawa, the young woman who's curator of the exhibit. She's concerned about the success of the exhibition, while Nakasugi is more of a sexual predator chasing after various women on his staff. He cancels the night shift installation of the exhibit, then tries to use this to put pressure on Ogawa, but the ghost intervenes.

The ghost is Higashi Narita, a graduate student who unearthed the artifacts as well as Ogawa's boyfriend at the time of his death. Nakasugi is persistent, however, hinting that Ogawa has to keep him happy to ensure that the exhibition opens. Ayaka, meanwhile, forms a pact with Narita, who sacrificed his life to find the Egyptian ruins. Narita goes after Nakasugi, who's getting grabby with Ogawa; Nakasugi isn't killed, but suffers an equally bad fate: he's caught embezzling from the corporation and fired—which is also bad news for Ayaka and the Phantom Quest Corp, since they won't get paid.

Vampire Princess Miyu: Himiko Se[104]

Vampire Princess Miyu started out as a series of four OAV episodes produced in 1988. Directed by Toshiki Hirano, these moody and

---

[104] This is a loaded name for the series' spiritualist. It invokes Himiko, the first recorded female ruler of Japan; Himiko, who was a sorceress and a shaman, was born about the year 175 C.E. and died in 248, although there is very little known about Himiko and even these dates are disputed. As a shaman, she reportedly left the actual day-to-day government of ancient Japan to her brother.

atmospheric episodes tell of a vampiric princess, apparently frozen at age fourteen. She doesn't behave according to traditional western vampire lore, although she does suck the blood of the living. Her actual task is to search for *shinma*, "divine demons" who have escaped from the spirit world into the human world. Miyu, accompanied by a companion shinma named Larva, must find and dispel the shinma while a spiritualist, Himiko Se, crosses Miyu's path in the OAV. (A 26-week television series, also directed by Hirano, was broadcast in Japan in 1997-1998, but its *shinma* are clearly demonic; only the one appearing in the third OAV episode behaves like a ghost. In this episode, Miyu and Himiko set out in search of a huge antique suit of Japanese armor, a prized family heirloom. This armor, however, has been possessed by one shinma on orders from another, Lemures, who knew Larva. As Himiko tries to exorcise the spirit from the armor, the shinma try to turn Larva's loyalty away from Miyu. They fail, and Lemures is banished.)

One of the fascinating aspects of the OAV series is Himiko Se, the professional spiritualist. She's statuesque, sophisticated, and very beautiful; however, much of what we see is a façade. She knows that spiritualism isn't paying the bills, and seems rather mercenary at times. We also see her in several episodes conducting arcane Buddhist exorcism rituals, with a skill that impresses even Miyu. From beginning to end, Himiko is portrayed as neither good not bad.

Like Miyu herself. In the OAV Miyu explains that her father was a human while her mother was a vampire; she came into her heritage as a shinma-fighter after World War II when her parents died. While Himiko chases after vampires, possessed suits of armor, and a variety of spirit assignments, Miyu's work is very specific. The overlap occurs only in the OAV series, at the end of which we learn that Miyu and Himiko have met before, years ago . . .

xxx

Muyo to Roji no Mahouritsu Soudan Jimusho

A more benign bunch of juvenile ghosthunters are featured in Nishi Yoshiyuki's manga *Muyo to Roji no Mahouritsu Soudan Jimusho (Muyo & Roji's Bureau of Supernatural Investigation)*. There's a bit of artistic influence of Hino Hideki in Muyo Toru, the shorter senior of the spirit-chasing kids who have their own third-floor office. The diminutive and somewhat creepy Muyo is a "magical lawyer"; this isn't about exorcism, after all, but about justice, for both the quick and the dead. Roji is the enforcer; tall, thin, friendly-looking, and (in keeping with lawyerly fashion) wears suspenders. His real name is Jiro, but he reverses the letters and calls himself Roji. This duo, which has appeared in *Shonen Jump* and a sister publication since 2004, has already been discussed in the Spirit Photography chapter; they'll return with our look at Train Ghosts.

xxx

Looking at *GS Mikami* above, we note that one of Mikami's assistants, Meiko Rokudo, has access to a dozen spirit helpers called shikigami. There's a pretty large body of literature just on these (literally translating the name) ceremonial spirits who do the bidding of onmyouji, shamans who are practitioners of this Shinto-related magic. Most shikigami are invisible, but they manifest to onmyouji in a variety of animal shapes, or as child-sized demons.

Shikigami should not be confused with shinigami, who are the focus of the next manga/anime series:

Yami no Matsuei (Descendants of Darkness)

This manga series first appeared in the girls' manga magazine *Hana to Yume* from 1996 to 2002; an anime version appeared in 2000. Officially, the manga by Yoko Matsushita is on hold, and was supposed to start up again in 2010, although the first release in 2010 involved episodes that were first published a decade earlier but have been redrawn.

Shinigami are death spirits, of a type that actually first appeared in western literature; they took root in Japan during the 19th century, although there is some overlap with Shinto shikigami. One aspect of the goddess Izanami, when she appeared to her brother after she was burned to death while giving birth to fire according to the *Kojiki* (Shinto's creation mythology), is as a shinigami. Other shinigami-like spirits include Enma, the King of Hell (who puts in an appearance in *YuYu Hakusho*) and Ryuk, the keeper of the notebook in the manga *Death Note* by Tsugumi Oba and Takeshi Obata, also the artist of the very different *Hikaru no Go*.

The shinigami of *Yami no Matsuei* are very different from any of their classical counterparts. The central actor in this comedy-drama is Asato Tsuzuki, who has been active for seven decades with the Second Division of the afterlife, sorting out proper and improper human deaths. Tsuzuki's death was apparently proper; he's a spirit, which doesn't stop his ravenous sweet tooth. His beat is Japan's southern island of Kyushu, which happens to be the homeland of manga artist Matsushita.

As part of the series he picks up a partner, a moody teenager named Hisoka Kurosaki. As they chase various evil spirits around Kyushu, sometimes they have a senior/junior relationship akin to Batman and Robin; at times, though, Kurosaki follows his own agenda, since he's convinced that he was never told the whole truth about his own death.

XXX

Rasetsu no Hana

One of the more recent manga in the ghost-busting genre, *Rasetsu no Hana* was created by Chika Shiomi, who also has another supernatural manga, *Yurara no Tsuki*, to her credit; *Rasetsu no Hana* is actually the sequel to *Yurara*. Serialized in *Hana to Yume*, this is the story of yet another young female exorcist; in many ways, it covers familiar ground, but there are a few unique features.

Like Misaki in *Vulgar Ghosts' Daydream*, Rasetsu Hyuga is a minor, eighteen years old, yet works full-time as an exorcist. She dropped out of junior high school because she could see spirits—too many of them. But one spirit in particular left its mark on her—literally. The mark resembles a tattoo of a rose on her chest, and the romantic implications are pretty obvious.

This spirit appeared to her when she was fifteen, declaring its love for Rasetsu, and that it would come for her and take her away when she reached adulthood at age twenty—if she did not find love before then. Meanwhile, she seems to be having trouble in that department. Besides being drop-dead beautiful, she's a bit on the crude side and, like the ghostly detective in *Yami no Matsuei*, has an insane sweet-tooth. She works in a ghostbusting agency in Tokyo, where "there seem to be more and more evil spirits that need banishing." The agency director, Hiichiro Amakawa, detects things about the clients by hugging them; this can get a bit awkward, since he's very *bishonen*. Another ghostbuster can control people with his voice, and one client, a librarian who can block spirits by casting a water barrier, joins the team after Rasetsu gets him fired from his day job. Here, too, are romantic implications, since this is a young good-looking librarian. This has all the earmarks of the *Ghost Hunt* cute-meet between Mia and Naru-san.

CHAPTER 25: MODERN GHOSTS

At the opening of the manga *Black Bird* by Kanoko Sakurakoji, the heroine Misao, having just reached her sixteenth birthday, talks with friends about (no surprise) boys—one of whom asked for Misao's e-mail address. She refused to give it to him, because she could see the guy was possessed by the spirit of an aborted child.

Misao is hardly the only manga character with the ability to see past the surface into the spirit world, or to be influenced by a spirit. However, Japan's culture has undergone countless changes since World War II. While there is often consistency between old and new, it's sometimes very hard to achieve.

A scene from an episode of Jyoji Akiyama's popular manga of the 1970s, *Haguregumo*, sums up the distressing state of folk medicine in the mid 1800s: a young girl has been raped and impregnated, and an elderly relative has tied the girl down and is beating on her abdomen in order to induce a miscarriage. The Meiji era brought an emphasis on western medicine, which in turn brought in some new spirit situations.

Life in any nation on Earth is precarious, and Japan is no exception. Miscarriages happen; infants die of illness or accident. The conscious termination of a pregnancy, however, carries with it a degree of guilt that would be hard to understand in the west. In *The Life of an Amorous Woman*, written in 1686 by Saikaku Ihara (1642-1693), a prostitute has nightmares of being confronted by the ninety-five pregnancies she had terminated. This is about as extreme an example as can be found of *tatari*, the retribution carried out by the spirit of the fetus. (LaFleur, William R., *Liquid Life: Abortion and Buddhism in Japan.*, 1992. Princeton: Princeton

University Press, p. 152) Those who believe in such things would state that the fetus is sufficiently aware, perhaps by virtue of having lived before and being reincarnated, to understand what has been done and resent the living for unnaturally terminating the soul's return to life. (p. 172) On the other hand, some Japanese deny the reality of fetal *tatari*, for a variety of reasons. Tadasu Iizawa, for one, considers it exploitation and compares religious practitioners who make money off of memorializing aborted fetuses to extortionists connected to Japanese organized crime (*yakuza*). (p. 166)

In any case, this is a type of Japanese ghost we've encountered before: resentful at the way it was treated in life, even if that life was *in utero*, and motivated by a desire for retribution that is not subject to rational thought, much less to negotiation. Misao did well in not giving her e-mail to someone possessed by the spirit of a mizuko—literally, a water child, and a euphemism for an aborted fetus. In modern times, rituals and systems have been developed through which the living can apologize to the dead; these include the erection and maintenance of memorial plaques and statues, and even charitable donations of what would have been "child support." (pp. 221-222)

xxx

Vampire Princess Miyu

Ten years after their stylish and creepy quartet of OAVs appeared, creators Toshihiro Hirano and Narumi Kakinouchi put together a 26 week TV series based on the teen vampire, her companion Larva, and their battle against *shinma*—demigods and demons who must be banished from the earth. Overall, the series was less successful than the OAVs, in part because of the need to come up with one *shinma* after another each week, and also because the series set Miyu in a Japanese high school, rather than having her play against the jaded spiritualist Himiko Se.

83. Taxi?

The sixth TV episode begins with Miyu hailing a taxi at night, and asking to be taken to a cemetery. When the cab gets there, however, she's gone. What started out as a simple joke by Miyu turns serious when her double turns up and starts biting cabdrivers' necks.

The "ghostly passenger" motif isn't just a Japanese urban legend. My hometown of Chicago boasts one of the most illustrious of such ghosts: Resurrection Mary.[105] Her story sounds rather similar to this Japanese version:

It was a stormy autumn night, near Aoyama Cemetery, where a taxi driver picked up a poor young girl drenched by the rain. It was dark, so he didn't get a good look at her face, but she seemed sad and he figured she had been visiting a recently deceased relative or friend. The address she gave was some distance away, and they drove in silence. A good cabbie doesn't make small talk when picking someone up from a cemetery.

When they arrived at the address, the girl didn't get out, but whispered for him to wait a bit, while she stared out the window at a second floor apartment. Ten minutes or so passed as she watched, never speaking, never crying; simply observing a solitary figure move about the apartment. Suddenly, the girl asked to be taken to a new address, this one back near the cemetery where he had first picked her up. The rain was heavy, and the driver focused on the road, leaving the girl to her thoughts.

When he arrived at the new address, a modern house in a good neighborhood, the cabbie opened the door and turned around to collect his fare. To his surprise, he found himself staring at an empty back seat, with a puddle where the girl had been sitting moments before. Mouth open, he just sat there staring at the vacant seat, until a knocking on the window shook him from his reverie.

---

[105] See Troy Taylor's website, http://www.prairieghosts.com/resurcem. html, accessed January 18, 2007.

Patrick Drazen

The father of the house, seeing the taxi outside, had calmly walked out bringing with him the exact amount for the fare. He explained that the young girl had been his daughter, who died in a traffic accident some years ago and was buried in Aoyama Cemetery. From time to time, he said, she hailed a cab and, after visiting her old boyfriend's apartment, asked to be driven home. The father thanked the driver for his troubles, paid him his fare, and sent him on his way.

xxx

Outer space is one of the last places we expect to offer up a ghost story. These stories, especially in Japan, are often tied to a specific place and the events that happened there, and space is still too much of a frontier. However, manga artist Katsuhiro Otomo created a cosmic ghost story when he wrote a film, *Memories*, that is actually three short films, with a different director and a different style for each segment. The first of these stories, called "Madame's Request" in Japanese and renamed "Magnetic Rose" for the English subtitled version, was directed by Satoshi Kon, who went on to become one of the greatest anime directors of the new generation, with a half-dozen modern classics to his name before his untimely death from cancer in 2010. His feature work includes *Perfect Blue, Millennium Actress, Tokyo Godfathers*, and *Paprika*, as well as the *Paranoia Agent* TV series.

84. Diva

Late in the 21st century,[106] the four-man crew of a salvage vehicle is slowly picking its way through the space equivalent of the Sargasso Sea; instead of seaweed, though, this patch of the cosmos

---

[106] For some reason, the salvage crew has its encounter with Madame on October 12, 2092—the 600th anniversary of Columbus' discovery of the western hemisphere.

230

is crowded with derelict spaceships and various kinds of junk. It's nothing but scrap metal, so the men were surprised to get a signal from one of the derelict ships. It seems to be a distress signal, and, as an even bigger surprise, the ship was the home of a retired opera soprano, around whom a great many rumors circulated.

Although it's impossible for the diva to still be alive after all these years, two of the crewmen enter the ship to investigate—and that's when the haunting starts. Lights come up as if on a stage, and the spacemen see the diva: sometimes onstage in costume, sometimes in an open field. One man, Heinrich, sees something that couldn't possibly have been in the ship's database: how he bought his daughter Emily a miniature spacesuit for her birthday one year, and how she put it on, climbed up onto the roof, and lost her footing . . .

There are old films and newspaper clippings suggesting that the diva's young paramour, believed to have run off, may well have been killed by the jealous soprano. When the ship starts trying to attack the two spacemen, it's all they can do to try to escape.

The music for this short film was written by Yoko Kanno, one of the greatest modern writers of music for animation. Her score repeats, recycles, and sometimes distorts excerpts from the operas of Giacomo Puccini, notably *Tosca* and *Madama Butterfly*. You don't need to know the scores to appreciate the extra dimension they add to the anime, but their inclusion is one of the creepy delights of *Memories*.

XXX

Most ghost stories start with the death of someone, and the consequences of their spirit not traveling on to the afterlife. *Maburaho* takes a bit of a different tack: a situation is set up in which everyone knows that someone is going to die, then it happens. It's a romantic comedy set in a high school.

Specifically, *Maburaho* was begun as a series of novels written by Toshihiko Tsukiji, with illustrations by Eeji Komatsu. The stories were serialized in *Gekkan Dragon* magazine and reprinted in book form between 2001 and 2006. The novels were adapted into a manga and the manga was adapted to an anime in 2003. While writing the stories, Tsukiji was asked by the *Gekkan Dragon* editors to change the rules and extend the life of the hero, Kazuki Shikimori. Tsujiki decided to keep with the plan, killing off the protagonist after six episodes; or, after killing him off, having his ghost keep hanging around.

85. Only eight times

Kazuki Shikimori was a second year high school student, but his old school wasn't a typical high school. He transferred from Aoi Academy, one of Japan's premier magical academies. (No points for guessing which series of books about a young British wizard was as popular in Japan as in the rest of the world.) Kazuki is rather shy and retiring, but he has a good heart and generally does the right thing. Unfortunately, being a nice guy doesn't get you extra years in the magical world, and Kazuki is at a major disadvantage. In the universe of *Maburaho*, some people can only cast a few hundred spells in their lifetime, and some a few thousand. When you hit your limit, though, you don't just become a Muggle: you die. Actually, "die" isn't accurate enough; the magician's body turns to dust. And Kazuki only had eight spells left in him.

At this point, other members of the student body take an interest in Kazuki's well-being, and these other students tend to be girls. Yuna Miyama was a childhood friend of Kazuki's, and as children they informally agreed to marry each other when they grew up; Yuna, being the "nice" girl in Kazuki's life, seems the strongest candidate. This being a "harem comedy," a genre in which one guy is enticed by a bevy of attractive females, there are at least a couple of others whose interest in Kazuki is more mercenary. In fact, two other girls are competing for Kazuki on behalf of two warring families. Kuriko Kazetsubaki and Rin Kamishiro are descended from prestigious magical families, and want to keep Kazuki alive since, if he turns to dust, they can't get to his genes. He's a physically weak example of a powerful magic family, and would be expected to father a very powerful magician—if he can be kept alive.

Unfortunately, he can't: he uses his final spell to rescue his childhood friend Yuna from a magical virus. Kazuki's body may be gone, but his ghost continues to hang around, and even meets with another ghost, who also becomes another member of the "harem": Elizabeth, whose family goes back centuries. She died during the Holy Roman Empire, where she met a soldier who bore a resemblance to Kuriko Kazetsubaki; eventually Elizabeth's spirit takes up residence inside Kuriko, who has made peace with Rin in their attempts to restore Kazuki's body and retrieve his genes.

He's ultimately brought back, but with a comic twist. With the wish that he have ten times his old life-span, the series ends with . . . ten different Maburahos, each with the same old life-span.

xxx

Maburaho represents at least one piece of the manga audience: high school boys. Let's take a quick look at the other side of the gender divide.

CHAPTER 26: GIRLY GHOSTS

We've already met with a number of ghosts who were created in the realm of *shojo*—manga and anime created with adolescent girls in mind. Even within this limited demographic, the stories, and the ghosts within them, have been all over the map, from the sentimentality of *Ai Yori Aoshi* to the gruesomeness of *Ghost Hunt*. The titles just keep rolling out of the manga magazine publishers, and most are destined never to be seen in the west except over the Internet in scanslation (amateur, do-it-yourself renderings into English, German, or whatever the fan's language might be). These are lucky enough to have found an official outlet in the west:

xxx

Heaven's Will
Satoru Takamiya is writer and artist of this short series that begins outside a "haunted house". The heroine, Mikuzu, a high school student, is being teased by her friends who try to convince her that there's no such thing as ghosts. But, as Mikuzu reflects: "Ghosts don't exist for people who can't see them; but, to people who can, ghouls and ghosts and fairies exist all over the place!" As if to prove her point, we see her dragging the ghost of a medieval soldier who won't let go of her ankle.

Meanwhile, Mikuzu has her own troubles: a guy who can't seem to take his eyes off of her; Mikuzu and her friends refer to him as a "stalker." As far as Mikuzu's concerned, there's no difference between a ghost and a creepy guy.

86. The Possessed Piano

Things get more intense for Mikuzu when she meets Seto (a boy) her age) and Seto (his deceased sister who died seven years before and whose identity he wishes to adopt). Mikuzu is asked to help Seto in an informal ghost-busting company (strictly for the money, which Seto needs for his sex-change operation to "revive" his sister). Woven through the story is their one serious case of exorcism: they are approached by the Student Council President of a prestigious boy's high school, who has purchased a piano that he cannot play. "Rather," he says, "while I am playing it, I become possessed by something and lose consciousness." He lets Mikuzu and Seto live in his house for a week while he takes a quick vacation, during which time he expects them to exorcise whatever's wrong with the piano.

Things start out complicated, with Mikuzu and Seto being given matching negligees (the President not realizing Seto is a boy) and their assistant Kagari playing the piano for hours to no effect (because he's a werewolf). Mikuzu and Kagari go to interview the grandson of the piano builder (in part so that Mikuzu find a quick solution, limiting the fee and keeping Seto from sacrificing himself to the sex-change). The piano builder, however, died just before finishing the instrument.

One day when Seto is out of town, Mikuzu actually meets Seto's kid's sister's spirit, trapped in a fan. She says to call her brother by his name, but we don't learn what it is. When Seto returns, he finds that the demon possessing the piano seems to be getting stronger and needs to be exorcised. The exorcism itself seems to be an easy procedure involving the fan containing the sister's spirit, but the demon isn't subdued so easily and swallows Seto. Mikuzu follows him into what looks like a completely different house; she finds Seto; identifying the one note sounded by the piano, touching it with the fan and stating "Be released from your despair," the piano is healed and the two are returned. The only problem is that the Student Cuoncil President doesn't pay cash for the exorcism, but plays to Seto's weakness for pastries.

Like many shoujo manga, this one is rather vague, complicated and seems to be unfinished. The issue of Seto's sister and his death-wish are left unresolved, as are relations between Seto, Mikuzu and Kagari. This unresolved state of affairs is considered poetic and aesthetic, focusing on emotion expressed through the action.

Bound Beauty (Shibariya komachi)

The Japanese view of the universe depicts destiny as, among other things, a scarlet thread tied around one's little finger, linking one (especially romantically) to someone else. This is part of the *yubikiri* "pinky swear" gesture still common in Japan. The manga by Mick Takeuchi centers on a high school girl named Chiyako who can actually see these threads; not only that, she does a little "insider trading" with this information, making money by telling romance fortunes.

Haruka

Toko Mizuno's manga *Haruka—Beyond the Stream of Time* (a translation of *Harukanaru toki no Naka de Hachiyoo Shoo*) has appeared in Japan's *LaLa* and America's *Shojo Beat* magazines. The manga's been criticized as a recycling of Yu Watase's similarly plotted *Fushigi Yugi*. However, this manga was inspired not by another romance manga but by a romantic video game. The series runs to fifteen tankobon volumes in Japan; only the first two volumes are available so far in America, and animated versions in both countries.

87. A Killer Koto

The lead character, Akane Motomiya, starts out as a modern high school student who's goodhearted, a bit naïve, and who gets an increased scope to use her abilities when she is carried back a thousand years to the Heian period of Japan's history. This means that she gets involved with the war between the Taira and Heike clans. She also gets involved with the Eight Guardians—a bevy of young good-looking guys.

She meets one of the guys under special circumstances. Akuram, of the Oni (Demon) clan, summoned Akane back to Heian-era

Kyoto, and has caused other problems to keep her and her Guardians busy. In one plot enacted over two manga episodes, Toji temple finds itself in possession of a Japanese table-harp or koto. Even though koto come in a variety of sizes, this one has eight strings, is deemed to be too heavy in the lower register, and its music actually kills the monk who sets out to play it. It doesn't end there, however; the monk's ghost, filled with anger at being killed, continues to play the koto, intent on killing others.

Akane cannot help this time, having been stricken with a sleeping curse by the sound of the koto. Before this, however, she meets a monk playing an elegy for the dead monk on a flute; this monk flutist is Eisen. The Guardians (not all eight of them have appeared at this point) need to play the koto themselves, to establish which string is the problem. The focus this time is on Eisen, the younger brother of the Heian Emperor, who abandoned his claims on the throne to become a monk. As an accomplished musician, he's the Guardian who solves the problem of the eight-stringed koto by preparing to play it, even though it may cost him his life to do so.

XXX

Phantom Dream (Genei Musou)
One of the early works of Natsuki Takaya, better known for the wildly successful manga *Fruits Basket*, this 1994-1997 story, serialized in *Hana to Yume Planet Zōkan* has some of the comedy but all of the drama of her later work. It tells of Tamaki Otoya, high school student and Shinto priest in training. The latest in a line of such priests, Tamaki doesn't merely help disturbed souls to find peace after death; he knows that these spirits could do some serious damage if driven by frustration and vengeance. For backup and general guidance, Tamaki can look to his mother and his girlfriend Asahi. His mother is the last remaining member of the family (his father and grandfather having passed on), leaving Tamaki as the head of the shrine.

88. The Twins Who Weren't Alike

A third person comes into the picture in the first chapter: a tall and statuesque girl named Mitsuru. Growing up, she had been a friend to both Tamaki and Asahi, but now she is aloof and standoffish. The reason becomes obvious pretty quickly: somewhere along the way, her body has become home to a *jaki*, a spirit that feeds on negative emotions like jealousy or anger. It's tied to Minoru, Mitsuru's twin sister who recently died after spending most of her life sickly, in bed, and alone. At first, Tamaki and Asahi assume that Minoru was the source of the negative spiritual energy, resentful of her isolation and her sickly condition. However, the resentment is from Mitsuru herself, feeling the guilt of getting the life that should have been shared with her sister. Asahi volunteers to take Mitsuru's bitterness and jealousy into herself, because "I'm just bubbling over with love inside." Minoru appears to actually move the dark feelings from Mitsuru to Asahi, who volunteered to ease her friend's heart because "Minoru-chan won't be able to rest in Heaven if you don't find peace here."

The bottom line: this series is based less on any internal rules of supernatural cause and effect than it is on the traditional notion that girls are supposed to be *yasashii* (kind, generous, compassionate). Sometimes, guys manifest these behaviors (see Seto in *Heaven's Will*, above, or Ichiro in the suicide chapter).

CHAPTER 27: TRAIN GHOSTS

More accurately, this isn't the ghost of a train, but a ghost that has come into being because of a train.

xxx

89. Got legs?

In this story from the 90s manga *Jigoku Sensei Nube*, the spirit of a girl cut in half by a commuter train has become a teketeke, which gets its name from the sound it makes getting around with half its body missing.

One of Nueno-sensei's fifth grade students, Makoto Kurita, has been listening to some high school kid telling tales about the teketeke. It started out as a young girl who tried beating a train across the track, and lost; she was cut in half at the waist. Now, her ghost wanders the streets looking for her legs, and it's said that anyone who even hears the legend of the teketeke is doomed to die in three days. Makoto is pretty frightened by this story, but the high school student offers to help . . . for ¥100 (about a dollar). The older student gets the money, tells Makoto "You're on your own," and takes off.

Makoto then enlists the help of his teacher and some of the other students; they keep watch and, sure enough, late one night the monstrous teketeke appears; torso cut off at the waist, dragging her entrails on the ground, wanting to cut off Makoto's legs to replace her own. Nueno steps in, protecting Makoto with his demon claw while asking, "Listen, Makoto; why can't this person rest in peace? Why is she saying these things?" Makoto looks, and sees tears on the horrible face of the teketeke. He realizes that this monster was once just a kid who wanted to live like a kid; she got caught up in the bitterness of her fate. Makoto prays for her to find peace, and she vanishes.

The prayer hasn't healed the teketeke; it merely spared Makoto. In the apartment of the high school student, we see him counting the money he took from Makoto, among others, laughing at the younger students for believing in ghost stories. He stops laughing when the teketeke appears . . . and the final scene shows the ghost moving through the alleys of the city, dragging the older boy's bloody pair of legs behind her.

2009 appeared to be a big year for the teketeke, with two Japanese feature films due out featuring this particular ghost.

xxx

We've already met the crew from Yoshiyuki Nishi's manga *Muyo to Rouji no Mahouritsu Soudan Jimusho (Muyo & Rouji's Bureau of Supernatural Investigation)*. In this, their first case, they tackle a variant of a teketeke, and find that (no surprise) the best weapon to use against it is, again, compassion.

90. The Girl on Platform 5

When a troubled, taller than average young girl named Rie comes to their office, Muyo deduces that she has ghostly parasites attached to her legs. Sure enough, he makes visible a pair of fox-spirits wrapped like furry snakes around Rie's lower legs. This is a violation of spirit law, and Rouji carries out the punishment: banishment.

Rie's case, which has her disturbed enough to lose sleep over, is based on a rumor. If one goes to platform 5 of the Hashiki Station on the JR line, the ghost of a girl appears. This is bad enough, but the ghost is also reputed to grab people by the ankles and pull them off the platform, into the path of an oncoming train. Rie in fact can put a name to the ghost: she's convinced that it was once her classmate, Taeko Okazaki. They befriended each other when they made the transition from junior high to high school; they became very close friends. Yet Rie says, "I killed her."

Her explanation is a bit complicated. On the one day Taeko caught a cold and stayed home from school, Rie was invited to join the girls' volleyball team. Before this, most of the school apparently avoided speaking to Taeko and Rie, suspecting that they were "too close" and "sick" (meaning, they were suspected of being lesbians). Taeko was fond of holding Rie's hand, however, and Rie didn't mind at first. By being on the volleyball team, Rie tells Muyo and Rouji, "suddenly my world changed." She got more involved in sports and other students, and consequently had less time for Taeko, who had no other friends. Rie didn't want to let down the team, but Taeko argues one day on the train platform, rather pathetically, that Rie is her only friend. During the argument Taeko fell backward off the platform, into the path of an oncoming train.

Although Taeko has been repeatedly to Rie's grave, she refuses to step onto Platform 5. Yet this is exactly what Muyo wants her to do, preferably at two in the morning. While the two ghostbusters are intercepted by police (and have to subdue them), Taeko confronts the spirit on Platform 5—which appears to be a large centipede-like creature. Muyo diagnoses the spirit as a jibakurei made up of the hatred and sorrow of all of the train death victims of that station. He opens a portal to Hell to swallow up the jibakurei; however, Rie is still determined to try to save her friend, whose death she still feels she could have averted. Rie is even willing to be pulled into Hell with her friend, but Taeko at the last tells her, "You can't, Rie, but I'm happy; thank you." And after having this chance to hold Rie's hand one last time, Taeko's ghost is pulled into the underworld. Specifically, Muyo announces that the lord of the underworld has indeed sent Taeko to the River Sanzu rather than directly to Hell. (This more satisfactory resolution is the way stories in this series usually end up.)

As an epilogue, Rie tries to meet with the psychic detectives again to thank them, but they avoid her; it seems that they have a rule never to meet with a former client, for fear of getting the person involved with other spirits. Rie leaves a note anyway, thanking them on behalf of herself and "Taeko, who should be in Heaven by now."

Even though this series ran in *Shonen Jump*, a magazine aimed at adolescent boys, and as a result stresses action, this story sets the tenor of the entire series by mixing magic spells with compassion. Rie had been properly penitent and tried repeatedly to apologize to Taeko's spirit for breaking her promise of lifelong friendship. However, Taeko's spirit was overwhelmed and subsumed into the centipede-like jibakurei. Once the other spirits had been peeled away, Taeko was able to speak with Rie directly. This episode also shows the reader what disasters could have been avoided if Rei had thought more about Taeko, and tried to balance the two aspects of her new life—the team and her friend—instead of going from one to the other.

xxx

The *Gakkou no Kaidan* anime series has its own connection to a railroad ghost, although it starts out and ends up in a taxicab.

It's two in the morning on a rainy night, at a railroad crossing on a lonely country road. A taxi driver is thinking of going home and calling it a night. Suddenly, a type we're familiar with by now appears directly in front of the cab: a pale-skinned woman whose long black hair is hanging in front of her face. The taxi driver jams on the brakes and goes out to check on the woman he's sure he hit. But there's nobody in front of the cab. When he gets back behind the wheel, the woman is sitting in the back seat. The title of the episode: "The ghost photograph that takes lives: The Railroad crossing of evil."

Once it's established (see chapter 20 on spirit photography) that this particular crossing is haunted, the fifth grade student named Leo notices that an offering has been made there: a vase of flowers, rice balls and a juice box have been set up on the spot by, as it turns out, the victim's mother.

CHAPTER 28: LIVING DOLLS

In Japanese, a doll is called ningyo (人形), which means human-shaped. A listing of all the kinds of dolls that were ever used in Japanese society would be a separate book. They are children's playthings, and mementos of visits to temples or other pilgrimage sites, funeral dolls, cell phone strap trinkets, and the legless Daruma dolls (named for Bodhidharma, who created the Zen sect of Buddhism and was said to have meditated until his limbs fell off). Dolls have their own holiday: the Hinamatsuri (Doll Festival, also known as Girls' Day), celebrated on March 3; the centerpiece is a group of dolls representing the Emperor, Empress, and the imperial court of the Heian period.

There were also dolls which were not mere playthings. During the Heian period dolls began to be used for religious purposes, by taking on the sins of the person they represented. During the past one thousand years, other dolls have served other, less beneficial purposes, and they figure as well in Japanese stories of the supernatural—on both the good and evil sides of the equation. (These dolls, by the way, go beyond those who get possessed according to legend, such as the "visible boy" in classrooms and the Ninomiya statue that used to be in front of every school.)

91. Minnie

Volume two of the manga *Ghost Hunt* is much more chilling than the first, with a little girl and her doll at the center of poltergeist activity. Exorcisms don't seem to work, and the mystery doesn't begin to unravel until Naru uncovers the history of the house: six children under the age of ten had died in connection with that house. The question is, where to search for the ghost: in the house, in the child named Ayami who lives there now, or in Minnie her doll?

The doll is the center of Ayami's attention, and supposedly has told the girl a number of strange things. Minnie told her that she shouldn't repeat what she says to anyone or else she'll hurt Ayami; that her mother is an evil witch and her father is the witch's servant; that the doll has her own servants, consisting of the ghosts of children about the same age as Ayami.

It turns out that one little girl disappeared years before the present house was built, only to turn up dead months later. The girl's mother in her grief threw herself down a well; the new house was built over the well, but the mother's spirit continued menacing other children roughly the same age as her dead child. Searching for her own child, she caused the other deaths of those about the same age. In the end, Naru succeeds where the exorcists can't by creating a doll; specifically, a hitogata. Using a different pronunciation for the same kanji that make up the word "doll" (the symbols for 'human' and 'shape'), the hitogata is a small wooden doll with a piece of paper attached; the paper bears the name and age of the person needing protection[107]—in this case, Tomiko, the daughter of Hiro Oshima, the ghost of the grieving mother who committed suicide. By uniting Hiro's ghost with the spirit of her dead daughter in the hitogata, this not only caused the mother to stop attracting other children's spirits, but allowed those spirits she'd already trapped to move on as well.

One interesting parallel between *Ghost Hunt* and *Lagoon Engine*: in both, getting through to the spirit world involves several different methods. First, there's a process of negotiation and persuasion, which has to give way to force when all else fails. The approaches are described in *Ghost Hunt* as "jōrei" and "jorei." The manga's celebrity exorcist Masako Hara explains the distinction: "Let's say you know

---

[107] http://www.geocities.com/Tokyo/7731/hitogata.htm, accessed October 29, 2006.

someone who is a troublemaker. Jōrei would be to try to talk to them so that they could reform . . . Jorei would be to just kill them mercilessly." Hara feels too much compassion to perform jorei, since "humans and spirits are the same in her eyes." The exorcism of Minnie is thus left to John Brown, the Catholic from Australia.

This creates a double-distancing between the intended reader (teen Japanese girls) and violence, even psychic violence, since the exorcism is conducted by someone who may be a handsome blond hunk, but is also of an alien race and faith, and it doesn't work as well as the creation of the hitogata. Once again, in the character of Hara, who always appears in traditional kimono, to be a young, quintessentially Japanese girl (*Yamato nadeshiko*) is to be *yasashii* (gentle, kind and compassionate), but being male is defined as being effective.

Hitogata are also used in a major case in books 4 & 5 of *Ghost Hunt* (see the story "I am not a dog" in the "School Spirits" chapter). A high school is flooded with various psychic problems, from poltergeists setting fires to ravenous dog spirits. It eventually becomes clear that all the supernatural activity started with the suicide of a student, named Sakauchi. However, his grudge-holding ghost would not have been enough to cause all of the problems. Naru, Mai and the others find out that Sakauchi was driven to suicide by an especially abusive administrator named Matsuyama. As a result, an interest grew among the students in *kokkuri-san* for the sole purpose of cursing Matsuyama to death. All that this activity accomplished, however, was to summon a wide variety of malevolent spirits who set about devouring each other; if left unchecked, the surviving spirit would be so large and so evil as to pose a major threat.

Unable to attack all of the spirits in the school at once, Naru decides to turn the evil spirits against the students who summoned them by destroying the students; actually, by fashioning hitogata for the students and letting the spirits attack them. When this happens (and we can tell because the wooden dolls are broken into splinters), the school is cleansed.

How did Naru suspect the use of kokkuri-san? He noticed, and mentioned to the others, that the students at this school, under the heavy disciplinary hand of Matsuyama, didn't show even the slightest sign of rebellion. Most Japanese high schools have a dress code but don't insist on it; boys' tunics are sometimes open at the collar, girls wear excessively baggy knee-socks that bunch up around their ankles, students dye their hair in the bizarre colors of anime characters. Students can thus push at the edge of the rules without actually breaking them, letting off steam and keeping the all-important harmony (*wa*). At this school, however, Matsuyama was so heavy-handed in his scorn of psychic phenomena, dismissing anyone who believed in it as escapists and the young exorcists of Shibuya Psychic Research as con-artists, that the students went to extremes, and came close to bringing disaster to their school. Averting disaster only cost a few wooden dolls.

Mystical Detective Loki Ragnarok

The provenance of the manga *Matantei Roki Ragunaroku (Demon Detective Loki Ragnarok)*, which ran from 1999 to 2004, is a bit jumbled, since, after its serialization began in *GanGan Comics*, the first seven tankobon were published by Blade. The manga, by Sakura Kinoshita, was picked up by *Blade* magazine, and was released in a total of twelve volumes. It was animated in a 26-episode series by Studio Deen, with an occasionally edgy style. "Edgy" in this case means evoking video "snow", simulated hand-held camera shakiness, and other techniques of current Japanese horror movies (many of which were developed originally for Italian horror movies by directors like Dominic Argento and Mario Bava). Overall, though, the look of the series is mainstream anime.

The title suggests the central plot: the action centers on the Norse god Loki, whose mischief in this story got him into trouble once too often; he was banished from Valhalla to Earth in the body of a young boy, but with all his wits intact. Charged with ridding the earth of evil spirits, he and his servant Yamino set up the Enjaku "psychic detective agency" to make it easier to find them. He also quickly finds a partner in Mayura Daidouji, a high school student and daughter of a Shinto priest. Mayura loves mysteries and the occult; however, she has no sixth sense at all, neither she nor her father can see spirits, and she tends to get in Loki's way as often as not.

92. The Lonely Doll

In her first case with Loki (also the first episode in the anime series), she meets a child's doll which has come to life. Her first visit to a reputedly haunted house introduces her to the doll, which laughs, calls Mayura "o-neesan" (big sister), then launches itself at Mayura. Even though the doll is fueled by a vengeful spirit, Mayura actually imagines herself and the possessed doll as potential media darlings. The doll was one of the few items that survived a fire twenty years before; however, not knowing about the fire, it feels abandoned and consequently lashes out at people. It's about to attack Mayura, accusing her of abandoning the doll and levitating knives and furniture against the girl, when Loki intervenes. After telling the doll about the fire, he puts an enchanted protective bracelet on Mayura and removes the vengeful spirit by having Mayura hold the doll. (We know the doll has lost its vengeful nature by one of the oldest conventions in Japanese pop culture: the doll, despite being a doll, sheds a tear.) In this case, among many others, simple compassion expressed through "skinship" is all that is necessary for the bitter spirit inside the doll to change and move on.

It's interesting to note that, the first time we see the doll, during an attempted exorcism, a few of its synthetic hairs have strayed in front of its face. A few hairs are hardly enough to make the doll look like Oiwa of *Yotsuya Kaidan* or like Sadako in *Ringu*, but the hint is certainly there for the savvy viewer. The doll indeed turns out to be a *jibakurei*—a vengeful spirit—despite its blonde hair and frilly dress.

Gakkou no Kaidan

Two episodes of this series, based on a collection of rumors and ghost stories from contemporary Japanese schoolchildren, feature two very different dolls.

93. Doll of Return

It's common for schools, as part of their science curriculum, to keep animals as pets. It's less common for one person to repeatedly volunteer to take care of the animals; the ideal in Japanese education is to give everyone the chance to experience an activity. Satsuki finds that her classmate Hajime has "volunteered" her to tend to the animals, over the objections of the animals' perennial caretaker, an otherwise shy and unassuming girl named Imai. Their teacher settles things by saying that both Satsuki and Imai need to tend the animals together.

In time a litter of rabbits is born, increasing the rabbit population to six; however, one day, the students notice that a seventh rabbit is in the pen. Imai names it Shirotabi (White Stockings), after a previous rabbit who had died and was buried in the improvised pet cemetery behind the school. What nobody realizes until later is that the new rabbit isn't just a stray who wandered in from the woods; this is the original Shirotabi, brought back to life by Imai with the aid of an enchanted doll buried with the rabbit. Unfortunately, at night, Shirotabi turns into a demonic rabbit bigger than a human, a monster more like the raptors in *Jurassic Park* than a rabbit. It breaks out of its pen, kills all of the other rabbits (and a couple of people), then chases the children (including Imai) who were trying to find out what was happening. In this case, seeing the damage she's caused just because she wanted her friend back, Imai is able to reverse the curse.

In the end, the teacher brings the class some new rabbits from a local farm; descendants of the original Shirotabi, as it turns out. The teacher explains, in a simultaneously scientific and Buddhist manner, that a time comes when everything must die, and life is passed on to the next generation; "it's been like this for hundreds of millions of years." However, Imai, an otherwise friendless and very forgettable girl, learns this lesson the hard way. She regarded Shirotabi as her only friend, and crafted the doll to resurrect the rabbit because she missed him. This episode suggests that Imai will now be able to reach out to her classmates, perhaps through her abilities with a sewing needle to stitch together cute little keychain dolls.

94. Mary

The teaser opening is on a rainy night at the city garbage dump. Among the few identifiable bits of refuse is a blonde doll in a frilly pink dress and a red hair ribbon. Given the progress of the series, it's not surprising when the doll opens its eyes . . .

We next see the doll sitting on top of a trashcan where the children are walking home from school. Keiichiro asks his sister if they can take the doll with them; she says that boys aren't supposed to be interested in dolls. However, that night, the doll shows up in their home by the front door; Satsuki assumes her brother brought it in anyway. After all, it's just a doll, and couldn't have entered by itself.

Things start to escalate late that night; Mary starts making phone calls to Satsuki. The doll also calls her the next day at school, first at the school office, then through Leo's cell phone. The children are then called out of school on a real emergency: their father is in the emergency room of a hospital. It's nothing serious, but he'll be there overnight. When they find the doll in the hospital, Satsuki's teacher takes the doll to a temple with a reputation for housing dolls of those who have died. They hope that the temple will cancel out whatever evil spirit possesses the doll.

However, as soon as they get back home, Mary's phone calls start up again. Hajime takes Satsuki and Keiichi to an old abandoned martial arts dojo. While Hajime takes Keiichi to an outhouse, Mary reappears, curtsies to Satsuki, and suggests that they play. Other ghostly dolls start appearing, suggesting that they do to Satsuki what was done to them, which involved losing limbs, or eyes, or getting run over. Before the torture can start, a handkerchief falls out of Satsuki's pocket. Satsuki had used the handkerchief to clean a smudge of dirt off of Mary's face, before the doll started harassing the family. Mary suddenly announces the game is over, that she'll keep the handkerchief as a souvenir, and disappears.

While we've already seen magical or ceremonial dolls like the hitogata which are supposed to take on human attributes, Mary was literally just a child's plaything. In theory, she wasn't supposed to have any supernatural powers at all. However, such things can happen—in the pop culture, anyway. In the second feature anime based on Osamu Tezuka's manga character Unico, titled *Unico on Magic Island*, the title character, a magical baby unicorn, encounters a wooden marionette come to life. The marionette, named Kuruku, was maltreated and ultimately just thrown away. This ill treatment inspired in Kuruku hatred toward all of humankind; it sought dark magic with a desire to turn people into puppets for his amusement. The only thing that undoes Kuruku's hatred is Unico's offer of friendship; once he has returned to being just a marionette, he is found by the young girl at the center of the story. She has already been established as kind and compassionate, so we know that history will not repeat itself.

This episode of *Gakkou no Kaidan* is a capsule version of the Unico movie: a castaway doll treats people callously, but is redeemed by a single act of kindness. Karma, after all, goes both ways. Good deeds live on, as do bad deeds.

95. The Ghost of Moga-chan

This story isn't about a traditional Japanese doll or a western baby-doll. The name Moga-chan is a brand name, a contraction of "modern gal"; it was Japan's answer to the Barbie doll. In the *GS Mikami* manga episode titled "Noroi no Ningyouteikoku" (Curse of the Doll Empire), we get a look at a ghost-doll that touches Mikami personally.

Returning to the office from an assignment, Mikami and company see a child waiting outside the office. The little girl, Aya-chan, says that her Moga-chan doll is missing; it was taken by a large and scary-looking doll. Mikami, who never works for nothing, still didn't want to just turn the girl down; however, forecasting the future, she's warned that she'll have bad luck if she accepts any money at all for this assignment. The cosmos wants this job to be a freebie.

In Aya-chan's room Mikami discovers a portal to another dimension; she, Okinu-chan, and Yokoshima pass through to discover an army of Moga-chan dolls, led by a doll who asks, "Aren't you Reiko Mikami? It's been a long time." The doll then takes off its clothes to reveal the name Reiko Mikami written on its back; the doll was once Mikami's! The doll goes on to say that humans will soon kill each other off, and dolls will survive to play with them. They attack the humans, who defend themselves but cannot stop the dolls, which cannot die. Mikami wishes that she'd gotten at least a token payment from Aya-chan's mother. At this, the Moga-chan that used to belong to Aya-chan grabs the doll possessed by part of Mikami's soul; Mikami then can easily capture the soul in an ofuda. As Aya-chan's doll dies, her last words are to tell Aya-chan "I love you."

Again, this story plays out like the Unico story mentioned above. Dolls are mirrors, reflections of the best and worst in people.

96. "Stalker"

The most modern doll in the ghost realm is also one of the smallest and least likely to offend: a strap doll that's meant to decorate a cell phone. One of these dolls is featured in a 2004 episode of Yoshiyuki Nishi's manga *Muyo & Roji*.

The two youthful psychic "attorneys" are visited by Kaya Onodera, who has been having haunted-house problems for the past six months. Doors open and close by themselves, curtains rustle when there's no breeze, objects start flying around; it gets worse whenever she has company. These things started happening after she got the strap doll (although she doesn't recall how she got it), but its appearance coincided with the accidental death of a classmate. The boy, Nobuo, was regarded as creepy and dismissed as a stalker, shunned and beaten. He had, for example, numerous photos of Kaya on his cell phone. Kaya made a couple of friendly overtures to Nobuo before his death.

Muyo realizes that the strap doll once belonged to Nobuo and was stalking Kaya, as its owner had once obsessed over her in life: "spirits hang around in objects to protect those they love and can't forget," Muyo says, but Nobuo's spirit didn't understand Kaya's feelings. Muyo declares that Kaya's feelings are at best conflicted: "She put on a gentle face, but her heart said, 'stalker.'" While both were set to be punished by a railroad trip through Hell for eternity, Nobuo throws Kaya from the train, saying that he merely wanted to be her friend. A tearful Kaya hopes that this can happen someday if they are both born again. This was all that was necessary to break the curse: Nobuo got the chance to state how he honestly felt, which still isn't easy in Japanese culture, as the train takes Nobuo to the River Sanzu. The story ends on the following Obon, when Kaya has a picture taken (she's wearing a floral yukata) with the ghost of Nobuo, who, like so many ghosts, returns to the world for Obon.

CHAPTER 29: A FEW WORDS ABOUT

VAMPIRES

Vampires have appeared in Japanese pop culture for decades. Osamu Tezuka created a comic 26 episode series about Count Dracula being transplanted—castle and all—to Japan, with his prepubescent daughter Chocula(!), published in *Shonen Champion* manga magazine in the 1970s. He was inspired by the Hollywood vampire parody *Love at First Bite,* which was shown in Japan as *Dracula Miyako e Iku (Dracula Goes to Town)*; the pun works in both English and Japanese.

A few years after *Don Dracula* came *Tokimeki Tonight,* a romantic comedy manga by Koi Ikeno. It started appearing in *Ribon Mascot* magazine in 1982 and ran until 1994. It's the story of Ranze Eto, a chipper teenaged girl with more than a few problems getting between her and her crush on classmate Shun Makabe; those problems include her father the vampire and her mother the werewolf.

Mamoru Oshii's Production I.G. studio in 1999 created a gory anime special, which ran just under fifty minutes and was supposed to be part of a trilogy. Instead, it reached the status of instant classic: *Blood the Last Vampire.* Set in 1966 at Yokota Air Base in Japan, this film used the birth and spread of vampires in Asia as a metaphor for America's war in Vietnam. In this case, the vampires were not truly human except in their ability to pose as humans; they were actually monsters called chiropterans, who could only be dispatched by Saya, a schoolgirl wielding a samurai sword, a girl who was set apart from the rest of the population by being an "Original" (a category which is never explained). The film later begat a 51-episode TV anime series, *Blood +*, and in 2009 a live action version of *Blood the Last Vampire* appeared, directed by Chris Nahon, trying to expand Saya's backstory.

The sheer number of shojo manga based on vampire stories, especially recently in the *Twilight* era, is impressive, from *Millennium Snow* (a comedy-romance between a dying girl who seeks to live and the vampire who can oblige her) to *Chibi Vampire* (a comedy about a little girl vampire who suffers from having too much blood) to *Vampire Knights* (a high school divided into day and night classes, and guess who's in the night group).

These stories, and many others, draw in part on the novel *Dracula* by Bram Stoker, and the various Hollywood films based on the novel, but feature a distinctly Japanese take on the proceedings. In the Buddhist context, the vampire's search for eternal life is somewhat superfluous, since the soul is in a cycle of death and rebirth anyway. Preserving the same soul and the same body, however, is unnatural, and the vampire who kills others to selfishly prolong his or her own life is a monster.

xxx

La Portrait de Petite Cossette

This 3-part OAV begins by directly referencing the "In a Cup of Tea" story in Hearn's *Kwaidan*. A teenaged painter, Eiri Kurahashi, works in an antique store, where he finds a Venetian wineglass. Within it is the spirit of a girl, Cossette d'Auvergne, with whom Eiri has fallen in love. Cossette is a blond-haired blue-eyed doll-like beauty with an unusual request. She tells Eiri that she cannot be reborn unless someone loves her enough to give up their life for her sake. In time Eiri sees other things in the wineglass, including Cossette being murdered by a man even as she declares that she loves him.

Directed in 2004 by Akiyuki Shinbo, written by Mayori Sekijima, and based on a manga by Asuka Katsura, *La Portrait de*

Petite Cossette has a twist on the Hearn story by making this ghost undeniably foreign, even down to the overly French name, Cossette of the Auvergne. The Auvergne region in central France is known for cheeses, Michelin tires, and mineral water. However, the name was chosen deliberately by Katsura, I think, because of a more modern association. Cossette lived in the Auvergne in the 1700s, as did Lestat de Lioncourt, the vampire protagonist of the popular series of books by Anne Rice.

Xenophobia—the fear of the outsider, the Other—isn't the private property of any country, and Japan has had its share over the years. There was the Tokugawa period, when Japan closed itself off from the world for two centuries. There is a long history of Japan disrespecting its neighbors in Korea and China, in forums ranging from textbooks to newspapers to manga.[108] The *Ghost Hunt* manga has Naru assisted by a tall, bishonen-looking young man named Lin or Rin; born in Hong Kong, at one point he tells Mai that he dislikes the Japanese because of the way they've treated Chinese in the past. Americans, often black Americans, have come in for the same disrespect, although the pendulum has also swung the other way in recent years, with Japanese pop bands adopting the clothes, slang, and mannerisms of hip-hop.

When it comes to western women, though, there seems to be a love-hate relationship. The blond-haired blue eyed ideal represented by Cossette has been a Hollywood staple for generations, and it's not surprising that it should have influenced the Japanese culture when a large part of that culture includes American media, whether magazines or movies, pop stars or politicians. The blonde baby-doll ideal has been attractive in Japan (as we've seen in the previous chapter on dolls), yet has also served in some anime/manga as a way of denoting the villain.

---

[108] One relatively mild example occurred in the *Don Dracula* manga by Osamu Tezuka, when the vampire tells his daughter Chocula, "I don't like Koreans; they cook with too much garlic."

xxx

The "Bloodstained Labyrinth" case of the *Ghost Hunt* manga features a bizarre old house haunted by a ghostly vampire, who's actually a composite of two historic European "vampires."

97. "I don't want to die"

Shibuya Psychic Research becomes part of a group of psychics investigating the haunting of an old western-style mansion at the request of no less than the Prime Minister of Japan. Four people have disappeared near the house recently, and no trace of them was ever found; similar disappearances have happened since the mansion's construction began in 1877. The mansion's owner, Kaneyuki Miyama, made a fortune in the 1800s in silk and then became a philanthropist, even opening his own charity hospital; however, other, darker rumors circulated around him when he was alive; he was reported to have died in 1910, but lived as a recluse in failing health long before that. Despite the high-powered psychic investigators, the business is being kept low-key lest the media find out what's been going on, and Naru goes so far as to assume an alias and let Yasuhara-san, who assisted in the investigation of Ryokuryo High School (see "I am not a dog"), pose as the head of Shibuya Psychic Research. One thing Mai and her female colleagues agree on: the mansion faintly yet definitely smells of blood.[109]

In the course of their investigations, three of the visiting psychics disappear, and they have one thing in common: they're young adults. Since Mai, Naru and the SPR group is between ages fifteen and thirty, they're also at considerable risk. Mai dreams at one point that she is kidnapped, taken by two men to a room buried in the heart of the old house, and bled to death. Masako is likewise

---

[109] Do I really need to explain why the women would be more sensitive to this?

spirited away, and, in a trance, Mai finds her and tries to protect her until the others arrive.

Masako narrowly misses being killed by the ghost of the previous owner of the house. Old documents refer to him under what seems to be the nickname "Urado", but during a séance which contacts one of the disappeared psychics, the name is spelled out on the mansion's walls in blood (along with phrases like "Help," "It hurts," "I'm afraid," and "I don't want to die") as "Vurado." Because of the nature of the Japanese alphabet, this is as close as the language gets to the name of Prince Vlad, the historical model for Dracula.

Sidebar: The real Dracula

The historical Dracula was a nobleman, and lived in the part of Romania known then and now as Transylvania ("Beyond the Forest"). Beyond that, there's much that's troubling but little vampiric about Dracula.

He was born about the year 1431, one of two sons of a nobleman who was awarded the Order of the Dragon, an honor from the King in recognition of the father's actions during the Crusades. The father highlighted the award by calling himself Dracul ("Dragon"). His son took the name "Dracula," meaning "Son of Dracul."

Prince Vlad, however, earned another name before his death in 1476: Vled Tepes ("Vlad the Impaler"). He was known to mount the bodies, or body parts, of anyone who displeased him on the tops of long poles, letting the flesh rot as a warning to the citizens: behave. By most accounts, the citizens did. It was said that one town had a well with a goblet of solid gold for anyone to drink from; the people knew what would happen if the goblet were stolen.

According to another famous story, Dracula met with a delegation from Turkey that refused for religious reasons to uncover their heads. Vlad declared that he would strengthen the religious beliefs of the delegation—and had their hats nailed to their heads.

xxx

In this story, however, Vlad is conflated with another historical "vampire," the Countess Erzsebeth (or Elizabeth) Bathory

(1560-1614). The owner of the story's mansion in the 1800s, Kaneyuki Miyama, tried to cultivate a reputation as a philanthropist, but had a much darker side. His health was always feeble and, when he started to decline, he apparently adopted the "cure" of Countess Bathory, who reputedly kept herself young and beautiful by bathing in the blood of between eighty and six hundred young women. Urado would similarly kidnap young servant-girls, among others, some of whom worked in the charity hospital he established, or patients. He and his two attendants would bleed them to death, then cremate the bodies and keep the bones in a storeroom, well organized and almost respectfully treated; the blood was destined for Urado's bathtub. Ironically, these victims were not haunting the house, because their remains had been properly treated. Those who were killed later, whose bodies had simply been dumped in haste in a spare room, like the missing psychic contacted by Misato, could still be reached by a medium.

The bloodletting continued even after the old man died; his ghost and the ghosts of his two assistants saw to that. As Naru points out, Miyama wanted to survive; he lacked the regret and sorrow toward this world that drives other ghosts. "They're no longer just spirits of the departed; they're now monsters." Some ghosts keep their integrity in Japanese lore, such as Fujiwara no Sai in *Hikaru no Go*, who survived a thousand years of haunting without turning into a monster.

After Urado's spirit was temporarily suppressed by a Daoist spell cast by Rin (who nobody knew at this point was anything but an assistant to Naru), they realized the only way to solve the problem was to burn the house to the ground. Urado didn't dare leave the house when he was alive; it was a maze that kept him safe and contained his victims; in the end, the house that sheltered him would also be his trap.

CHAPTER 30: IN A HAUNTED HOUSE

We've already seen examples of a haunted house; in the movie *Kwaidan*, the first story featured a man returning to his traditional house, which is rundown and full of foreboding shadows. It turns out to be as haunted as it looks.

The *Ghost Hunt* account of Urado provides a western-style haunted house, although, with its endless revisions and additions and pointless remodeling, with windows looking at nothing and stairs climbing nowhere, it might make more sense to look back to a word used in Shirley Jackson's classic novel *The Haunting of Hill House*. In that book, Hill House is described as "deranged." The house itself was disordered, sick.

The creators of *Ghost Hunt* drop one hint about their own sick house in the "Bloodstained Labyrinth" story, which takes up tankobon volumes 6 and 7 of the manga. It takes a while for blueprints of the house to turn up, but, when they're examined, it turns out that the mansion has 106 rooms. However, there has to be at least one room not on the blueprints where the ghostly outrages take place, plus a way to access the hidden room. In short, the house actually has 108 rooms, and 108 is a magically loaded number in Japan. (see *Anime Explosion*)

When Takashi Shimizu, writer and director of *Ju-On*, said that "In old Japanese houses, even during the day, it is dark deeper inside," he didn't just mean the architecture. He also meant the ever-present reminders of death within life, reminders which Shimizu considers uniquely Japanese. These can include the Buddhist altar and/or Shinto shrine in the home, ancestral poems on the walls next to teacups, portraits of departed ancestors. Certainly the annual Obon festival is itself a reminder of the departed members of the family.

Ironically, Shimizu's definition of an "old" Japanese house is one built after World War II. In his film *Ju-On* (remade in the west as *The Grudge*), the house itself is modern concrete and wood, and perfectly mundane, but has more than its share of weirdly lit corners and closets, where anything can be lurking at any time. (In the *Ghost Hunt* manga, one character comments that it's possible to create a scary moment just by leaving the door to a storage closet slightly ajar.)

Volume 3 of *Lagoon Engine* by Yukiru Sugisaki is an account of a case in which the Ragun brothers have to deal with a haunted house. There are definitely surprises along the way, as well as scares.

98. A child's feelings

The volume begins with a statement that makes sense only at the end: that "a child's feelings can only be fully understood by other children." We've seen this already in stories involving the ghosts of children: the *Ghost Talker's Daydreams* OAV, volume 2 of the *Ghost Hunt* manga, and others. In this case the two tween-age Ragun brothers are put in charge of investigating a haunted house.

Mr. Kanuma approaches the boys' father, Hideaki Ragun, who was reported to be one of the best at getting rid of the spirits haunting his house. Mister Ragun says that he trusts the judgment of his sons, who have been trained in the family business since infancy. Mister Kanuma explains that his family had built a new house and was trying to sell their western-style mansion. However, any realtor who tries to show the house gets injured, either by losing their footing or by having something fall on them. Only Mister Kanuma can enter and leave the house safely.

On their first day in the house, Yen and Jin notice that the walls are covered with pictures of birds, which Mr. Kanuma doesn't particularly like. They also find that the house is filled with a variety of spirits, that they've put up a barrier to keep the boys from roaming through the house, and that one of the Ragun boys' familiar spirits has been injured by the house spirits. They get the spirit healed after school (at a doctor whose practice doesn't exactly exist in three dimensions) and they return to the Kanuma house. This time, they get sent on a wild chase throughout the house, although they seem never to leave one room. Amid all the pictures of birds, they find one picture of a boy.

This provides the answer, especially when they talk to the spirit of the boy in the painting. The boy was Susumu, son of the owners of the house. About the time he was seven years old, one day his mother was simply gone. He repeatedly asked his father about her, but he would only tell the boy that they can't be together; the boy retreated into his picture books of his beloved birds. Mister Kanuma tried to move his son to a new home, but the boy slipped at the top of the stairs . . .

"I kept waiting here because I thought, if I wait here, dad and mom will come back." In time, though, the memories of his parents faded and the spirits of the birds began to mean more to him. He gave the Ragun brothers a message for his father, who was still apologizing for the death of his son: "Tell my dad that it's okay." This story reminds us that "people try to avoid facing their pain. They hold it deep inside. For living things, as well as for things that have died, the greatest relief, apparently, is to forget." Susumu was able to Become One with the Cosmos once he had delivered his message for his father. Mister Kanuma, however, needed a bit more persuasion, since he had forgotten to mention one other important piece of information: he was dead, too. In a twist that again recalls M. Night Shyamalan, the spirit of a dead man had approached the Raguns for help with the house. He and his wife had divorced when Susumu was seven; then father and son had died. Of course, the elder Ragun's confidence in his son was justified; the boys tell Mister Kanuma's ghost, "That was obvious right when we first met; you'd be surprised how many people we get like that."

xxx

It may not be orthodox Japanese beliefs in ghosts, but the notion of forgetfulness, of not realizing one is even dead, has gained currency in recent kaidan. It seems that, the younger the ghost, the more likely it is to forget, as in several cases of *Ghost Hunt* that involve the ghosts of children. We also saw this in the case of Sayo in *Negima*: the girl who seemed to forget that she was a ghost, or at least for whom it no longer seemed to matter.

FINALE

In Japan, ghosts are (a) Evil, (b) Good, or (c) None of the above?

In this book we've met some ghosts who were scary, homicidal, driven by vengeance, and others who were cute, sweet, or harbingers of good luck. The deeper we look into Japanese ghost lore, the more kinds of ghosts we seem to find. This is as it should be: in the Japanese perspective, being freed from life also frees the spirit from earthly consequences.

Yuko the witch from CLAMP's *xxxHolic*, put it this way: "Good and evil are concepts that humans decide. Those concepts don't apply to non-humans." In one of the *Ghost Hunt* stories the same confusion applies: the spirits inhabiting one site are described as "a swirl of something extremely evil and something extremely good." Although this described a seacoast site in Japan, the character said that she'd felt the same conflicted swirl at a Native American sacred site.

Yet the humans affected by the hauntings certainly can end up feeling that they're on one side or the other of a line between good and bad, between curses and blessings. Watanuki finds a girlfriend (of sorts) in the zasshiki, even as Okiku's ghostly search for the tenth plate drove her beloved master to madness.

But are mere mortals stuck with the ghosts and their desires to have an effect on this world from beyond?

The most common strategy we've seen is to pray for divine intercession, so that the spirit may find the peace it lacked. But there are other ways as well of keeping peace between this world and the next. One way was set down by Lafcadio Hearn in his classic collection *Kwaidan*; a short story originally titled "Diplomacy" shows how even a vengeance-seeking ghost can be undone, simply by an understanding of human nature:

99. The Ghost Who Did Nothing

A man was sentenced to death by beheading. He was forced to kneel in the central courtyard of a mansion; the courtyard was criss-crossed with stepping-stones. The man's hands were tied behind his back, and canvas bags full of pebbles kept him from moving. As the preparations were being made for the beheading, the condemned man shouted out: "My Lord, I am being killed for a crime which I did not choose to commit. I did what I did because of bad karma and stupidity. What I did was wrong, but killing a man like me over a mistake would be just as wrong. Killing me will provoke resentment on the part of my spirit."

The owner of the mansion, a high-ranking samurai, knew that this was how ghosts worked, so he said, "I am sure that your spirit will threaten us all after your death. However, do you think that you can demonstrate the power of your spirit before your death, if you are feeling resentful now?"

"My Lord, I am sure that I can, but there is little I can do now."

"Then let me propose something. Directly in front of where you're kneeling is a stepping-stone. When you have been beheaded, try to grasp the stone with your teeth. That would certainly scare us and convince us of your power."

"I will bite it!" the condemned man said angrily. "I will bite it! I will bite it!"

The sword flashed in the sunlight; two long jets of blood sprayed from the neck where the head used to be. The head rolled upon the ground. Suddenly it seemed to leap up and grasped the edge of the stepping-stone between its teeth. It hung there for a few seconds, then fell back to the ground.

The samurai seemed unconcerned by all this. As he held out his sword, an attendant poured pure water on the bloody blade, which he cleaned with several sheets of paper.

For days thereafter the servants of the household lived in a state of fear. They saw the disembodied head grasp the stone in its teeth, and felt that it was only a matter of time before the dead man's vengeful spirit manifested itself. The samurai, however, continued to act as if nothing was wrong.

Finally, the servants, after jumping at every rustle of wind and every movement of a bamboo plant, asked their master to say a special service on behalf of the vengeful ghost.

"There is no need," the master replied. "Nothing is going to happen."

The leader of the servants wanted to ask how this was so, but didn't want to contradict his master. The samurai, being a wise man, anticipated the question:

"The reason is simple enough. When I gave him something to do with the last of his spirit, it took his mind away from thoughts of vengeance. He died focused on grasping the stepping stone, which meant that he had to clear his mind of thoughts of revenge. Don't worry about it."

And the samurai was right. Nothing at all happened.

xxx

The book is almost finished. The game is almost done; in our *hyaku monogatari* session there's one candle left burning, one tale left to tell. How does it end?

In a cemetery, or a crematorium? With the ghost of a man, or a woman? Perhaps of a child who doesn't quite understand what's going on? The ghost of a criminal consumed by resentment? Or of a priest, wanting to do one more good act in the world?

This is your chance. You get to make up the final story. It could be something that actually happened to you; even if it didn't, try your best to convince the audience that it really did happen.

If you really need at least one clue, here's one sentence from the middle of a ghost story. It actually comes from an episode of Ken Akamatsu's popular manga *Negima!*, about a British boy-wizard teaching at an all-girl junior high school in Tokyo (among other tasks). At one point the wizard and his students take the traditional field-trip to Kyoto; at the inn one night, some of the girls have gotten together to (yes) tell ghost stories. The manga looks in on the girls and catches one in mid-story, with an appropriately chilling line:

100. The Ghost Story You Write

. . . The next night, that comic-book artist was working by himself when, from the radio that he knew he had turned off, came a voice . . . a woman's voice . . . a voice that was not of this world . . .